Amoral Gower

Series Editors

Rita Copeland

Barbara A. Hanawalt

David Wallace

*Sponsored by the Center for Medieval Studies
at the University of Minnesota*

Volumes in this series study the diversity of medieval
cultural histories and practices, including such
interrelated issues as gender, class, and social
hierarchies; race and ethnicity; geographical
relations; definitions of political space; discourses
of authority and dissent; educational institutions;
canonical and noncanonical literatures; and
technologies of textual and visual literacies.

AMORAL GOWER

LANGUAGE, SEX, AND POLITICS

DIANE WATT

Medieval Cultures, Volume 38
University of Minnesota Press
Minneapolis
London

An earlier version of chapter 2 appeared as "Literary Genealogy, Virile Rhetoric, and John Gower's *Confessio Amantis*," *Philological Quarterly* 78 (1999): 387–413; reprinted by permission of *Philological Quarterly*. An earlier version of chapter 3 appeared as "Sins of Omission: Transgressive Genders, Subversive Sexualities, and John Gower's *Confessio Amantis*," *Exemplaria: A Journal of Theory in Medieval and Renaissance Studies* 13, no. 2 (2001): 529–51; reprinted by permission of Pegasus Press, University of North Carolina, Asheville, NC 28804; copyright 2001 Pegasus Press. An earlier version of chapter 6 appeared as "Oedipus, Apollonius, and Richard II: Sex and Politics in Book VIII of John Gower's *Confessio Amantis*," *Studies in the Age of Chaucer* 24 (2002): 181–208; reprinted by permission of *Studies in the Age of Chaucer*. Part of chapter 6 also appeared as "Consuming Passions in Book VIII of John Gower's *Confessio Amantis*," in *Consuming Narratives: Gender and Monstrous Appetite in the Middle Ages and the Renaissance*, edited by Liz Herbert McAvoy and Teresa Walters (Cardiff: University of Wales Press, 2002), 28–41; reprinted by permission of University of Wales Press.

Published by the University of Minnesota Press
111 Third Avenue South, Suite 290
Minneapolis, MN 55401-2520
http://www.upress.umn.edu

Library of Congress Cataloging-in-Publication Data

Watt, Diane, 1965–
    Amoral Gower : language, sex, and politics / Diane Watt.
        p.   cm. — (Medieval cultures ; v. 38)
    Includes bibliographical references (p.   ) and index.
    ISBN 0-8166-4027-0 (alk. paper) — ISBN 0-8166-4028-9 (pbk. : alk. paper)
    1. Gower, John, 1325?–1408. Confessio amantis.   2. Politics and literature—Great Britain—History—To 1500.   3. Gower, John, 1325?–1408—Political and social views.   4. Gower, John, 1325?–1408—Language.   5. Gower, John, 1325?–1408—Ethics.   6. Ethics, Medieval, in literature.   7. Courtly love in literature.   8. Politics in literature.   9. Sex in literature.   I. Title.   II. Series.
    PR1984.C63W37   2003
    821'.1—dc21   2003007851

Printed in the United States of America on acid-free paper

The University of Minnesota is an equal-opportunity educator and employer.

12 11 10 09 08 07 06 05 04 03   10 9 8 7 6 5 4 3 2 1

Contents

Acknowledgments

The research for this book began in 1996, and in the ensuing years I have incurred many debts. It is impossible for me to name everyone with whom I have discussed ideas and problems related to this project. Nevertheless, special mention must be made of Siân Echard, Ruth Evans, Simon Gaunt, Douglas Gray, Diane Purkiss, James Simpson, David Wallace, and Nicholas Watson. All of these scholars have given me advice, encouragement, and support in various ways, and I am extremely grateful to them for their efforts.

I wish to express my thanks to the English Department at the University of Wales, Aberystwyth, for granting me research leave in the second semester of the academic year 1998–99. Thanks are also due to the Master and Fellows of St. John's College, Oxford University, for electing me to a visiting scholarship in the summer of 1999. Early completion of this project was made possible by the Leverhulme Trust, which awarded me a research fellowship for the academic year 2001–02.

This book is dedicated to Heike, Rufus, and Floyd, and to Hengwrt, much missed.

A Note on the Texts

All references to *Confessio Amantis* are to *The English Works of John Gower,* ed. G. C. Macaulay, EETS e.s. 81, 82 (London: Kegan Paul, Trench, Trübner, 1900–01; reprint, Oxford: Oxford University Press, 1979). According to Macaulay's system of classification, *Confessio Amantis* exists in three recensions. He uses Oxford, Bodleian Library, MS Fairfax 3, which he labels a third recension manuscript, as his base text. Using a split page format, he also includes variant lines from the first recension of the poem. Following Macaulay, quotations from the first version of *Confessio Amantis* are here indicated with an asterisk.

Unless otherwise stated, translations from the Latin verses of *Confessio Amantis* are taken from *The Latin Verses in the Confessio Amantis: An Annotated Translation,* ed. and trans. Siân Echard and Claire Fanger (East Lansing: Colleagues Press, 1991). All references to the Anglo-Norman text of *Mirour de l'Omme* are to *The French Works of John Gower,* ed. G. C. Macaulay (Oxford: Clarendon Press, 1899). Translations of Gower's Anglo-Norman are taken from *Mirour de l'Omme (The Mirror of Mankind),* trans. William Burton Wilson, rev. Nancy Wilson Van Baak (East Lansing: Colleagues Press, 1992). All references to the Latin text of *Vox Clamantis* and Gower's other Latin poems are to *The Latin Works of John Gower,* ed. G. C. Macaulay (Oxford: Clarendon Press, 1902). Translations are from *The Major Latin Works of John Gower,* trans. Eric W. Stockton (Seattle: University of Washington Press, 1962).

All Chaucer references are to *The Riverside Chaucer,* ed. Larry D. Benson (Oxford: Oxford University Press, 1988). I refer to the text of Alain de Lille, "De Planctu Naturae," ed. Nikolaus M. Häring, *Studi medievali,* series 3, 19 (1978): 797–879. Translations are from *The Plaint of Nature,* trans. James J. Sheridan (Toronto: Pontifical Institute of Mediaeval Studies, 1980). I refer to the text of Guillaume de Lorris and Jean de Meun, *Le Roman de la Rose,* ed. Ernest Langlois, 5 vols., Société de Anciens Textes Français (Paris: Firmin-Didot, 1914–24). Translations are from *The Romance of the Rose,* trans. Frances Horgan (Oxford: Oxford University Press, 1994). I use the text of Ovid, *Metamorphoses,* ed. and trans. Frank Justus Miller, 2 vols., Loeb Classical Library (London: Heinemann, 1916).

PREFACE

From the late Middle Ages to the Renaissance and beyond, writing in the vernacular has been associated with daring intellectual experimentation. At around the same time as Geoffrey Chaucer began work on *The Canterbury Tales,* John Gower embarked on his own long poem in the vernacular, *Confessio Amantis* (completed 1390–93). Medieval literary scholarship has traditionally focused on the works of Chaucer, at the expense of those of his contemporary and friend, Gower. One of the main aims of this study is to make readers aware of the intellectual sophistication of Gower's *Confessio* and to demonstrate ways in which Gower's writing lends itself to the current critical and theoretical climate. The epithet "moral Gower" (originally coined by Chaucer) has proved sufficient to dissuade many from exploring his poetry, but Gower's examination of language, gender, and sexuality, as well as the questions raised by his poetry about the ethics of reading and writing, are still relevant today. While, in an era that celebrates literary "subversion," Gower's reputation as both morally and politically conservative may seem off-putting, it is crucial that we acknowledge that in overtly criticizing as well as describing current affairs, Gower intervenes in politics in a way Chaucer did not. Although Gower is not overtly opposed to either the traditional social hierarchy or the monarchy, his text often challenges the readers' ethical and political expectations. While ostensibly concerned with the promotion of morality at the levels of both macrocosm (of society) and microcosm (of the individual), Gower's *Confessio* betrays a fascination with loss of control, abuse of power, and the dangers of knowledge gone astray.

To begin, I should explain and justify the title of the book: *Amoral Gower.* Gower's *Confessio Amantis* has often been read as a poem that attempts to reach a loftily abstract and ethical view of the sinful (or in Gower's own terms, divided) human condition. I would not dispute the claim that *Confessio Amantis* is profoundly concerned with the related issues of good government and personal conduct (indeed, according to

medieval classifications, poetry was a branch of ethics).[1] Yet while it may
initially seem unreasonable to suggest that Gower, or his poetry, rejects
or even sidesteps ethical principles, I argue that the tensions, contradictions, and silences in Gower's text expose the limitations of the ethical
structures available to him and open up his text to multiple interpretations. A central argument of this study is that the poem destabilizes accepted categories of gender and sex, and that this has a profound impact
on Gower's treatment of ethics and politics, as well as language and
rhetoric, and knowledge and power. Elizabeth Allen suggests that Gower,
following the medieval Aristotelian tradition, represents morality not in
terms of a body of doctrine or commands but as a question of choice
and as a process.[2] A number of critics have taken the view that the poem
teaches both its own protagonist (the lover, Amans) and its audience
about themselves and about how to live. James Simpson, for example,
believes that as *Confessio* progresses, we mirror Amans's own develop-
ments and move toward an "integrated" reading.[3] Ethics, writing, and
reading certainly intersect in the poem. Medieval thinkers were aware
that fiction, and especially vernacular fiction, has a transgressive potential; that texts can be read and misread. Hugh of St. Victor, for one, was
conscious that readers, as they reflect upon texts, go beyond the precepts
of the texts themselves.[4] Thus texts are open to interpretation and misinterpretation, and truth becomes contingent and relative rather than uni-
versal and transcendent. Lee Patterson makes the following observation:

> If medieval readers were capable of anticipating the modern
> taste for ambiguity, the temptation of misreading was also avail-
> able to them. And as we might expect of a culture of the book,
> medieval misprision brought with it little but anxiety.[5]

Yet, whereas Patterson contends that Gower, unlike other writers of his
time, did not make reading "a dangerous exercise,"[6] I am of the opposite
opinion. I conclude that the poem deliberately encourages its audience
to take risks in interpretation, to experiment with meaning, and to offer
individualistic readings. Indeed, insofar as it does not always give satis-
factory answers to the moral questions it raises, and at times obfuscates
rather than clarifies, it can be seen to pursue a negative critique of ethical poetry. Gower can be described as amoral because, insofar as he leaves
the reader to make her or his own decisions, or, as Allen puts it, to take

"responsibility for creating resolution—or for tolerating irresolution,"[7] he does step outside of his own ethical system. In so doing, Gower offers his readers (medieval, modern, and postmodern) an imaginative participation in the sinful condition of humanity and an aesthetic experience of the disorder of the world.

Reading Gower's *Confessio Amantis* in the twenty-first century invites self-reflection, as it must have done in the late fourteenth century and the fifteenth century. More specifically, it encourages us to consider the ethics, if not of living (it is surely too much of its time for that), then of our own reading processes. Ethical criticism has received considerable attention in recent years.[8] Here I am not interested in ethical criticism in the sense of reading literature as moral philosophy, or even, and more accurately (remembering the medieval classification of poetry as ethics), in reading moral philosophy as literature. I am, however, interested in ethical criticism in the sense of the ethics *of* criticism, or the responsibilities of interpretation.[9] In a useful essay, Karlheinz Stierle argues that the critic or interpreter is bound by a double contract with the text and the reader. The role the critic adopts is that of mediator. For the critic, "understanding is . . . a way of giving presence to the text for readers who, without the interference of the interpreter, would not reach the text any more or would not reach it in all its dimensions."[10] Consequently, the critic must have certain qualifications:

> The interpreter as a mediator must be, as it were, an inhabitant of the work, knowing it in detail and also having experienced its more remote aspects. As an interpreter he [or she] must not only know the work itself, but also its language and how it is grounded in the language of a historical moment, in its particular cultural and social reality.[11]

In mediating the text, in building a bridge between text and reader, the critic subscribes to the notion that "interpretation is always part of an ongoing discourse . . . [and] a professional and institutionally bound activity which has to keep standards of reliability."[12] In other words, the critic is also obliged to work within established traditions and theoretical paradigms. One dimension of this must be that the interpreter assumes a certain sort of receptive and informed readership, addresses a particular and largely academic community.[13] I would suggest that the interpreter as mediator has a further responsibility: to demonstrate to her or his readership why the text is worthy of study at the given moment, to forge connections between the past and present, and thus to make the text live in the here and now.[14]

This study offers a detailed reading of Gower's *Confessio Amantis* and is informed by queer and feminist theory, as well as textual criticism, linguistic and narrative theory, and historicist and psychoanalytical approaches to literature. From my own perspective, it is my sense of my role as interpreter and the responsibilities it entails that justifies my eclectic theoretical approach. In reading Gower's *Confessio Amantis* closely, in considering it in terms of its cultural and social reality (including its textual history), I hope to make the poem more comprehensible by conveying a sense of how it might have been received by its author's contemporaries. In drawing on feminist theory and psychoanalysis, I am able to address issues relating to the construction of gender and sexuality in the poem (albeit in terms that Gower and his contemporaries may never have considered). These are likely to be urgent concerns for my own contemporaries, for my own interpretative community.[15] Thus I also hope to make the poem more accessible by suggesting how it can be read today. My debts to deconstruction and queer theory are more problematic and require a different sort of justification. This is because both approaches, with their shared emphases on surface effects and reading against the grain, have been dismissed not only as unhistorical and apolitical but also as irresponsible, risk-taking, amoral, even unethical.[16] Stierle's defense of deconstruction can be applied equally to queer theory. Deconstruction and queer theory are invaluable as interpretative strategies, or as "methodological device[s] for approaching the complex reality of the literary text in its concreteness and immanent contradictions . . . [for helping] resist a simplifying and commonplace form of reception."[17] Until relatively recently, Gower's *Confessio Amantis* has certainly suffered from what Stierle calls "the simulacrum of stereotyped reception."[18] The present study, by drawing attention to the inconsistencies, ambiguities, and absences in the poem, all of which I believe to be integral to its self-critical and relativistic ethical project, attempts to break this down. Ultimately, I agree with Stierle's conclusions that, "if interpretation has to take radical risks in order to approach the radical risk of literature and poetry, it has to be controlled and counterbalanced by that responsibility which the contract of interpretation implies."[19]

Lynne Pearce has written about the implicit gendered opposition of the masculine rational critic and the feminine intuitive reader, the opposition of the objective academic interpreter who keeps her or his distance and what Pearce terms the lover of the text who engages fully with it, responds personally to it.[20] The former always takes precedence, the latter has little or no place in scholarly discourse. In the context of Gower's *Confessio Amantis*, I am reminded of Simpson's argument that within the world of the poem's framework—the confession of a lover to his priest—the lover (Amans) is a reader, driven by the will or desire, while the priest (Genius) represents the imagination.[21] According to Simpson, by the end of *Confessio* reason has replaced desire, making the integrated and ethical reading possible for both Amans and the actual reader of the poem. In my own twenty-first-century ethical reading, I have tried to reconcile the demands of reason and desire, "disinterestedness" and involvement, wisdom and seduction, by communicating the sense I have made of this poem and why it moves me. In offering a new interpretation of *Confessio Amantis*, then, I do not attempt to offer a final interpretation. My principal aim is to engage more readers, and thus to stimulate more interpretations.

Unlike many previous monographs on *Confessio Amantis*, this study does not provide a book-by-book commentary. The combined evidence of medieval literary theory and of manuscript production suggests that late medieval texts were not always designed to be read cover to cover. The (possibly authorial) Latin summaries and glosses of *Confessio*, whatever other functions they fulfill, serve as mnemonic aids, which help the reader to move around this encyclopedic work. Consequently, I read thematically, making my own connections between narratives, verses, and glosses that are not necessarily located in close proximity to one another, or connected by the poem's penitential taxonomy. I also read across different levels of the narrative, moving between the frame and the exemplary stories, and across different versions, looking at both the Ricardian and the Lancastrian texts. This study neither slavishly follows the original order of *Confessio* nor attempts to analyze every narrative or even every book of the text. Such an undertaking would be mammoth and repetitive. What this study does do is to identify three central and interrelated concerns in Gower's major English poem and to explore and to contextualize his treatment of them: language, sex, and politics. This detailed analysis of Gower's *Confessio* will enable me to make larger points about the representation of sex and gender at the end of the Middle Ages. It will also enable me to address issues such as the instability of England in the realm of Richard II and the status of the vernacular at the end of the fourteenth century.

Before directly addressing the treatment of language, sex, and politics in *Confessio Amantis,* I consider in the Introduction the questions of Gower's background (especially his class and social position), of his intellectual circle and changing political affiliations, and of the relationship between the implied and actual audiences of *Confessio.* In so doing I reconsider Gower's literary relationship with Chaucer. I go on to outline briefly the reception of *Confessio* in the fifteenth century and thereafter before considering, in the second half of the chapter, what we might term the material reality of the poem. Part I is concerned primarily with issues of language and style. The link between language, gender, and ethics was well established in the Middle Ages. Chapters 1 and 2, for example, make a connection between Gower's writing and that of Alain de Lille, who famously argues in *De Planctu Naturae* that grammatical barbarisms detract from masculinity. According to Alain, errors in grammatical gender are associated with immorality and sodomy, and rhetorical language has the power to corrupt. This text, with which Gower was clearly familiar, had a profound impact on his writing. Chapter 1 investigates the language and gender politics implicit in *Confessio Amantis* in relation to Gower's Latin and Anglo-Norman writings. I argue that what might be characterized as the queer gender play of *Confessio* links sexual confusion to linguistic indeterminacy and associates both with division and sin. Chapter 2 continues my exploration of Gower's politics of language and style by focusing on the subject of rhetoric and connecting this to Gower's own construction of his authorial role. In this chapter, my primary concern is the way in which Gower's construction of rhetoric can be seen to be both gendered and sexualized, especially when read alongside other classical and medieval discussions of the subject. In both chapters, the immediate historical context of the poem is relevant to the discussion. The linguistic play in *Confessio* betrays the author's anxieties about the instability of language and the communication of knowledge. One context for these anxieties is the Peasants' Revolt of 1381, another is the Oxford Translation Debate and the intense disputes that preceded it about the role of the vernacular. Equally significantly, hostile critics attributed the vices with which rhetoric was associated—insincerity, mas-

querade, effeminacy, even sodomy—to the court of Richard II. I suggest
that the elision of the Ricardian Prologue may reflect Gower's concerns
about patronage and reputation.

Part II concentrates on the relationship between gender, sexuality,
and personal ethics in *Confessio*. In line with current feminist theory, I
see gender as central to hierarchies of power. This section is concerned
with ethical self-control, or self-government, and the exercise of power
over others in the field of erotic love. Chapters 3 and 4 look at some of
the ways in which gender and sex distinctions are constructed and de-
constructed in the text through stories of effeminacy, transgendering,
transsexuality, female homosexuality, incest, and rape, and through their
corresponding morals (in English and in Latin). Chapter 3 focuses initially
on the frame narrative of *Confessio*—specifically the relationship between
Genius and Amans—and on a series of exemplary narratives embedded
within the text of *Confessio* which are centered around problems of gender confusion. This analysis reveals that although Gower does not shy
away from discussing some forms of gender transgression (including
female masculinity) and sexual subversion, male sodomy remains taboo
throughout. I examine the meaning of Genius's silence on this subject
and relate it to prohibitions against discussing the topic found in confessional literature more generally, and to the political aspects of the
poem. *Confessio* contains a surprising number of stories about incest,
rape, and seduction. Indeed such stories could be said to be central to
the work as a whole. Nevertheless, they are complex and often contradictory. In Chapter 4, I examine the accounts of Venus's birth and her
union with her son, alongside the Tales of Tereus, Mundus and Paulina,
and Nectanabus. Here I am concerned with accountability for sexual sin
and with the question of how this is gendered: while women have to
take responsibility for their own actions, men are condemned for taking
advantage of others. I am also concerned with the inconsistencies in the
depiction of such sin: both incest and rape, it appears, can be simultaneously reprehensible and redemptive.

In Part III my main focus is the exercise of power in the field of politics. Chapter 5 takes as its starting point the apocalyptic opening of
Confessio and the monstrous image of Nebuchadnezzar's statue. I am
principally interested here in Gower's depictions of kingship and go on
to consider Gower's portrait of Alexander the Great and, in this context,
to think about the instruction that Alexander the Great received from

Aristotle, which is related in Book VII. I link this discussion to an analysis of the Tales of Lucrece and Virginia, both of which draw clear parallels between rape and bad government. Gower condemns tyranny and argues for self-regulation and self-reform on the part of the king, but offers no challenge to the existing political structures. Chapter 6 focuses on the climax of *Confessio:* Book VIII and Genius's Tale of Apollonius of Tyre. This narrative is on one level concerned with the satisfaction of "legitimate" male appetites and the frustration of appetites judged to be illegitimate or feminine, while on another it admits the possibility of an autonomous female sexuality. Gower's version acknowledges the importance of women—as wives and as mothers—within the patriarchal household and points to the indispensability of women and femininity in ethics and politics. The tale offers criticism of the monarch in its portrayal of Apollonius, who is implicated in the crimes of incest and sodomy, and who, like Alexander and other political characters discussed in the previous chapter, misuses his knowledge and power. The chapter concludes by revisiting the narrative framework and considering the ethical and political implications of the author's decision to merge his own authorial persona with the figures of Amans, Alexander, and ultimately Richard II himself.

The Epilogue examines some of the ways in which Gower represents himself and his literary project. Gower's poetic persona in *Confessio* is notoriously divided between the serious and the playful: he is prophet, teacher, political commentator, philosophical poet, and (at the end of the poem at least) aged and unsuccessful lover. Here I argue that the disunities and internal contradictions (including the failure to prioritize lore over love) that mark the poem as a whole undercut its moral project. In the final analysis, the poem may be political, but it is not ethical, because, while it may warn against unreasonable conduct, it fails to give straightforward and coherent guidance about either how to govern or how to live one's life. Gower's treatment of language, sex, and politics is symptomatic of his perception of the division of the world. Gower's *Confessio* is therefore less an examination of human sin than a literary and intellectual engagement with it. While on many levels appearing to stand for truth and order, the poem partakes of the world's inevitable disorder.

INTRODUCTION

SOCIAL GOWER

SOCIAL GOWER

Relatively few documents relating to Gower's life have survived.[1] His birth is generally dated to 1330 or thereabouts. He may have been born in Yorkshire, but was brought up in Kent and West Suffolk. His social background was similar to Chaucer's in that he was from an affluent middle-class family and connected in some way to the royal court.[2] Like Chaucer, he held the rank of *esquier.* However, unlike Chaucer, he does not seem to have been a member of the king's household, or to have been in the employment of the government. Gower himself was most probably a lawyer by profession, and consequently he was no doubt more able than Chaucer to choose and to switch his political loyalties. Gower was also a country landowner. Records of his property transactions have come down to us, and one of these seems to have been of dubious legality, although his claim was ultimately upheld.[3] In the 1370s, he became involved in the rebuilding of the Priory of St. Mary Overeys in Southwark, where he lived in his old age. In his last years Gower, whose eyesight had been declining for some considerable time, suffered a great deal of infirmity. On 23 January 1398, in other words when he was almost seventy years of age, he married Agnes Groundolf. He died ten years later between 15 August (the date of his will) and 24 October 1408 (when probate was obtained).

Gower's literary career spanned most of the second half of his life, although he was most active between around 1374 right up until 1400, when he went blind. In this period he was writing and revising his major works in Anglo-Norman, Latin, and English, which were, in roughly

1

chronological order (the revisions complicate this pattern somewhat),
Mirour de l'Omme, Vox Clamantis, and *Confessio Amantis.* This period coincides with his connection with the Priory of St. Mary Overeys, which
John Fisher believes provided Gower with a library and scriptorium, although this idea has been convincingly challenged.[4] This period begins
in the final years of the reign of Edward III (1327–77) and spans the
reign of Richard II (1377–99). Major national and international events
that took place in these years include the death of Edward's son and heir,
Edward the Black Prince, and crisis between the king and Commons in
the Good Parliament (both in 1376), and the start of the Great Schism
(1378). The following decade saw the Peasants' Revolt (1381), the condemnation of John Wycliffe's views (1382), the Wonderful and Merciless Par-
liaments (1386 and 1388), and the assertion of Richard II's majority in
1389. The relative peace of the first half of the 1390s did not last, and
that decade culminated in Richard II's "tyranny," and in the death of
John of Gaunt, deposition of Richard II, and accession of Henry IV (in
1399). One of the aims of this study is to demonstrate how contemporary political affairs impinged on Gower's writing, and especially how
Gower's changing views of Richard II are reflected in *Confessio.*[5] Equally
significantly, however, the period 1374–1400 coincides with Gower's
interaction with an intellectual and literary group of friends. This circle
included Chaucer, as well as the philosopher and lawyer Ralph Strode.[6]
Connected to it were the poets Thomas Usk and, somewhat later, Thomas
Hoccleve, both minor civil servants.[7] It has been posited that Gower's
circle was active at least until Chaucer gave up position as Controller of
the Customhouse and his lease of his London dwelling in 1386. With
Strode's death in 1387 and Usk's execution for treason in 1388 (following the Merciless Parliament), any remaining members of the group
may well have drifted apart.[8] However, Chaucer returned to the city in
1389, when he was appointed Clerk of the King's Works. Hoccleve, who
was too young to have been an active member of the group in the mid-
1380s (he did not actually take up his position in the Privy Seal until
1387–88) probably joined a reconstituted group at around this time. As
we shall see, there is strong evidence to support the hypothesis that the
exchange of ideas between Chaucer and Gower continued well into the
early 1390s.[9] It is likely that in the last decades of Gower's life, his circle
was, if not identical to that of Chaucer (before his death in 1400), at
least comparable to it in terms of the occupations and social positions of

some of its members. It may, for example, have included figures such as John Hend or Hende, a wealthy draper who became mayor of London in 1391–92 and again in 1404. Gower's will provides us with the names of his wife and other close friends, two of whom have been identified.[10] One executor was William Denne (or Donne or Doune) who, like Hoccleve, had been a Clerk in the Privy Seal in the late 1380s and 1390s. He was appointed canon of the King's Free Chapel of St. Stephen within the Palace of Westminster in 1399. Another executor was Sir Arnald Savage. He had been a member of Richard II's household, became Speaker for the House of Commons in 1401 and 1404, and later joined Henry IV's continual council.

Although the *Mirour de l'Omme* exists in only one manuscript, suggesting that it was not widely circulated, and is often taken to be a work of private meditation, Gower's oeuvre as a whole implies an extremely wide readership.[11] *Vox Clamantis*, for example, asserts at VII.1469 that what is written is the voice of the people. Yet, it would be a mistake to identify too readily the implied and the actual audience of the poem;[12] at any rate Gower's commonality should not be taken to include the lower and peasant classes that he castigates so vociferously.[13] Likewise, the first version of *Confessio Amantis* claims to be penned at the request of and for Richard II himself, and the poem as a whole undoubtedly "bespeak[s] a courtly ambience," as Michael Bennett expresses it.[14] Nevertheless, in Anne Middleton's opinion, Gower's poem is intended to have a wider appeal and "the king is not the main imagined audience, but an occasion for gathering and formulating what is on the common mind."[15] Indeed, although *Confessio* is in part (Book VII) an advice to princes, it is conceivable that the dedicatees of the poem are not actually any more than "fictional" readers. The consistent juxtaposition of political macrocosm and social microcosm in the poem makes it clear that at some levels at least the figure of the prince or king is everyman, and the counsel offered in the book is directed at the citizenry at large. It is significant that the poem in its revised form not only develops its praise of the future Henry IV, but also addresses the English nation itself. Nonetheless, it seems that by the end of Gower's literary career, his intended and also his actual audience had changed, perhaps gradually, but significantly.[16] In the last decade of the fourteenth century, Gower certainly benefited from his transferral of political allegiance. In 1393 Henry of Derby presented Gower with a collar, possibly to acknowledge a gift of a presentation copy of the newly rededicated *Confessio*. Shortly after his accession to the throne in 1399, the new king awarded Gower an annual grant of two pipes of wine at the port of London. Gower's Latin poem, *Cronica Tripertita*, which was written shortly afterwards, is clearly a work of Lancastrian propaganda. Kate Harris's study of the ownership of late-fourteenth- and fifteenth-century manuscripts of *Confessio Amantis* reveals that the poem was highly regarded by the House of Lancaster.[17]

I propose however that at the time when he began composing *Confessio Amantis* (around 1386 or 1387), Gower was writing, in the first instance, not for the king and higher court circles or the realm of England as a whole, but for the members of the group described above. It was this circle that was intended to provide Gower with his immediate, although not, of course, his only, readership. Gower's circle of the mid-1380s corresponds to the assumed audience of *Confessio Amantis*, which included educated men of the gentry class as well as the aristocracy. If Gower's revisions of *Confessio* reflect his increasing dissatisfaction with Richard II, his expectations of his core readership remained constant. Like Chaucer, when he wrote *Troilus and Criseyde* and the *Canterbury Tales*, Gower was writing primarily for an audience of near social-equals and an audience of literary competence, an audience capable of reading with sensitivity and sophistication. Like Chaucer, then, he wrote for readers with "an implied literary 'horizon' of some refinement."[18]

The centrality of Chaucer to Gower's circle is evidenced by the close personal and literary relationship that existed between the two poets. In 1378, in preparation for his second diplomatic journey to Italy, Chaucer named Gower as one of his legal attorneys. Then, sometime around 1386, Chaucer completed *Troilus and Criseyde*, which included in the penultimate stanza the famous dedication:

> O moral Gower, this book I directe
> To the and to the, philosophical Strode,
> To vouchen sauf, ther nede is, to correcte,
> Of youre benignites and zeles goode. (V.1856–59)

I will return shortly to consider the full implications of these lines, which entrust the preservation and interpretation of the poem to two men whom we can take to be among the author's closest friends. Here, however, I wish simply to place them in the broader context of the literary relationship between Chaucer and Gower. Around 1390, Gower was to return Chaucer's compliment in the first version of *Confessio Amantis,* in which he has the goddess of love praise Chaucer as her own disciple and poet for, in his youth, filling the land with "Ditees" and "songes glade" (*VIII.2945). Gower also has Venus instruct him to give Chaucer this message:

> "That he upon his latere age,
> To sette an ende of alle his werk,
> As he which is myn owne clerk,
> Do make his testament of love,
> As thou hast do thi schrifte above,
> So that mi Court it may recorde." (*VIII.2952–57)

Gower's *Confessio Amantis* and Chaucer's *Legend of Good Women* have long been recognized to have been produced in a spirit of what Lynn Staley terms "collaborative competition,"[19] and Fisher believes that with these lines Gower seriously intended to encourage Chaucer to bring *The Legend* ("his testament of love") to completion.[20] Given the current critical consensus that Chaucer did not simply abandon *The Legend* out of boredom, in order to move onto his next and more inspiring project, *The Canterbury Tales,* this view is hardly tenable.[21] If Gower was indeed referring to *The Legend,* he must have been aware of Chaucer's intentions concerning that work. More provocatively, Elizabeth Allen contends that these lines constitute "a specific challenge to Chaucer's notorious political reticence," that Gower "now charges his fellow-poet to take a personal stance."[22] But however we take it, as intended seriously or humorously, we can be sure of one thing: that the reproach of Chaucer implicit in Gower's eulogy contributed to the legend of a feud between the two poets.[23]

Traditionally, the strongest evidence for the view that Gower and Chaucer quarreled sometime in the 1390s is the fact that Gower cut the lines in praise of Chaucer from *Confessio* in his rewritings of the poem. Gower, supposedly horrified by *The Canterbury Tales,* and especially by its more coarse narratives, expressed his disappointment in and disapproval of his fellow poet's new literary enterprise through his silence.[24] It has also been suggested that Gower recognized in Chaucer's poem a number of far-from-complementary allusions to himself and his own

work. The least contentious of these occurs in the Introduction to the Man
of Law's Tale, in which the sententious pilgrim famously dismisses what
are taken to be Gower's versions of the stories of Canace and Machaire
and of Apollonius of Tyre (both incest narratives) as "swiche unkynde
abhomynacions" (88). In the course of the Tale itself, he then implicitly
criticizes Gower's retelling of the Constance legend.[25] Some critics have
identified other references to Gower in *The Canterbury Tales*. Fisher, for
example, sees a possible allusion to Gower in Chaucer's portrait of the
Man of Law himself.[26] More convincing, perhaps, is Steven Justice's recent
argument concerning the Nun's Priest's Tale. It has been acknowledged
for some time that this fable may include a passing snipe at Gower's
representation of the revolting peasants of 1381 in the first book of *Vox
Clamantis* in the fable's description of the commotion of the farmyard
animals.[27] Justice goes much further and posits that Chaucer actually offers a caricature of Gower in the depiction of the uxorious dreaming
cock, Chauntecleer.[28] Interesting though these ideas may be, they can
however be little more than hypotheses. Even if we accept that Chaucer
did make a series of references to Gower in his *Canterbury Tales,* we can
never be certain how Gower reacted to them. Pearsall possibly under-
states the case in his succinct summation that "the quarrel of Gower
and Chaucer makes a good story, but it may well be fiction."[29] A more
feasible explanation for the deletion of the Chaucer eulogy from *Confessio* is that offered by Anne Middleton: that as the *Confessio* reached a
wider audience, such "coterie" references were no longer appropriate to
the poem.[30] One of the influencing factors in his revisions to *Confessio*
then may have been that Gower began to envisage his poem being circulated among the wider populace.[31] In other words, he saw it moving
beyond the readership that he had addressed in the first instance and
reaching one unacquainted with members of his own group, their interaction with one another, their politics, and their literary politics. Furthermore, as I will suggest in the next chapter, this more remote and
less predictable audience could have been one whose response may have
been less sophisticated and less "safe."

My interpretation of the literary relationship between Gower and
Chaucer is rather different from those accounts offered hitherto. Gower's
ostensible celebration of Chaucer in the first version of *Confessio* has to
be understood in terms of competitive anxieties about authorship and
influence that pervade his poem (a point developed in Chapter 2 in rela-

tion to Gower's debt to Brunetto Latini). Gower, in including a message (however flippantly intended) to Chaucer concerning his literary output, represents himself as a poet who has completed his life's work. At the same time, Chaucer is figured as his successor, a poet who is expected to follow Gower's own example. On the evidence of the passages discussed so far, there can be no doubt that, as Paul Strohm suggests in relation to Chaucer, both poets consciously establish themselves as part of the same interpretative community.[32] Yet I would disagree with Strohm's opinion that the allusion to Gower at the end of *Troilus and Criseyde* is simply intended to anchor the final meaning of the text by orientating it to a specific audience. If we look again at the terms Chaucer uses to describe Gower and Strode, his two ideal readers ("moral" and "philosophical"), and the virtues he conjures up in them ("benignites and zeles goode"), we can see his anxieties being betrayed, anxieties that concern the text and its interpretation. It is evident that Chaucer, or his authorial persona, is fully aware that his poem could reach another kind of reader altogether, a reader not informed by morality and philosophy, a reader *not* motivated by kindness, generosity, and mercy; in other words, a reader motivated by "zeles badde."[33] It is even possible that Gower and Strode themselves, driven by the wrong sort of enthusiasm, could misread the poem. Chaucer, in entrusting his text, at the end of *Troilus and Criseyde,* to two "actual" members of his fictional audience, and two of his closest and presumably most sympathetic and receptive literary associates, acknowledges the instability of meaning. He does this because he knows that "real" readers—no matter how moral or philosophical—are beyond his intervention and cannot be so easily controlled. In the preceding stanzas, Chaucer expresses unease about reading and misreading (as he does throughout the poem), reflecting on the possibilities either that mistakes will be made in the transmission of his verses or that they will be misunderstood (*Troilus and Criseyde,* V.1793–98). Furthermore in surrendering himself in his concluding lines to the mercy of the "sothfast Crist" (*Troilus and Criseyde,* V.1860), the only reliable source of truth, he admits the futility of any earthly attempt to control interpretation.

It is timely, then, to remember that the community evoked by both Chaucer and Gower is as likely to be united by interpretative disagreement as by interpretative harmony.[34] The implied or intended and the actual audiences of Gower's *Confessio Amantis* are similar to those of *Troilus and Criseyde,* and perhaps especially *The Canterbury Tales,* even though the text produced is very different from either of these poems. In his conflicting descriptions of Gower as both "moral" in the sense of being "an author concerned with morality,"[35] and also, in his retellings of tales of incest, "immoral," Chaucer is responding on a sophisticated level to the ethical ambiguities in his fellow poet's writing. These were, as I will argue throughout this study, ambiguities of which Gower himself was aware, and that he consciously intended. As Allen puts it, Gower offers his audience "a profound aesthetic and moral challenge."[36]

RECEPTION

In the context of a consideration of Gower's audience and readership, it is useful to follow through audience responses to *Confessio*, to examine briefly the reception of Gower in the late fourteenth and early fifteenth century and beyond, and to compare it to constructions of Chaucer and his texts. To begin, let me look in more detail at what Chaucer's Man of Law actually says in his apology for Chaucer's poetry—the "Seintes Legende of Cupide" (61), usually taken to be *The Legend of Good Women*—and his dismissal of Gower's *Confessio Amantis:*

> "But certeinly no word ne writeth he [Chaucer]
> Of thilke wikke ensample of Canacee,
> That loved hir owene brother synfully—
> Of swiche cursed stories I sey fy!—
> Or ellis of Tyro Appollonius,
> How that the cursed kyng Antiochus
> Birafte his doghter of hir maydenhede,
> That is so horrible a tale for to rede,
> Whan he hir threw upon the pavement.
> And therfore he, of ful avysement,
> Nolde nevere write in none of his sermons
> Of swich unkynde abhomynacions,
> Ne I wol noon reherce, if that I may." (77–89)

This is clearly a comic and self-ironic passage.[37] The Man of Law's account of Gower's tale attributes to it a scene that does not take place:

Antiochus in the *Confessio* does not rape his daughter on "the pavement."
Similarly the preceding description of the contents of *The Legend of Good
Women* is not exactly accurate.[38] The Man of Law is clearly figured as a
misreader, and also, in the narrative that follows, as a blinkered storyteller.[39] But what the Man of Law does succeed in doing is isolating two
of the tales of *Confessio* that were to become particularly familiar to late-
twentieth-century readers: the Tale of Canace and Machaire and the Tale
of Antiochus. That he should comment on the Tale of Antiochus, which
occupies most of Book VIII, should come as no surprise to us: this is
the last and the longest narrative in the whole collection. But the Tale of
Canace and Machaire (III.143–336) comes early in the collection and
does not stand out in structural terms. Indeed the reason this tale has
gained more attention in recent years than many others in *Confessio* is
the gap between the exemplum and its moral: the narrative describes
the sexual relationship between brother and sister, while the moral condemns the uncontrolled anger of the father on its discovery.[40] (Similar
problems emerge in the Tale of Apollonius, as is revealed in my own
analysis in Chapter 6.) Outside the comments of the Man of Law, there
is little other evidence to suggest that the Tale of Canace and Machaire
was particularly remarked upon in Gower's own time or in the century
after his death. Strohm has written about the "narrowing" of the Chaucer tradition in the fifteenth century, which coincided with the broaden-
ing of his "secondary" audience to include the emerging middle-class
reading public.[41] Strohm argues that the most popular of Chaucer's poetry
in this period—advice to princes, moral works, and poetry concerned
with *fin amour*—was that which was least experimental, reflecting the
conservative taste of the audience of the time. In an earlier article, David
Lawton makes a similar observation, commenting that "the Chaucer of
the fifteenth century is unusually austere."[42] It is plausible that a similar
narrowing of the Gower tradition occurred, and that its influence on modern perceptions has been greater. Certainly, Gower's audience widened
socially, and also geographically, throughout the fifteenth century. Pearsall
notes that copies of the poem appeared in the libraries of monasteries
and the collections of London merchants and country gentry, as well as
those of the aristocracy.[43] At the same time, the Latin elements of the
poem were increasingly minimized, and consequently some of the more
difficult and intriguing aspects of the poem were lost to generations of

readers.[44] While Chaucer may have been aware of the sophistication of Gower's *Confessio* (the Man of Law's choice of such problematic tales is itself evidence of this),[45] many of his successors evidently were not.

Fisher laments that "it has been the fate of John Gower to appear to succeeding ages almost constantly in the company of Geoffrey Chaucer."[46] From the fifteenth century through to the eighteenth, from James I in *The Kingis Quair* to Philip Sidney and on to Samuel Johnson, both poets were praised for their rhetoric and eloquence and celebrated for their innovation as the first writers to compose in the vernacular.[47] Yet, it is far from clear that for many of the writers who mention him, Gower was anything more than a name with which to conjure. While poets such as Usk, Hoccleve, and Lydgate may have been indebted to his poetry in various ways, either directly or indirectly, Gower simply did not have Chaucer's followers and imitators.[48] His *Confessio* was mainly celebrated not as a poem about love, but for its moral value because, as William Caxton put it, it was "ful of sentence."[49] Yet there were real readers whose response to Gower's poetry was closer to that of the Man of Law. John Walton of Osney, in his ca. 1410 translation of Boethius, had his reservations about *Confessio* and especially its concern with pagan deities. He warned the reader:

> For certaynly it nedeþ noght at all
> To whette now þe dartes of cupide,
> Ne for to bidde þat venus be oure gyde
> So þat we may oure foule lustes wynne
> Onaunter leste þe same on us betide
> As dede þe same venus for hire synne.[50]

I will discuss in a later chapter Alexander Barclay's condemnation (written around 1523) of *Confessio* as a "thing wanton, not sad but insolent."[51] George Puttenham (1589) also dismissed the substance of Gower's poetry, in part because "the applications of his moralities are ... many times very grossely bestowed."[52] Other later readers, albeit largely responding to Gower's perceived political opportunism, have also opposed the dominant construction of "moral" and even "manly" Gower with accusations of instability and what amounts to effeminacy.[53] Furthermore, while the excerpted manuscripts and anthologies containing tales from *Confessio* may reveal little about patterns of reader response to the poem,[54] Kate Harris has suggested that annotations of manuscripts to *Confessio* often indicate a heightened interest in the more racy narratives.[55] This pattern may also be reflected in the illustrations of New York, Pierpont Morgan Library MS M.126 (dated ca. 1470), which tend to be of a violent and salacious nature.[56] The response of Gower's readership as a whole seems to have been a divided one, reflecting (often perhaps subconsciously) the complexity of both the poem itself, which invites conflicting interpretations and contradictory reactions, and its textual history. This a point to which I will now turn.

THE POEM

There is not one late medieval English poem, *Confessio Amantis*, by John Gower, but there are many *Confessiones Amantis*. There are forty-nine complete or near complete manuscripts of *Confessio*.[57] Although one manuscript, Oxford, Bodleian Library MS Fairfax 3, is often considered to be Gower's "final official version" of the poem, the textual history of *Confessio* is nonetheless a fairly complicated one.[58] Leaving aside for a moment the finer points of bibliographic and manuscript traditions and focusing instead simply on content, the most obvious way of classifying the poem is in terms of its changing dedications. There are, in summary, two principal forms: that version of the poem that praises Richard II and claims to be written at his request, and that which celebrates Henry of Derby, the future Henry IV. These are commonly known as the Ricardian and the Lancastrian texts, respectively. It is fairly clear that having written the poem for King Richard in the first instance, Gower himself subsequently revised the poem, and that the changing dedications reflect in some way the poet's own changing political allegiances.[59] Peter Nicholson has contested this view, believing that "Gower's political concerns had little to do with the rededication; that his relationship with both men at the time of the presentation was literary rather than political in nature."[60] While I do not share Nicholson's opinion on this point, I nonetheless agree that we have, as Nicholson puts it, "two equally authoritative versions to choose from."[61] One is certainly, as Nicholson states, "closer to the original moment of composition," but the other (and here

I borrow James Simpson's formulation) reflects "Gower's final, and certain disillusionment with Richard."[62] Neither version should, I suggest, automatically take precedence over the other.

It would be misleading moreover to think of the Ricardian text of the poem as in any concrete sense "earlier" than the Lancastrian one. In actual fact some of the earliest surviving manuscripts of *Confessio* (San Marino, California, Huntington Library MS Ellesmere 26.A.17, known as the "Stafford Manuscript"; and MS Fairfax 3), which were probably produced during or immediately after the reign of Richard, are dedicated to Henry, earl of Derby. Meanwhile, most of the manuscripts copied in the early fifteenth century, after Richard's overthrow and Henry IV's accession, preserve the dedication to the deposed king (indeed this version of the poem continued to be copied in the mid- and late fifteenth century).[63] Three deluxe manuscripts of the Ricardian version of *Confessio* (including the Stafford Manuscript, thought by some to be a presentation copy given to Henry of Derby in 1392–93)[64] were actually owned by princes of the House of Lancaster.[65] In other words, the very labels Ricardian and Lancastrian are useful but potentially misleading.

Running alongside this two-text system of categorization is Macaulay's three-recension classification.[66] Macaulay argued that the changes to the prologue of the poem are not the most reliable indicator of textual tradition. He contended that Gower's process of revision was in fact stepped, taking place over the period ca. 1390–93. He proposed that the first recension of the poem is best distinguished by its inclusion of praise of Richard II in its epilogue.[67] The second recension adds passages to Books V and VII, rearranges Book VI, replaces praise of the king in the conclusion with a prayer for the state of England, and, in some versions, changes the prefatory dedication to Henry. The third recension has the revised prologue and conclusion, but in other respects follows the original form of the poem. As mentioned above, most manuscripts in the second and third recensions also cut a *coterie* reference to Chaucer found in Book VIII of the first recension. For Macaulay however the first recension can be further subdivided into three stages: unrevised, intermediary, revised; and the second recension has at least two distinct forms. MS Fairfax 3 is classified by Macaulay as third recension, but is, as he notes, a revised first recension manuscript.[68] Just as the once widely held view that Gower oversaw the production of copies of the poem in a personal scriptorium at the Priory of St. Mary Overeys in Southwark is no longer completely tenable, so the three-recension system has now been challenged in a series of articles by Peter Nicholson.[69] Nicholson is surely correct to argue for a large degree of scribal intervention, that some of the most important second- and third-recension manuscripts are composite texts, and that the third recension is in many ways "merely the accidental product of several different layers of textual history."[70] Nevertheless, provided that we do not assume that all the changes are authorial, Macaulay's method of organization of the manuscripts is still a serviceable and no doubt necessary tool.[71]

A third way of classifying the texts of *Confessio Amantis* is by examining what Joel Fredell has termed its "design strategy" or the layout of the Latin and English elements of the poem.[72] Derek Pearsall lists four different types of Latin in this "vernacular" poem.[73] First, there are the Latin verses, which introduce sections and subsections throughout the poem, and which Macaulay prints in italics in the text column.[74] Second, there are the prose commentaries or glosses (the latter a slightly misleading term, which I nonetheless adopt out of convenience), which serve a variety of functions, and which Macaulay (following the layout of MS Fairfax 3) prints in the margins.[75] It is usually assumed that Gower himself wrote not only the verses but also the commentary.[76] The status of the remaining two categories is less clear. The third is made up of other occasional glosses, principally speaker markers (indicating different stages in the poem's dialogic frame), and these Macaulay also prints in the margins.[77] The fourth is made up of the Latin verse, rubric, and colophon, which appear at the end of many manuscripts of the poem, and which conclude Macaulay's edition of the poem itself (often alongside other appended material, which Macaulay edits in his volume of Gower's Latin works).[78] Siân Echard adds to these four categories of Latin other types of manuscript apparatus, which she refers to as an "indexing tool," some of which Macaulay reproduces in some form alongside his own editorial innovations.[79] Richard Emmerson has recently challenged the tendency of scholars "to overemphasize the 'marginal' nature" of the poem's Latin elements, and especially of its prose commentary.[80] He explains, for example, that many manuscripts of *Confessio Amantis,* and indeed most of those unrevised and intermediate first-recension manuscripts, locate the Latin commentary as well as the Latin verse within the text columns.[81] In contrast, revised first-recension, second-recension, and third-recension manuscripts tend to place the commentary in the margins ("Gower's

own design for the poem" according to Emmerson[82]) or even to omit it
altogether. Such manuscripts he believes represent "a more English
Gower."[83] Emmerson speculates that the different treatments of Gower's
Latin in *Confessio* reflect changes in reading practices and in readership.[84]
In his analysis, certain early, illustrated, manuscripts (which marginal-
ize the commentaries) were designed to aid public reading. Other manuscripts (which place the apparatus in a dominant position) were more
probably intended for private silent study. And he suggests that "with
the passing of public reading and in the more modest circumstances of
merchant-class readers . . . manuscripts came to emphasize the English
poem."[85]

The fourth (related) way of classifying the texts of *Confessio Amantis*
is to examine the illustrations. Of the manuscripts of *Confessio Amantis,*
some twenty are illustrated.[86] These illustrations take two principal forms.
Eighteen illustrated manuscripts include near the beginning of the poem
either one or both of the following two miniatures:[87] one illustrates the
frame narrative of *Confessio Amantis* and represents the confession of
the lover, Amans, kneeling before the priest Genius; the other illustrates
the biblical story of King Nebuchadnezzar's dream concerning the destruction of a statue by a rock (Daniel 2; recounted and explicated in
Confessio Amantis Prol.602–1052). The latter is often referred to as the
Dream of Precious Metals. A number of critics have postulated that
Gower himself may have had some influence over these illustrations.[88]
The confession miniature is, at least at first glance, fairly static in its
subject matter, although the details of representation vary,[89] and it can
either appear as a kind of frontispiece at the beginning of Book I or as
an illustration within it.[90] Nonetheless, John Burrow has pointed out
that the appearance of Amans differs markedly in the various examples
of this miniature.[91] Some represent Amans as a fashionable young lover,
as he arguably appears for much of the poem. A bizarre and unique example of this type occurs in London, British Library MS Add. Harley
3869, in which Amans appears as an elaborately dressed figure in a
large brown hat, engaged in earnest conversation with his priest (Figure
1). Others depict Amans as Gower himself and anticipate the climax of
the poem, which centers on the revelation that Amans/Gower is too old
for the pursuit of love (first mentioned by Venus at VIII.2367–71).
Jeremy Griffiths shares Burrow's opinion that Gower was not responsible for the confessor miniature, on the grounds that "to decide to illus-

Figure 1. Amans and Genius. London British Library MS Add. Harley 3869, fol. 18r (detail).
Reprinted by permission of the British Library, London.

trate the Lover in a Confessor miniature is to have to commit oneself
to the question of his age" and thus to spoil the suspense of the poem,
although this is a view that has its opponents.[92] The dream miniature
can also take one of two quite distinct forms.[93] The first represents
Nebuchadnezzar in bed, alongside a depiction of the statue, the subject
of his dream. According to Emmerson, manuscript evidence indicates
that this "must represent the original design of the miniature."[94] This
form of miniature also often appears as a frontispiece to the poem as a
whole. The second form of the miniature omits the king and includes
only the statue. This form is usually integrated into the text column,
placed close to the passage illustrated.

　　Recent critics have tended to agree that manuscript reception largely
dictates the different forms and positions of the miniatures, but diverge
as to the exact causes. As we will see in Chapter 5, Fredell believes that
political factors influenced the change in the form of this miniature
(an argument for which I have considerable sympathy).[95] Emmerson
disagrees, contending that the shifts in reading practices outlined above
are sufficient to account for it, the frontispiece illustrations being appropriate for display at a public reading.[96] Whatever we decide on this
issue, it is surely fair to conclude, as Emmerson does, that the two main
types of miniature "do not so much illustrate the poem as introduce
and highlight its major concerns," whether these be macrocosmic or

microcosmic, concerned with history or with love.⁹⁷ A further tradition of
manuscript illustration is the author portrait, which is found in two manuscripts, and which seems quite distinct despite the obvious relationship in terms of subject representation with those confessor miniatures
that depict Amans as a *senex amans*.⁹⁸ There are also two unique later
manuscripts that include a whole series of miniatures: New York, Pierpont Morgan Library MS M.126, and Oxford, New College MS c.266.⁹⁹
Emmerson observes that the former links the miniatures to the Latin
commentary, and illustrates the entire poem (including the mirror for
princes' section, Book VII), while the latter "treats the *Confessio* primarily as an English collection of love stories to be read privately."¹⁰⁰

It must be apparent from this albeit oversimplistic account of the
poem's textual and manuscript history that critical opinion concerning
the extent of Gower's control over his own text and its production varies
greatly. There is a school of critics that has worked under the assumptions that the poet maintained a tight control over the design and the
copying of *Confessio,* and over the establishment of his own authoritative
voice within the text itself.¹⁰¹ More recently however, the research of A. I.
Doyle and Malcolm Parkes, Siân Echard, Jeremy Griffiths, and others
has questioned sometimes one and occasionally both of these hypotheses, with varying degrees of ferocity and conciliation. We have already
seen, for example, that scribes, illustrators, readers, as well as changes
in reading patterns may have had their impact on the content and appearance, indeed the physical makeup, of the text. In her provocative
and convincing essay, "With Carmen's Help," Echard puts forward the
suggestion that what she refers to as the "vagaries of manuscript production" only serve to highlight and to intensify tensions within *Confessio
Amantis* itself.¹⁰² She also remarks that the *Confessio Amantis* "appears to
be about control—of interpretation of texts, of tongues," and goes on to
state that "this appearance of control *is* merely appearance."¹⁰³ Echard's
main concern in this particular essay is with the competing and often
conflicting English and Latin voices in the poem. It is certainly true to say
that with a text like *Confessio Amantis* it is impossible to read the poem
apart from its textual tradition, because we "read through the interpretative lens created by the layout of a particular witness."¹⁰⁴ And it is important to acknowledge that this is equally applicable to those of us who
rely on Macaulay's edition (which emphasizes the Lancastrian frame
over the Ricardian one, for example) or a modern classroom text,¹⁰⁵ and

to those who read early-modern printed texts, or relied on translations or extracts of *Confessio Amantis* or selections reproduced in sixteenth-century commonplace books.[106]

Having said this, it is equally important to acknowledge that the early-twenty-first century reader, who is aware that there is no single definitive text of *Confessio Amantis* and who (with the aid of the insights of others) has some understanding of its textual history and traditions, does in a sense create her or his own mental hypertext. Indeed, it seems that the actual hypertext simply makes a virtual reality of the mental processes of centuries of readers of a certain type. (I would include here those scribes who found themselves working from a number of exempla, and alongside other copyists and illuminators and so on.) In many respects *Confessio Amantis* is not dissimilar to other medieval texts with complex manuscript traditions and/or that survive in two or more recognizably distinct versions. Here, prominent examples are *The Canterbury Tales, Piers Plowman,* and also the *Divine Revelations* of Julian of Norwich (though the problems each of these texts present are unique). Like these works, *Confessio* invites the following questions. What text(s) are we reading? Whose text is it anyway? Is the text the author's or the reader's (editor's), both or neither? And following Echard's lead, I suggest that it is not only the textual history of *Confessio Amantis* but the poem itself, with all its multivalency and tensions, that invites these questions. Like the study of any medieval text, modern scholarship on *Confessio Amantis* depends upon and could not exist without editorial and bibliographical research. Such research not only provides us with a text to work with, but also gives us essential information about the production, circulation, and reception of that text from its inception to the present day. But just as there is no single definitive authorial text of *Confessio Amantis,* so there cannot and should not be one single definitive reading of the poem. What the present study intends to do is to offer the sort of *speculative* reading of *Confessio Amantis* that has been so lacking in recent years. Fundamental to my argument are my convictions that *Confessio Amantis* actually invites multiple interpretations, and that author, text, and reader collaborate in the production of complex, often contradictory, and sometimes "perverse" (mis-)readings.

PART I

LANGUAGE

1

GOWER'S BABEL TOWER

LANGUAGE CHOICE AND
THE GRAMMAR OF SEX

It is appropriate that a reading of *Confessio Amantis* should begin with a broader investigation of the gender politics implicit in Gower's poetry. Gower wrote substantial works in Anglo-Norman and Latin before turning to the vernacular. Here I will argue that, within Gower's corpus as a whole, the authority of prestige and vernacular tongues alike is undermined by queer gender play that connects sexual indeterminacy with linguistic confusion. An immediate context for Gower's anxieties concerning language is the contemporary dispute about the role of the vernacular in communicating truths, especially religious truths, to lay and nonaristocratic readers. Gower is concerned to communicate rather than to withhold learning, and his decision to write a major work in the vernacular is crucial to the fulfillment of that aim. At the same time, he would certainly have been sensitive to its political and ethical ramifications and to the risks he might be taking in the process. There is at the heart of Gower's writing a contradiction that he does not and cannot resolve. Although in many ways a deeply conventional thinker and writer, Gower, or his writing, betrays a cognizance of the plurality of language in general, and the indeterminacy of translation and disruptive potential of the vernacular in particular.[1] Gower's writing raises questions about how the text should be read and by whom.

A SLIP OF THE TONGUE

Gower begins *Confessio Amantis*, generally thought of as his "English" poem, with a Latin verse:

> Torpor, ebes sensus, scola parua labor minimusque
> Causant quo minimus ipse minora canam:
> Qua tamen Engisti lingua canit Insula Bruti
> Anglica Carmente metra iuuante loquar.
> Ossibus ergo carens que conterit ossa loquelis
> Absit, et interpres stet procul oro malus.

> (Dull wit, slight schooling, torpor, labor less,
> Make slight the themes I, least of poets, sing.
> Let me, In Hengist's tongue, in Brut's isle sung,
> With Carmen's help, tell forth my English verse.
> Far hence the boneless one whose speech grinds bones,
> Far hence be he who reads my verses ill.) (Prol.a–f)

In these lines Gower implicitly likens his own role as poet to the status of the vernacular as the language of poetry. Both, it seems, have similar limitations, and English, he suggests, cannot stand on its own: it requires the support of the Latin verses and glosses that he includes in the work as a whole. But Gower's depreciation of his own intelligence, education, effort, and, indeed, status as writer is as conventional as it is insincere.[2] The inference we are forced to draw from the parallel between author and vernacular is that the English language has greater potential than the poet is willing to admit openly. Clearly Gower's learning is revealed in these very verses in which he alludes to the history of the Anglo-Saxons and to the pseudo-classical mythology of the origin of writing. Hengist was legendary leader of one of the first bands to invade and to settle in Britain; somewhat ominously he was also known for his treachery. According to Isidore, the goddess Carmentis was responsible for the invention of the Latin alphabet.[3] There may even be a faint allusion to Virgil in the second line; if we accept this to be the case, Gower likens himself to the Latin author even as he belittles his own theme of love as so much lesser than that of arms and the man.[4] Furthermore, Gower's punning in Latin demonstrates his virtuosity in what was, of course, the language of authority and power in the later Middle Ages. As Siân Echard and Claire Fanger point out, the reference to the "boneless one" is a riddle to which the answer is intended to be the "tongue" with its capacity for uttering wicked words. Yet they also observe that "Gower has clearly worked to make the sense of the line available only to the reader who is willing to consider it carefully."[5]

Now riddles are, in a sense, central to *Confessio Amantis*. The poem not only starts with one, but the Tale of Apollonius of Tyre, which occupies most of the final book, hinges upon another, that set by Antiochus (VIII.405–09), and its exact meaning, if not its general sense, is even more obscure.[6] The solution to the riddle at the beginning of *Confessio* may be even more complex than Echard and Fanger allow. The editors of the extract from *Confessio Amantis* included in the recent anthology *The Idea of the Vernacular* also comment on this riddle. They suggest that "The force of the phrase 'que conterit ossa' (that grinds down bones) is perhaps an ironic acknowledgment of the power of the reader's—or interpreter's—words to wrest meaning away from authorial intention."[7] In the very next line, Gower attempts to banish, but simultaneously evokes, the evil or perverse reader ("Far hence be he who reads my verses ill"). While he—or she—struggles for meaning, this sort of reader may well either willfully or guilelessly mistake "the boneless one whose speech grinds bones" to designate the male sexual organ.[8] It is something of a commonplace to note that medieval theories of writing are influenced by theories of reproduction.[9] The materials and matter of the text are seen as passive and feminine, while the author, because his role is viewed as active in that he generates the text and gives it form, is gendered masculine. But what of the recipient of the text; what role does she or he play in the production of meaning?[10] Is it an active or a passive one? The penis in the riddle has a symbolic rather than a physiological significance: it represents the potency to interpret independently of the poet's aims. The text and its creator are rendered feminine or effeminate because a reader whom the author cannot control threatens them with penetration. Such a reader could be described as the metaphorical rapist of both poem and poet. It is as if Gower were announcing at the start of the poem that despite its lofty themes, neither he nor it is inviolate. Gower conjures up the specter of an abusive and potentially sodomitical relationship between reader and text/author, only to dismiss it immediately.

The threat of the perverse reading may be repressed but Gower cannot escape its return.

It is exactly this sort of creative yet crude and disruptive "misreading" that will be the focus of my analysis in the next section of this chapter, in which I examine some examples of the troubled sexual politics of grammatical gender in Gower's English, Anglo-Norman, and Latin writings. Then, in the third and longest section, I locate this analysis within the broader context of the politics of language and style in late-fourteenth- and early-fifteenth-century England. My exploration of the implications of Gower's wordplay in the opening riddle of *Confessio* and elsewhere is influenced by Mikhail Bakhtin's work on discourse, which brings together linguistics and stylistics.[11] The relevance of Bakhtin's notion of polyglossia, which can be defined as "the simultaneous presence of two of more national languages interacting within a single cultural system," to the trilingual culture (Latin, Anglo-Norman, and Middle English) of late medieval England is manifest.[12] This active polyglossia serves to undermine the hegemonic status of Latin; as Bakhtin explains, polyglossia fractures "the myth of a language that presumes to be the only language, and the myth of a language that presumes to be completely unified."[13] Likewise within Gower's entire corpus there exists a polyglossia, a dialectic relationship between prestige and vernacular language, between "high styles" (sermon, advice to princes, estates literature, penitential literature, romance) and "low" (elements of farce, fable, and satire). Similarly, *Confessio* itself has a dialogic or polyphonic form insofar as there is a dialectic relationship between the English texts and the Latin verses and glosses. Linguistically then, the poem is divided; the various "voices" of the poem often contradict each other, or are at odds with one another in a number of different ways. In fact the *Confessio* as a whole might be viewed as an example of the carnivalesque, in which the lover's confession to a very secular priest (Genius, as the servant of Venus) is a semi-parody of a religious ritual, perhaps even a travesty of a Church sacrament.

Grammatical Gender-Benders

The penis riddle is just the first of many linguistic jokes in *Confessio Amantis*. In a Latin headnote in Book I, the pernicious vice of Hypocrisy is personified as one whose face is masked with made-up paleness, and frauds are hidden with mellifluous words:[14]

> Laruando faciem ficto pallore subornat
> Fraudibus Ypocrisis mellea verba suis.
> Sicque pios animos quamsepe ruit muliebres
> Ex humili verbo sub latitante dolo. (I.574e–h)

These lines are translated by Echard and Fanger as:

> Hypocrisy suborns sweet words to fraud,
> Bewitching face with pallor feigned. And thus
> She often hurls down faithful women's minds,
> With lurking trick beneath a humble word.

The word *hypocrisis,* like most Latin abstract nouns (Genius is a notable exception), is grammatically gendered feminine. We find a similar description of Hypocrisy as female in the final book of *Vox Clamantis* (VII.175–90). Nonetheless in the English verses in Book I of *Confessio* and elsewhere, the figure of Hypocrisy is clearly masculine. Like a self-interested and corrupt courtier, he masquerades as a loyal counselor and genuine lover, but is in fact the first minister of Pride (I.585). We are later told that "the derke untrewe Ypocrisie" is the counselor and constant companion of Falssemblant (II.1890–92), who is in turn a retainer in the service of Hate (III.963–65).

Helen Cooper argues that in *Piers Plowman,* Gower's contemporary, William Langland, exploits the evolution of English into an analytic language in making many of his personifications masculine.[15] It suits Langland's purposes to people his texts with masculine personifications because they function, to a greater or lesser extent, as projections of the dreamer Will's own state of mind and inner conflicts (and, by extension, the author's). So too Gower, or his fictive creation Genius, in the English text of *Confessio,* is able to rehearse Amans's psychodrama in front of him with the help of specifically male allegorical actors. Although Cooper suggests that "it does not seem to have worried anyone unduly that female personifications might sometimes do very unfeminine things,"[16] I would assert that, in the tension between the Latin and English verses of *Confessio,* Gower is indulging in deliberate syntactic gender play. Like everything else about Hypocrisy (who, by definition, always has a double signification), her/his gender and also sexuality is, if only fleetingly, indeterminate, polymorphous, and uncontrolled. What is more, in the English verses, Hypocrisy's masculinity and (assumed) heterosexuality are the result of grammatical error: they are barbarisms, the results of a mistake in the gender of a word. The homoerotic potential of *Ypocrisis*'s female gender is undeveloped in the Latin verses of *Confessio* and has consequently been largely overlooked by critics or dismissed as a grammatical accident (Eric Stockton in his translation of Gower's Latin text, *Vox Clamantis,* silently "emends" the gender of Hypocrisy to make it neuter).[17] However, this homoerotic potential seems to be quite consciously evoked by Gower; his gender play is perhaps reminiscent of Bakhtin's *grammatica jocosa* in which "grammatical order is transgressed to reveal erotic and obscene or merely materially satisfying counter-meaning."[18] Whereas Alastair Minnis, for example, contends that Gower's use of Latin in *Confessio* functions to "affirm the unifying moral intention of the work," I would argue the opposite: that Gower's Latin is not so "straight" as it seems.[19] Gower himself was aware of the gap between languages and their prestige, and sometimes his Latin, rather than authorizing the text, serves to undermine its ethical structure. In the Latin verse cited above, which describes a female *Ypocrisis* as a smooth-operating seducer of chaste ladies, the creative and disruptive power of misprision already seen in the penis riddle is once again demonstrated. Here it is the shadow of female homosexuality that is cast on Gower's writing, and the linguistic indeterminacy is made more visible through a juxtaposed translation that renders Hypocrisy as male.

Similar grammatical "problems" to those I have just discussed emerge in Gower's other major vernacular work, the Anglo-Norman *Mirour de l'Omme,* and would seem to disprove the received idea, summed up by John Fleming, that "ideas do not have 'sex', though in Romance tongues they do have gender."[20] In *Mirour,* we frequently find apparently feminine personifications—such as the figure of *Stupre* (Rape [or, perhaps more accurately, Debauchery]), who is the second daughter of *Luxure* or *Leccherie* (Lechery) (*Mirour de l'Omme,* 8665–8748)—acting in unexpected ways and swapping gender as the urge takes them. Here, however, Gower actually offers an explanation for what is going on. He tells the reader:

Entendre devetz tout avant,
Tous ceux dont vous irray contant,
Comme puis orretz l'estoire dite,
Naiscont du merveillous semblant;
Car de nature a leur naiscant
Trestous sont mostre hermafodrite:
Sicome le livre m'en recite,
Ce sont quant double forme habite
Femelle et madle en un enfant:
Si noun de femme les endite,
Les filles dont je vous endite,
Sont auci homme nepourquant.

(You should understand in advance that all these I am going to tell you about, as later you will hear the story told, were born with strange appearance, for at birth by nature all were hermaphroditic monsters. As the book tells me, these are when a double form, female and male, lives in a child. If I lay on them the names of female, the daughters of whom I am telling you are nonetheless also males.) (*Mirour de l'Omme*, 1021–32)

Yet to some extent this explanation—like the book Gower suddenly and cryptically refers to as his authority (does he mean the source of his story about the seven daughters of sin, or the source of his information on hermaphrodites?)—is a smoke screen. It comes too late—after our curiosity has been aroused and our appetites have been whetted. Because even before this the reader has encountered a feminine *Char* (Flesh) sighing for love of the devil's daughter, *Pecché* (Sin; this noun is normally masculine) (*Mirour de l'Omme*, 613–25). Equally unsettling are the curious antics of Sin's gender-bending son and brother and lover, *Mort* (Death; normally feminine).[21] In a particularly striking passage *Mort*, wrapped in a worldly mantle and lurking in a closet, exposes himself (or herself as Death—"*La* Mort"—suddenly now appears) to the inquisitive/voyeuristic eyes of *Char* (*Mirour de l'Omme*, 697–732).[22] *Char* is of course horrified, but we might wonder what exactly it is about the physical appearance of *Mort* that is so shocking. Is it, at least in part, the fact that Death now appears as female before an unsuspecting, if not innocent, female spectator?

All of this gender confusion led George Macaulay to the conclusion that "no doubt the feeling for gender had been to some extent worn away in England."[23] This generalization seems unlikely to be applicable to someone as educated as Gower, someone who was so closely acquainted with Alain de Lille's *De Planctu Naturae*. In this text we find a detailed, if not exactly coherent, discussion of the grammar of sex in which barbarisms are seen to detract from masculinity and errors in gender are associated with immorality and sodomy (see especially metrum I and prosa 4).[24] Gower adapts Alain de Lille's ideas freely. In his Tale of Iphis and Ianthe, which appears in Book IV of *Confessio Amantis* (451–505), discussed in more detail in Chapter 3, Gower forges a link between grammatical and sexual or gender confusion and ethical complexities which may explain his inconsistent use of the third person pronouns. Here the narrator refers to Iphis (born female, brought up male, married to a girl, and transformed into a man) as both "him" and "sche." Gower's manipulation of grammar can be disruptive, at times even anarchic. It is unlikely then that he lacked a "feeling for gender," whatever language he chose to write in at a given time. Nonetheless, if we think about Gower's readership, the generalization that gender rules were pretty lax in late medieval Anglo-Norman possibly strengthens rather than undermines my argument that Gower is playing with grammatical gender in *Mirour* since it would allow him greater stylistic freedom. This is not to say that Gower does not expect or intend his readers to get his jokes; in other words, we find here further evidence that he is being disingenuous in *Confessio* when he banishes the one who "misreads" his verses. Gower's jokes are not simply examples of linguistic play; rather, the ludic quality of Gower's writing disturbs the status quo, and, within his work, polyglossia and heteroglossia function as resistance to Latin and Anglo-Norman and French dominance.[25] Gower's attitude to the vernacular is individual and at times somewhat inconsistent, reflecting the fluidity of the linguistic hierarchies of late-fourteenth-century England. Like many other writers of the time, Gower hoped to improve the status of learning. He saw in the vernacular, which he associated with his idea of the English nation, the potential to harmonize social differences. Nevertheless, he also recognized that the vernacular was the language of the illiterate masses and of heresy. Perhaps it is as a consequence of the complexity of his views that his writing is not univocal but riddled with internal contradictions and conflicts.

POLITICS AND QUEER POLITICS

When Gower (or his authorial persona) announces, in the Prologue to *Confessio,* that "And for that fewe men endite / In oure englissh, I thenke make / A bok for Engelondes sake" (Prol.22–24), he immediately embroils himself in the language politics of late medieval England. In the fourteenth and fifteenth centuries, the nation was expanding its intellectual horizons. New forms of knowledge were manifested in the emergence of vernacular theology, and they resulted in anxieties that centered on the dangers of making certain forms of learning accessible to a lay readership. The Oxford debate on Bible translation (1401–ca. 1407) provides one context for Gower's writing. In the later Middle Ages, defenders of vernacular translation attacked the clergy's attempts to restrict the circulation of knowledge to the Latinate elite.[26] Gower was writing *before* the Oxford translation debate. Nonetheless, biblical translation of even single verses could evidently be considered problematic, and many of the issues raised in the debate were anticipated much earlier, with the dispute over vernacular theology in general dating back at least as far the beginning of the fourteenth century.[27] Gower does not openly intervene in this debate: the major sources of *Confessio* are secular texts (such as Ovid's *Metamorphoses*), and only parts of the work could be described as biblical translation, even in the broad medieval sense of exegesis or interpretation.[28] In his Prologue and elsewhere, he claims that his text serves a didactic function (instructing the king and his advisers, the clergy, and the commons). However, at the beginning of the work in its revised form he stresses that his poem falls somewhere between "lust" and "lore" (Prol.19); and at the end he goes so far as to state that he undertook "In englesch forto make a book / Which stant betwene ernest and game" (VIII.3108–09). Gower seems concerned to undercut the high seriousness of his vernacular work. In the revised Prologue to *Confessio,* he takes the potentially radical step of representing himself as a "burel"—that is, "coarse," "simple," or perhaps "lay"—clerk, concerned with creating a new vernacular authority (Prol.52).[29] Yet within the frame narrative, this blurring of roles takes on some ludic qualities with Genius playing clergy to Amans's layman. In other words, there is some irony in the fact that Genius polices the transmission of knowledge of the vices and virtues when, as a pagan priest, he could hardly be more laicized.[30]

Gower's caution in this respect can be explained in part by his religious and political allegiances. His avowed loathing of Lollardy is well known. In the Prologue to *Confessio,* for example, he blames the emergence of "This newe Secte" (Prol.349) on the depravity of the Church that cultivated it, while in the fifth book heresy is personified as one who skulks about undermining people's faith (V.1810–12). Gower also observes that "It were betre dike and delve / And stonde upon the ryhte feith, / Than knowe al that the bible seith / And erre as somme clerkes do" (Prol.352–55), possibly a reference to the Lollard emphasis on the word of Scripture. Gower's anticlericalism and his attitude toward dominion have a certain amount in common with the views of the Lollards (Gower argues that one cannot serve both God and the world: Prol.860–64). At the same time, he implicitly condemns John Wycliffe in both *Vox Clamantis* (for example at III.1129–30, III.1819–20; VI.1267) and the later Latin poem "Carmen super multiplici Viciorum Pestilencia" (which dates to 1397). Although it cannot be assumed that Gower took the side of those who were opposed to translation of the Bible (he may in fact have approved of it, at least for readers of the aristocracy and gentry class), he did sympathize politically with individuals in that camp. In the Latin *Cronica Tripertita* (written ca. 1400), he wrote a defense of a central figure in the debate, Thomas Arundel (II.232–50). Following the resumption of his office as Archbishop of Canterbury in the reign of Henry IV, Arundel was responsible for the Statute of Heresy *(De heretico comburendo)* in 1401 and for the legislation on preaching and teaching known as his Constitutions (1407–09). Praise of Arundel's learning can also be found in the dedication of a late but authoritative version of *Vox Clamantis* (Epistola.1–49).

To some extent, the caution and conservatism commonly ascribed to Gower in terms of his political stance (see Chapters 5 and 6) are reflected in his attitude to the vernacular, most obviously in his apocalyptic description—*in Latin*—of the horrible cacophony of the bestial multitude in Book I of *Vox* (783–830):

> Quidam sternutant asinorum more ferino,
> Mugitus quidam personuere boum;
> Quidam porcorum grunnitus horridiores
> Emittunt, que suo murmure terra tremit:
> . . .

Nec minus in sonitu concussit garrulus ancer
Aures, que subito fossa dolore pauent:
Bombizant vaspe, sonus est horrendus eorum,
Nullus et examen dinumerare potest:
Conclamant pariter hirsuti more leonis,
Omneque fit peius quod fuit ante malum.

(Some of them bray in the beastly manner of asses, some bel-
low the lowings of oxen. Some give out horrible swinish grunts,
and the earth trembles from their rumbling. . . . No less did the
cackling gander strike the ear with its sound, and even the graves
tremble with sudden anguish. Wasps buzz, and their sound is
fearful, and no one can count the swarm of them. Together they
make a roar like a bristling lion, and everything that was previously bad becomes worse.) (*Vox Clamantis*, I.799–814)

The immediate context of this text is not of course the 1401 controversy,
but the Peasants' Revolt of 1381.[31] However a connection between the two
may exist as similar descriptions of the laity as brute beasts are found in
antitranslation works.[32] David Aers follows Steven Justice in claiming
that, although in *Vox* Gower claims to speak as the common people, his
use of Latin firmly distances his narrator from the unruly rural masses
and the rebels, whose voices are dehumanized and linked to anarchic
violence.[33] Yet, in the passage just cited, we can hear the Latin sounds
actually mimicking the peasants' shouts; despite the difference in language, the two combine together to make the outcry even louder. The
weakness of Aers's reading is that it "resolves" the difficulties of the
text, and evades the questions it raises, in exactly the way he criticizes
audiences and readers of *Piers Plowman* of doing when they offer their
own "definitive" interpretations of the poem.[34] At the risk of the sort of
"interpretative violence" Aers associates with radical readers,[35] I would
suggest that the vividness and vitality of Gower's passage indicate a fear
of but also *a fascination with* the spread of learning amongst the lower
classes. (John Ball is portrayed as having been instructed by a malicious
spirit: *Vox Clamantis*, I.793–94.)

My reading of *Vox Clamantis* complements that offered by Eve Salisbury.[36] Salisbury observes that Gower's poetic method in *Vox* is that of
cento.[37] That is, the poem is a literary pastiche, a composition made up
of a patchwork of passages taken from the writings of earlier writers

(Ovid, Virgil, Godfrey of Viterbo, and many others). In agreement with R. F. Yeager, Salisbury thinks it likely that Gower's *cento* technique is derived from the poetry of a fourth-century Roman woman, Faltonia Betitia Proba.[38] Whereas Bakhtin sees *cento* simply as parodic,[39] Salisbury characterizes *Vox*, with its fragmented form and feminine origin, as the monstrous birth of Gower's maternal (rather than paternal) imagination. Like the monstrosities and prodigies described in Isidore of Seville's *Etymologiæ*, Gower's *Vox* serves a prophetic function, commenting on the ills of society and warning of the disasters that are to come.[40] But for Salisbury, the saturnalian aspects of Gower's *cento* link the poem to the bloody carnivalesque drama of the rebels' invasion of London on the Feast of Corpus Christi. This was when (to quote Salisbury's evocative description), "what began as a sacred celebration of the body of Christ, became instead an unholy parody attended by mock priests serving real pieces of human flesh upon a mock altar."[41] Just as disrupted syntax can cause as well as signal sexual or moral confusion, so textual fragmentation both parallels and is embroiled in social disorder. Gower may have hoped that his portrayal of contemporary horrors would serve as an admonition that would inspire reform within the established political and social framework. However the extent of his poetic engagement with the world of the violent mob and its leaders, and the power he attributes to their voices, indicates that his response to the changes of his time, social as well as linguistic, was a complex one. Paradoxically Gower's Latin text might be seen as adding its voice to that of the peasants whose asinine bellows and outrageous behavior he sets out to decry.[42]

Further evidence of Gower's attitude to the vernacular can be found in his depiction of the Tower of Babel in the Prologue to *Confessio Amantis*:

> And over that thurgh Senne it com
> That Nembrot such emprise nom,
> Whan he the Tour Babel on heihte
> Let make, as he that wolde feihte
> Ayein the hihe goddes myht.
> Wherof divided anon ryht
> Was the langage in such entente,
> Ther wist non what other mente,
> So that thei myhten noght procede.
> And thus it stant of every dede,

Wher Senne takth the cause on honde,
It may upright noght longe stonde;
For Senne of his condicioun
Is moder of divisioun
And tokne whan the world schal faile. (Prol.1017–31)

For Gower, Babel signifies the discord within society, and the division of languages is just one aspect of the confusion that results from sin. According to Copeland, the English verses function to undermine the imperialistic and hegemonic status of Latin in the medieval Western world by drawing our attention to "the limits of the power of Latinity to contain difference through an idealized linguistic order transcending time and place."[43] But as Copeland also observes, Gower's use of the myth of Babel must "inevitably call attention to the fact of vernacularity" while at the same time implicating *Confessio* within it.[44] Gower may have intended his writings as a response to Babel that would bring about some sort of social harmony, insofar as he no doubt hoped that his trilingual works would address an inclusive audience.[45] (Although his apparent failure to disseminate texts of the *Mirour* presumably reflects the decline in the prestige of Anglo-Norman at the time.) But by the time Gower came to write *Confessio,* that is, by the time he decided to write in the vernacular, he must also have been aware that his own poetic discourse had become a hybrid. A mixing of "high" and "low," prestige and vernacular languages, it was itself a cacophony, a confusion of voices, a veritable Tower of Babel.

Looked at from a rather different perspective, however, it might be that in implicating the multiplicity of languages, and thus his own verses in Anglo-Norman, Latin, and English (and his Latin glosses), in the Fall, Gower is again drawing a parallel between language and sexuality. In the discussion of division and sin in the lines immediately preceding his account of the Tower of Babel, Gower alludes to Noah's Flood (Prol.112–16). In the Middle Ages, this biblical event was often ascribed to God's anger at the prevalence of "perverse" sexual practices like sodomy.[46] Later on—in Book VII—Gower returns to Noah's Flood when he revisits the subject of diversity and corruption: here, the Flood brings about the division of the Earth and its peoples as each of Noah's sons is granted his own land (VII.521–600). The implied logic is that sexual "deviance" causes God's wrath, and that diversity in its various forms—

including linguistic diversity—is the consequence of it. This has important ramifications.

In his portrayal of the gender-bending personification Hypocrisy (who, as we saw earlier, is a women who seduces women in the Latin verses of *Confessio*, but a sly male courtier in the English text), Gower indulges in the sort of linguistic play that Simon Gaunt, in a reading of *Le Roman de la Rose*, has associated with queer writing.[47] According to Gaunt, Jean de Meun deliberately fosters grammatical (and consequently sexual) indeterminacy, creating tensions between the literal and allegorical narratives of homoerotic and heterosexual desire and relishing the contradictions within his text. Gower employs a similar strategy in *Confessio Amantis*. But one caveat must be kept in mind, and that is that Gower never actually mentions sodomy in this long poem about love and its perversions. Indeed, as we will see in Chapter 3, he sometimes goes to some lengths to avoid the subject. To give just one example, in Book VIII, the story of Lot begins at the point where Lot's wife has just been transformed into a pillar of salt (VIII.227–28). This is appropriate in its context, since the story of Lot sleeping with his daughters is being told to illustrate the ills of incest. Nonetheless, it is noteworthy that the sins of Sodom and Gomorrah and God's vengeance on them are written out of the narrative—even the backwards glance of Lot's wife (interpreted by St. Ambrose as a return to lust[48]) is omitted. Yet the moral of the narrative, that he who allows his lust "in other place falle / Than it is of the lawe set" (VIII.252–53) will sorely repent, would in this case be more applicable to the sodomite than to the incestuous father. Indeed Gower himself is guilty here of interpretative violence insofar as he has to change his source to make it fit the moral. Lot is represented as the instigator of the incestuous act, rather than as the victim of deception carried out by his daughters and in effect as a victim of a rape that occurs when he is drunk. Gower's text is not a queer text because it explicitly discusses homosexuality—it does not—but because it is undercut by a rich vein of linguistic gender play that involves its readers and that destabilizes its moral arrangement.

Gower's *Confessio* as a whole, and in particular the narratives about Hypocrisy that I discussed at the start of this chapter, teaches us that most familiar of lessons: appearance should reflect reality, and language truth.[49] In Book I, Genius warns Amans to "eschuie of thi manhiede / Ipocrisie and his semblant" (I.1212–13).[50] Hypocrisy, characterized by duplicity and falsehood and inspired by self-interest, is caused by and causes division. Like the depiction of Death in the *Mirour* (sometimes male, sometimes female), who is *literally* as well as allegorically the brother, son, and lover of Sin, the gender bending of Hypocrisy in *Confessio*—and the errors in grammar and tension between the Latin commentary and the English narrative this creates—reinforces the message that s/he is in the service of evil. Hypocrisy is, by definition, opposed to those virtues or qualities that raise mankind above brute animals and that are, in this text, associated with the ideal of stable heterosexual masculinity: honesty, humility, and truth (see I.3043–48 and VII.4215–32). But as Wetherbee has convincingly argued, Gower seems to represent division and instability as humankind's natural state (e.g., Prol.970–82).[51] Division is pervasive in the poem, from the duplicity of Hypocrisy to the two languages in which it is written and the two patrons to which it is dedicated. Even love is riven by the split between perfect and imperfect love, between romantic love and love of God. The degeneration of love into discord is caused by division, and is a further indication of our fallen natures (cf. Prol.115–21). In representing sexual indeterminacy as perversion and associating it not only with sin and death, but also with linguistic diversity, Gower may not seem to be resisting the established order. But by implicating everyone—not only himself and his readers but also the church (see the discussion of chastity and continence at Prol.470–80) and the monarchy (see the discussion of chastity at the end of Book VII, especially 4215–56; and also VIII.3089–95 of the later recensions)—his message is more challenging. Gower's poem, while overtly supporting the religious and political hierarchies, simultaneously undermines them, and in this interplay of order and disorder lies the key to its structure and meaning. Thomas Palmer was subsequently to argue, in his attacks on vernacular translation, that the lack of inflections in English and the apparent absence of grammatical rules and figures rendered it inadequate as a medium through which divine truths could be conveyed.[52] As we have seen in the case of Hypocrisy, Gower must certainly have been aware of the seemingly disordered nature of the English language, but this did not prevent him from writing in the vernacular. He knew that translation rendered possible grammatical and moral barbarisms, yet these are nonetheless exploited within *Confessio* to allow the audience an imaginative participation in and an aesthetic experience of the division of the world.

PLAYING SAFE

To conclude this chapter, I will return briefly to a consideration of the readership of Gower's *Confessio*. According to Bakhtin, every utterance is directed toward a listener, every text toward a reader, embodying "an orientation toward a specific conceptual horizon, toward [a] specific world. . . ."[53] I have already suggested in the Introduction that the implied reader (to borrow Wolfgang Iser's term) of the text is masculine, educated, and aristocratic or of the gentry class. (See especially the references in the revised poem to "som man" in Prol.21, and to "lered men" in VIII.3113; and see also Prol.86–87). I have also noted that the implied or assumed audience and the actual medieval readership seem to correspond. In other words, at least part of the audience of the *Confessio* was probably not so very different from that originally intended for the Anglo-Norman *Mirour* (which, however, as I have noted already, does not seem to have been widely disseminated and only survives in one manuscript).[54] Aristocratic and courtly book owners and readers would have largely been exempt from the early-fifteenth-century regulations governing vernacular teaching.[55] Members of Gower's own immediate circle may well have been more vulnerable, in theory if not in reality. Yet, unlike Chaucer's *Canterbury Tales*, ownership of a copy of *Confessio* was never taken as evidence of heresy in a trial for Lollardy.[56] Gower himself seems to have assumed that the vernacular theology, like the political and social commentary, embedded in his texts—the biblical quotations, translations, and expositions—was not fundamentally dangerous, presumably because it was directed at an upper-class or upper-middle-class lay audience rather than at society as a whole. If Gower's texts are congenial to perverse (mis)interpretation, Gower presumably did not intend them to reach truly radical readers. In inviting misreadings, Gower was merely acknowledging the divided nature of our postlapsarian existence. His poetry, born from and into sin, describes the state of the world but does not try to change the structure of society. While engaging with the confusions and contradictions of his age, Gower had no desire to inspire revolt. After all, only the Latinate would be able to read his Latin verses and glosses. Gower did not intend to throw his pearls before the swine of the peasantry. His jokes were aimed at the *litterati*, not the *ilitterati*. This would not however have prevented him feeling a certain unease, as well as an excitement about his own vernacular translations (susceptible as they are to perverse readings). This was not only because they seemed an appropriate—*the* appropriate—medium for examining humankind's sinful and sexual state, but also because on some level he was aware that such linguistic sport has its own disruptive force. This anxiety could well explain Gower's decision to cut from the later versions of the Prologue a reference to his intention to write a book in such a way that it might prove, not only wisdom for the wise, but also "pley to hem that lust to pleye" (*Prol.85).

2

WRITING LIKE A MAN

RHETORIC AND GENEALOGY

DANTE, BRUNETTO LATINI, AND GOWER

In one of the best-known passages of *Inferno,* Dante unexpectedly encounters the Florentine magistrate, rhetorician, and poet Brunetto Latini amongst the sodomites in the innermost ring of the seventh circle of Hell. The poignancy of this episode, in which Dante greets his former teacher, suggests a degree of sympathy with the sinner on the part of the narrator that the modern reader might well not anticipate:

> E io, quando il suo braccio a me distese,
> ficcai gli occhi per lo cotto aspetto
> sì, che il viso abbruciato non difese
> la conoscenza sua al mio intelletto;
> e chinando la mia a la sua faccia
> risposi: "Siete voi qui, Ser Brunetto!"

> (I, when to me he stretched his arm out, brought
> my gaze to rest so squarely on his baked
> appearance, that his scorched face stayed me not
> from recognizing him with my intellect;
> and *"You* here, Ser Brunetto!" stooping down
> my face to his, I said: and my heart ached.)[1]

In their ensuing conversation, Dante explains to Latini that he is overwhelmed by feelings of gratitude as he remembers "'quando nel mondo,

ad ora ad ora, / m'insegnavate come l'uom s'eterna'" (*Inferno,* XV.84–85;
"'when in the world you taught me early and late / the art by which
man grows eternal'"). In other words, Dante is indebted to Latini for his
instruction in the art of poetry.

The intimacy of the exchange between the two men, the absence of
censorious condemnation of the sinner on the part of Dante, has led a
number of scholars to question the exact nature of Latini's error and to
try to exonerate him from the taint of homosexuality.[2] Certainly there is
reason to think that Latini's transgression may be more complex than it
appears at first. Terms like *sodomy* and *sodomite* are notorious for their
instability and therefore had the potential to be used in quite unspecific
ways in the Middle Ages.[3] Although Dante classifies sodomy as a species
of violence against God (placing it alongside blasphemy and usury),[4] it
may be no coincidence that Latini's companions in suffering are all notable *litterati,* scholars for whom the love of learning was of paramount
importance. A causal connection between vanity and idolatry and both
female and male homosexuality was well established in the Middle Ages
and can be traced back to the teachings of St. Paul (Romans 1.21–27).[5] It
is this context that may help to explain Latini's final prayer, when he en-
treats Dante to

> "sieti raccomandato il mio Tesoro
> nel qual io vivo ancora; e più non cheggio." (*Inferno,*
>   XV.119–20)

> ("take good care of my *Treasure,* for in that
> I still live, and no more I ask of thee.")

Latini's concern for the survival of his book and seeming disregard for
the state of his own soul—his lack of penitence—can be seen as evidence of pride and self-adulation. As Eugene Vance explains, "as the
willing emblem of the classical rhetoricians, Brunetto is enacting all the
vices for which rhetoricians since Plato had been censured—love of appearances, love of money, opportunism, and so on—vices that persist in
Brunetto even though he is now suffering for them in hell."[6] Latini's
ambition reveals him to be at least equally guilty of narcissistic self-love
as he is of "spregiando natura" (*Inferno,* XI.48; scorning Nature). Dante
represents him as being concerned more with artistic creativity than
with procreation, with literary patrilineage rather than human genealogy.[7]

To some extent this canto as a whole can be read as a variation of the "outdoing topos,"[8] or of what Harold Bloom famously termed "the anxiety of influence," a type of literary competitiveness.[9] Latini predicts the literary success of the man he refers to as his son, "'Se tu segui tua stella, / non puoi fallire a glorioso porto'" (*Inferno*, XV.55–56; "'An thou pursue thy star, / thou canst not fail to reach the glorious port'"). At the same time, Dante ensures that his predecessor—safely trapped in eternal motion in hell—cannot challenge what is now his, Dante's, position of superiority. Yet Dante's benevolent, if condescending, appreciation of the favor formerly shown him by his master may well be misplaced. Latini implicates Dante as his literary (and therefore improper) heir and, insofar as Dante shares Latini's desire for literary immortality, it would appear that he has himself become corrupted by his sin. Certainly, Dante's response to Latini's flattery reveals him to be more concerned with his own future status, his metaphorical birthright, than with the survival of his master's text:

> "Ciò che narrate di mio corso, scrivo
> e serbolo a chiosar, con altro testo,
> a donna che saprà, se a lei arrivo." (*Inferno*, XV.88–90)

> ("What you narrate of how my steps shall fare
> I write, and keep with other texts to gloze,
> by a wise lady, if I attain her.")

But however one interprets Latini's error and his prayer, and Dante's response to them, it is evident that the latter's vivid description of Latini's punishment ensured that his name would indeed continue to be remembered, if not for the reasons that Latini had wished.

Brunetto Latini's book, *Li Livres dou Trésor*, written between 1260 and 1266, was not lost and otherwise forgotten.[10] One of those writers on whom it had a major impact was Gower. The extent of Gower's familiarity with Dante's *Commedia* is unknown,[11] and Gower does not at any point mention either Latini's crime or his compendium. However, Gower does draw extensively on the *Trésor* in Book VII of *Confessio Amantis*, in which there occurs what has been identified as the first discussion of rhetoric in English (VII.1507–1640).[12] This, the penultimate book of *Confessio*, interrupts the series of narratives structured around the lover's confession and his priest's exposition of the seven deadly sins. Exceptionally, it is not written "in the registre / Of Venus" (VII.19–20), but contains instead, as Alastair Minnis notes, "a veritable 'de regimine principum [sic],' a little treatise on the proper methods of ruling a country."[13] My own discussion of the political dimensions of Book VII of *Confessio* occurs in Chapter 5, below. Here my focus is restricted to the discussion of language that is embedded within Book VII. As Winthrop Wetherbee observes, Book VII "places the obligations of self-governance and kingship in the context of world history, natural philosophy, and an alternative, classical system of ethics."[14] Genius then follows the Aristotelian scheme articulated in Latini's *Trésor* in dividing knowledge into three categories, with the theoretical as the first, and the practical as the third. However, Genius diverges from Latini's scheme when he elevates "Rhetorique" to the second category; logic, which Latini has as his second category, is thus rendered subordinate to rhetoric and placed alongside the remaining art of the medieval trivium, grammar.[15]

Previous critics have discussed Gower's treatment of rhetoric in some detail, and I am particularly indebted here to the information they have provided about his use of his source material, and also to their explorations of the complex interrelations between rhetoric, ethics, and politics.[16] In this chapter, my primary concern will be with the way in which Gower's construction of rhetoric can be seen to be both gendered and sexualized, especially when read alongside other classical and medieval discussions of the subject. This is of particular significance within the confessional framework of Gower's text, since the fictive narratives of Amans and Genius are used for exploring the lover's inner psyche and ostensibly for bringing about his cure, and hence they are revealing about medieval notions of heterosexual masculinity in particular. Even within Book VII, where the focus is on the ruler (both in the person of Alexander, and in the notion of the ideal king more generally), not Amans, we learn a great deal about gendered and sexualized identity. In the Middle Ages, the definition of heterosexual masculinity was closely tied to issues of patrilineage and genealogy. Medieval authors like Dante (and, as we will see, Gower), seem to have been particularly anxious about the possibility of being tainted by the sins of their metaphorical fathers. The anecdote concerning Latini in *Commedia* reveals Dante's concerns about poetic inheritance, and also the link that exists in his imagination between literary pride, narcissism, and sodomy. It also suggests that the pursuit of writing, which can gain a man renown and honor, can at the same time render him vulnerable to corruption. In what follows, Gower's ambivalent attitude to rhetoric in Book VII and elsewhere is located in the context of classical and contemporary ideas that connected eloquence with insincerity, masquerade, cosmetics, effeminacy, sodomy, and other forms of "moral degeneracy." These vices were in turn associated, in contemporary texts, with the court of Richard II. I will conclude this chapter by explaining how the troubled character of Dante's relationship with his old teacher is reflected in Gower's own anxiety of influence.

THE GENDER OF RHETORIC

Rita Copeland argues that "For Gower, rhetoric is defined in almost entirely political terms."[17] Yet in *Lies, Slander, and Obscenity*, Edwin Craun notes that in Book VII, Genius actually "establishes an ethical foundation to rhetoric in the cognitive function of words *before* he turns to its use in political discourse."[18] Genius opens his explication of rhetoric with a brief account of how

> Above alle erthli creatures
> The hihe makere of natures
> The word to man hath yove alone,
> So that the speche of his persone,
> Or forto lese or forto winne,
> The hertes thoght which is withinne
> Mai shewe, what it wolde mene. (VII.1507–13)

Genius's account of the origins of language, with its resonances of the Book of Genesis and of St. John's Gospel (John 1:1–4) forges a strong link between God's gifts to humankind (language, but also Christ as the Word) and ethical and moral responsibilities. After stressing the importance of honesty and of avoiding any wicked abuse of language, Genius concludes:

> Whereof touchende this partie
> Is Rhetorique the science
> Appropred to the reverence
> Of wordes that ben reasonable. (VII.1522–25)

As Craun observes, "The play of sense in 'resonable' links the cognitive function of words to rhetoric: in rhetoric, words both 'pertain to the faculty of reason' (MED1b) and are eloquently expressed (MED 5)."[19] If, according to Aristotle, reason is humankind's principal distinguishing quality, by relating rhetoric to reason, Genius, or Gower, follows Latini and thus also classical authorities like Cicero in suggesting that rhetoric also places humanity above mere animals.[20]

Taking this further, it seems that in Gower, correct use of language is also gendered as masculine. If the ability to express one's thoughts in words "is noghwhere elles sene / Of kinde with non other beste" (VII.1514–15), proper speech is perhaps bestowed specifically on mankind, as opposed to mankind *and* womankind. While the word has a transformative power that can be used for good or evil (VII.1572–87), throughout *Confessio* the virtue of honest eloquence seems primarily to be a masculine rather than feminine quality. Indeed, when Genius explains how "Word hath beguiled many a man; / With word the wilde beste is daunted, / With word the Serpent is enchaunted" (VII.1564–66), we might well be reminded of Adam. The first man was deceived by the emotional, sensual, and irrational Eve, who in turn transgressed because she allowed herself to be charmed by the words of a snake, a lowly creature that had illegitimately claimed for itself the power of speech. Likewise in Book V, in the Tale of Jason and Medea, it is only through the woman's magical talismans and charms that Jason is able to slay the serpent and yoke the oxen and thus achieve his quest for the fleece. Nevertheless, Medea's powers appear primarily to be derived from the disruption rather than manipulation of rhetoric and speech:

> Sche made many a wonder soun,
> Somtime lich unto the cock,
> Sometime unto the Laverock,
> Sometime kacleth as a Hen,
> Somtime spekth as don the men:
> And riht so as hir jargoun strangeth,
> In sondri wise hir forme changeth,
> Sche semeth faie and no woman. (V.4098–4105)[21]

From the bathetic structure of this passage, it would seem that language and reasonable speech are even more alien to Medea, as a woman whose excessive and uncontrollable desire for her man is so typical of her sex, than is the cacophony of the birds. It is in fact at the moment when she speaks like a man that her "jargoun strangeth"—and, by implication, her transformation—reaches its ultimate realization.[22]

Gower assumes, then, that the power of speech reaches its true fulfillment in men alone. Nonetheless, according to Götz Schmitz, he does not follow Cicero's, and thus also Latini's, class-based distinctions between language (common to all men) and eloquence (the preserve of the few and an indication of true nobility). Schmitz states that Gower "levels both the distinctions between language and eloquence and between the few and the many by speaking of the 'word' as an ability conferred on every man."[23] It is evident throughout *Confessio* that Gower sees a plain style as ideal. For example, in Book VII, Genius explains that one may find in Tullius (i.e., Cicero) "in what wise he schal pronounce / His tale plein withoute frounce" (VII.1593–94).[24] If, according to Genius, rhetoric is related to reason, so eloquent words that do not correspond with reason are not truly rhetorical. The Latin verses that head this section on rhetoric in Book VII suggest that "Compositi pulcra sermonis verba placere / Principio poterunt, veraque fine placent" (Fair words at first are pleasing in a speech, / But in the end what pleases is the truth) (VII.1506a–b).[25] Gower also condemns outright the misuse of language:

> For if the wordes semen goode
> And ben wel spoke at mannes Ere,
> Whan that ther is no trouthe there,
> Thei don fulofte gret deceipte;
> For whan the word to the conceipte
> Descordeth in so double a wise,
> Such Rethorique is to despise
> In every place, and forto drede. (VII.1550–57)

The pairing of deceipte/conceipte (see also II.2311–12) draws our attention to the hypocrisy that may hide behind the mask of eloquence. Plain-speaking advisors like the ribald in the Roman triumphal procession (VII.2355–2411) or the unheeded prophet Micaiah (VII.2527–2685) are represented positively in their narratives. In contrast, in Book I, hypocrisy and trickery result in the deception of Paulina (I.761–1059) and the destruction of Troy (I.1077–1189), and in Book III, Cheste, or contention,

the second subspecies of Wrath, demonstrates in his loose talking another form of "croked eloquence" (III.440). As Craun puts it, "In the
Confessio, the deviant speaker is most often a more calculated and rhetorically savvy speaker."[26] Gower, then, makes it clear that he values clarity
and sincerity above false eloquence, which is artful and beguiling and
can be treacherous.

But despite the class leveling implicit in Gower's adaptation of Latini, it is nonetheless the case that in Book VII Gower is particularly
concerned with the conduct of the king rather than the common man.
Thus, we are told that Aristotle taught Alexander that truth was preemi-
nent amongst the virtues,

> So that his word be trewe and plein,
> Toward the world and so certain
> That in him be no double speche:
> For if men scholde trouthe seche
> And founde it noght withinne a king,
> It were an unsittende thing. (VII.1731–36)

Likewise, abuses of language are associated with the royal court. It is in
this context that Genius argues that the monarch should shun flatterers,
asserting that

> This vice scholde be refused,
> Wherof the Princes ben assoted.
> But wher the pleine trouthe is noted,
> Ther may a Prince wel conceive,
> That he schal noght himself deceive,
> Of that he hiereth wordes pleine. (VII.2338–43)

The historical background for such warnings is of course the reign of
Richard II:[27] at the time when Gower was first writing *Confessio* (1386–
90) the Appellants were attacking a number of the king's favorites, who
were seen to be giving him bad council. Amongst them was Robert de
Vere, Earl of Oxford, who was thought to be too young to be an influential councillor, and who was found guilty of treason in 1388. Gower's
choice of the word "assoted" may well refer to Richard's obvious and immoderate affection for de Vere, whom he created Marquis of Dublin in

1386 and Duke of Ireland the following year. But the play on words, "wel conceive," may allude to concerns about the monarch's failure to produce a male heir.[28] Writing before 1381, that is, even before Richard's friendship with de Vere had attracted public attention, Gower warned the king "sordibus implicitos falsosque cauebis amicos" (you shall beware of false friends involved in base behavior)[29] and urged him to avoid the sins of the flesh by marrying.[30] Gower's concerns about proper speech and about appropriate conduct for the king (as both an every*man* figure and as the head of the body politic) are inevitably tied in with worries about the failure of the royal line. As we have seen in the case of Dante, and will see later in the discussion of Alain de Lille's *De Planctu Naturae*, rhetoric, reasonable behavior, chastity, and the obligation to reproduce are interrelated.

For classical writers like Cicero, rhetoric referred to the art of speech. Although he gives it a clear moral slant, Genius interprets it in this way at VII.1630–40:

> Ther mai a man the Scole liere
> Of Rhetoriqes eloquences
>
> . . .
>
> Wherof a man schal justifie
> Hise wordes in disputeisoun,
> And knette upon conclusioun
> His Argument in such a forme,
> Which mai the pleine trouthe enforme
> And the soubtil cautele abate,
> Which every trewman schal debate.

On one level (that of rhetoric as persuasion), the famous men named by Genius to illustrate his discussion of rhetoric support this definition. They are Ulysses, who convinced Antenor to betray his city (VII.1558–63), and Julius Caesar, who successfully defended the traitors at the Catiline trial (VII.1595–1628); the latter example is borrowed from Latini's *Trésor*. However neither can be described as a true man contending against subtle tricks. By the time Gower was writing, in fact, rhetoric was understood less in terms of its practical uses and more in terms of its decorative role.[31] As Schmitz notes, "In ordinary speech, the ornamental concept of rhetoric . . . has been dominant ever since the Middle Ages: we still think of rhetorical figures or *colores* primarily when speaking of rhetorical style."[32] Even if, as Schmitz rightly suggests, Gower is indebted to the classical concept, his suspicion of rhetoric is closely related to the more narrow medieval sense of the word. Ulysses' "eloquence" and "facounde" (VII.1560) are only implicitly represented by Genius as a misuse of language, although few medieval readers would fail to recognize the ominous significance of any allusion to the fall of Troy, with its connotation of not only treachery, but also uncontrolled desire. Caesar is, however, explicitly contrasted with Cicero and his party who spoke "plein after the lawe" (VII.1623). It is said of Caesar that he "the wordes of his sawe / Coloureth in an other weie / Spekende" (VII.1624–26), and that his manipulation of language won the debate in the face of "trouthe" and "the comun profit" (VII.1608–09). In a detailed comparison of this passage with its immediate source, Schmitz draws our attention to differences between the two writers. Whereas Latini "accepts without scruples the purely instrumental character of rhetoric," Gower "alerts his reader to the fact that Caesar's use of rhetorical coloring obscures the truth and runs counter to the law."[33] Both the MED and the OED cite this example in their respective definitions of the verb "colouren"/"colour."[34] But it is perhaps indicative of the ambivalence with which Gower regards eloquence that their definitions are at odds with one another. The MED glosses the phrase "colouren wordes" as "to use words skillfully (to a certain effect)" and "colouren speche" as to "use figurative language." The OED, in contrast, gives the following definition: "To exhibit in a false light; to put an unfair or untrue construction upon; to misrepresent."[35] While Genius's discussion of rhetoric seemingly draws a careful distinction between the use and the abuse of rhetoric, the examples he cites serve to blur rather than to clarify.

Gower's use of the word "colour" in his discussion of Caesar's rhetoric alerts us to the gender play underlying this section of *Confessio Amantis,* and it may throw some light on this gender play if we examine the background to it in some detail. Commenting on the "connection of love in the 'modern' sense with fiction in the sense of disguise and deceit," Schmitz suggests that within *Confessio,* "the present world of love appears to be as superficial as a layer of make-up on an otherwise ill-favoured face."[36] Schmitz's choice of simile is both conventional and revealing. Schmitz echoes the classical writers and the church fathers in viewing cosmetics in a negative light. According to Marcia L. Colish, St. Ambrose

viewed the use of makeup "as one among a larger group of moral problems which all involve deception, cruelty, or dishonesty in one way or
another."[37] Such thinking continued into the Middle Ages. Alain de Lille's
Nature condemns the behavior of arrogant and insincere men who
adopt various modes of behavior in order to stand out from the crowd,
some of whom put on elaborate mannerisms, while "Alii uero sua cor-
pora femineis comptionibus nimis effeminant..." (others overfeminize
themselves with womanly adornments...).[38] In Guillaume de Lorris's
section of *Le Roman de la Rose*, Love advises Amant to keep himself well
groomed, but warns him against excess:

> Mais ne te farde ne ne guigne:
> Ce n'apartient s'as dames non,
> Ou a ceus de mauvais renon,
> Qui amors par male aventure
> Ont trovees contre Nature.

(but do not paint your face or wear make-up: only women do
that, and those of evil reputation who have unfortunately found
unlawful love.)[39]

Similarly Latin authors frequently likened the misuse, or overuse, of
rhetorical figures to false beauty. The influential Latin writer Quintilian
made the following criticism:

> non aliter quam distortis et quocunque modo prodigiosis cor-
> poribus apud quosdam maius est pretium quam iis, quae nihil
> ex communi habitu boni perdiderunt. Atque etiam que specie
> capiuntur, vulsis levatisque et inustas comas acu comentibus et
> non suo colore nitidis plus esse formae putant, quam possit
> tribuere incorrupta natura, ut pulchritudo corporis venire videa-
> tur ex malis morum.

(Similarly we see that some people place a higher value on figures which are in any way monstrous or distorted than they do
on those who have not lost any of the advantages of the normal
form of man. There are even some who are captivated by the
shams of artifice and think that there is more beauty in those
who pluck out superfluous hair or use depilatories, who dress

their locks by scorching them with the curling iron and glow with a complexion that is not their own, than can ever be conferred by nature pure and simple, so that it really seems as if physical beauty depended entirely on moral hideousness.)[40]

The use of makeup, the abuse of the figures of rhetoric, and an immoral disposition were seen to be closely interrelated. As Jacqueline Lichtenstein explains, "used to excess, ornament becomes makeup, which conceals rather than elucidates truth."[41]

Images of artificially colored or made-up faces combined with lying words haunt Gower's writing. One example in *Confessio* occurs in the Latin verses in the Prologue at line 92: "Nuncque latens odium vultum depingit amoris, / Paceque sub ficta tempus ad arma tegit" (Now hidden hatred paints a loving face, / And hides a time of war beneath feigned peace) (Prol.92g–h). Another occurs in Book I in the description of two-faced Hypocrisy, who "The colour of the reyni Mone / With medicine upon his face / He set" (I.692–94) in order to feign love-sickness.[42] Thus Gower's choice of the word "colour" to describe, apparently pejoratively, Julius Caesar's eloquence when he pleaded for mercy in a case of high treason clearly carries with it connotations of falsified appearances and verbal masquerade (see also I.606 and II.1874). "Peinte" is another word that recurs in *Confessio* in similar contexts to "colour" and with a similar range of meanings. It refers to the application of cosmetics (for example in I.1346) as well as to linguistic embellishment. Its rhyming pair is often "queinte" with its connotations of cunning and dissimulation (e.g., I.283–84; I.2729–30; II.2853–54; V.4623–24). Also relevant here is "coverture," meaning "a protective device, a refuge; a disguise or pretext" and, more sinisterly, "concealment; stealth" (I.645; II.1939; IV.1102).[43]

In the Latin tradition, (ab)use of rhetoric was not only associated with cosmetics but, by extension, also with effeminacy: Cicero's eloquence was dismissed as "emasculated" by Brutus, and in similar terms by Quintilian[44] who praised the manly vigor of the genuine orator, but condemned the modern taste for expressions that he describes as "impropria, obscura, tumida, humilia, sordida, lasciva, effeminata" (inappropriate, obscure, high-flown, groveling, mean, extravagant or effeminate).[45] The connection between rhetoric and effeminacy is perhaps most fully realized in one of Gower's primary sources for *Confessio Amantis*, Alain de

Lille's *De Planctu Naturae*. Alain's attitude to rhetoric is similar in some respects to Gower's (like Gower, Alain was suspicious of elaborate diction), but Alain is more direct in his criticisms. According to Jan Ziolkowski, Alain's attitude to the art of speaking is not one of outright condemnation, but rather one of "healthy skepticism."[46] Nature does not advocate the total avoidance of rhetorical figures, and indeed justifies her own use of them on more than one occasion.[47] Nonetheless, we are told that one of the flaws in rhetoric is the way in which the hypocrite can manipulate stylistic range to flatter or to detract, irrespective of true merit.[48] In addition, figurative language or literary devices are admissible only insofar as their use can be justified. Nature also relates to the narrator of *De Planctu Naturae* how she tried to teach Venus the difference between an excusable and an inexcusable figure of speech.[49] Right at the beginning of the text, Alain's narrator draws on the metaphors of the "tropus" (trope; an acceptable rhetorical usage) and "vitium" (defect, vice; an unacceptable stylistic device) to describe abuses of the laws of Nature.[50] These have resulted in men degenerating into the passive sex, in other words becoming like women or hermaphrodites:

> Se negat esse uirum Nature, factus in arte
> Barbarus. Ars illi non placet, immo tropus.
> Non tamen ista tropus poterit translatio dici.
> In uicium melius ista figura cadit.

(Becoming a barbarian by nature, he disclaims the manhood given him by nature. Grammar does not find favor with him, but rather a trope. This transposition, however, cannot be called a trope. The figure here more correctly falls into the category of defects.)[51]

In this text the personification of Nature characterizes the manifold perversities of humankind as those that are primarily concerned with nonreproductive forms of intercourse and issues of lineage, including sodomy in its narrow sense of sexual relations between men. Nature blames them on Venus and her persistent abuses of the trivium:

> Sed pocius se gramaticis constructionibus destruens, dialeticis conuersionibus inuertens, rethoricis coloribus decolorans, suam artem in figuram, figuram in uicium transferebat.

(On the contrary, destroying herself with the connections of Grammar, perverting herself with the conversions of Dialectic, discoloring herself with the colors of Rhetoric, she (Venus) kept turning her art into a figure and the figure into a defect.)[52]

Rhetorical vices, moral corruption, and perversity are inseparable from one another. Furthermore, sodomy and other forms of deviance seem to be represented in *De Planctu Naturae* as almost irresistibly attractive.[53] In the same way, Alain implies, people find effeminate rhetorical devices in general, and tropes or literary contrivances in particular, more pleasing than a virile, in other words masculine and potent, plain style, and their influences are consequently the more insidious. As Ziolkowski puts it, "Just as the serpent beguiles the quail, so the sophist misleads the uninitiated with a quick tongue and an impudent misapplication of the anvil of creation."[54]

The court satire and other literature of the later Middle Ages likewise reveal a nexus between rhetoric, dissimulation, effeminacy, self-indulgence, and all forms of lust including sodomy.[55] In Thomas Walsingham's *Chronicle,* we find courtly speech being linked to womanizing and idleness:

> Et hii nimirum milites plures erant Veneris quam Bellonæ, plus valentes in thalamo quam in campo, *plus lingua quam lancea præmuniti, ad dicendum vigiles,* ad faciendum acta martia somnolenti. Hii igitur, circa Regem conversantes, nihil quod deceret tantum militem informare curabant. . . .

> ([And surely] they were knights of Venus rather than knights of Bellona, more valiant in the bedchamber than on the field, *armed with words rather than weapons, prompt in speaking* but slow in performing the acts of war. These fellows, who are in close association with the King, care nothing for what a knight ought to know. . . .)[56]

Walsingham's claim that the advancement of de Vere was the result of his "familiaritatis obscoenæ" (intimate familiarity; i.e., sodomitical relationship) is now well known.[57] Furthermore, other writers of Gower's time were aware of an apparently fairly widespread identification of masquerade and effeminacy with the court of Richard II.[58] In other words,

even if, after possibly reading about the fate of Brunetto Latini in Dante's
Commedia, Gower did not make the connection between rhetoric, moral
degeneracy, and sodomy, Alain's concerns about the dangerous influence of corrupt language are as pertinent as Latini's *Trésor* to Gower's
discussion of rhetoric. It is plausible that this may have also been
"coloured" by contemporary writing and satire.

The conceptual link between false eloquence and sodomy (in its
most general sense of nonreproductive sexual intercourse) indicates that
it would be wrong to isolate Gower's discussion of rhetoric from Genius's
praise of "honeste" love and marriage, or from the extended account of
chastity as the fifth point of Policy (VII.4215–5397; esp. 4215). Effeminacy is a form of moral degeneracy that Gower condemns outright on a
number of occasions. Most notably, in his discussion of chastity in Book
VII, Genius states:

> Therfore a Prince him scholde avise,
> Er that he felle in such riote,
> And namely that he nassote
> To change for the wommanhede
> The worthinesse of his manhede. (VII.4252–6)

See also the Latin verses at VII.4214a–d; and the Tale of Sardanapalus,
VII.4313–43. In his discussion of the rhetoricians in VII.1558–1628,
Gower does not depict either of his silver-tongued orators as womanly.
Nonetheless, their masculinity was not unimpeachable. As Ad Putter
has pointed out, in medieval versions of the debate over the inheritance
of Achilles' armor in Ovid's *Metamorphosis* (XIII), Ajax accuses his eloquent opponent of effeminacy:

> Femineis Itacus nugis exuberat, expers
> Virtutis, Verres crimine, fraude Sinon.
> Oris pollicitis mens est contraria, belli
> Nescia, cum lingua disputat egra manus.

(The Ithacan [Ulysses] triumphs in feminine trifles. Without
prowess, he is a Verres in crime, and a Sinon in fraud. His pol-
ished speech belies his willpower, it does not want to know about
war; those with feeble hands must needs fight with words.)[59]

Gower, who elsewhere in *Confessio* associates Ulysses with both rhetoric and double-dealing,[60] also has Ulysses accused of effeminacy and cowardice in Book IV.1877–81. As we will see in Chapter 3, Ulysses is contrasted with the masculine and heroic Protesilaus.

Likewise, Julius Caesar had a reputation for effeminacy, although this had less to do with his eloquence and more to do with his sexual profligacy and rumors that he had played the passive role in his sexual relationship with Nicodemes, king of Bithynia. Suetonius states:

> At ne cui dubium omnino sit et impudicitiae et adulteriorum flagrasse infamia, Curio pater quadam eum oratione omnium mulierum virum et omnium virorum mulierem appellat.

> (But to remove all doubt that he had an evil reputation both for shameless vice and for adultery, I have only to add that the elder Curio in one of his speeches calls him "every woman's man and every man's woman.")[61]

Likewise, according to Catullus:

> Pvlcre convenit improbis cinaedis,
> Mamurrae pathicoque Caesarique.
>
> . . .
>
> morbosi pariter, gemelli utrique,
> uno in lecticulo erudituli ambo,
> non hic quam ille magis vorax adulter,
> rivales socii puellularum.

> (Well agreed are the abominable profligates,
> Maurra the effeminate, and Caesar.
>
> . . .
>
> Diseased alike, very twins,
> both on one sofa, dilettante writers both,
> one as greedy in adultery as the other,
> rivals and partners in love.)[62]

While Gower makes no reference to Caesar's reputation, it was widely known in the Middle Ages. Not only was Suetonius Petrarch's principal source for his *De viris illustribus,* but Dante has the poet Guido Guinicelli refer to the story in *Purgatorio,* XXVI:

"La gente che non vien con noi, offese
di ciò per che già Cesar, trionfando,
regina contra sè chiamar s'intese.
Però si parton *Soddoma* gridando,
rimproverando a sè com'hai udito,
ed aiutan l'arsura vergognando." (*Purgatorio,* XXVI.76–81)

("The folk who come not with us, used to err
in that for which Caesar, triumphing,
heard 'Queen' against him shouted: whence at their
departure from us they, to feel the sting
of self-reproof, shout 'Sodom,' as thou'st heard,
and on the fire their shame as fuel fling.")

Of course, the objection might be put forward that in his discussion of
rhetoric Gower does not actually refer to either Ulysses' womanliness or
Caesar's depravity. It might be argued therefore that, in *Confessio,* the
connection between rhetoric and effeminacy and sodomy is not established, that unlike Dante Gower does not represent the rhetorician as
sodomite. Nonetheless, we cannot isolate the text from its literary and
cultural contexts, and such connections did exist whether or not Gower
and his readers consciously made them. Furthermore, I would argue that
Gower might have been aware of the fact that Dante had represented
Latini—the immediate although unacknowledged authority for much
of Gower's discussion of rhetoric—as a notorious and unrepentant
sodomite, and also as a proud and narcissistic author. And like Dante, who
shared his disquiet about literary genealogy and inheritance, Gower must
have had a complex and highly problematic experience of the anxiety of
influence. It seems logical then to posit that Gower's ambivalence about
rhetoric—with its associations with makeup, masquerade, and effeminacy—forced him to question his own role as rhetorician and poet.

CONTAGIOUS DISEASES AND
INHERITED SINS

Having started with Dante's touching portrait of Latini, it seems appropriate to begin the final section of this chapter with Gower's own depiction of the great Italian poet. In the first recension of *Confessio* Book

VII, Genius inserts a brief narrative about Dante into his account of the evils of flattery. He recounts Dante's words to a flatterer with whom he had quarreled:

> "Ther ben many mo
> Of thy servantes than of myne.
> For the poete of his covyne
> Hath non that wol him clothe and fede,
> But a flatour may reule and lede
> A king with al his lond aboute." (*VII.2332–37)

Unlike Latini in *Commedia*, Gower's Dante does not exhibit false pride or vanity. Genius uses this story to illustrate the differences between a poor poet and a king—the latter is susceptible to the insincere and manipulative words of others in a way that the former is not. In line with the other changes to the text discussed earlier in this book, the later deletion of this passage may indicate that Gower identified the king with Richard II. At any rate, Gower aligns himself with Dante. Yet, at the same time, he distances himself from the actual authorities for Book VII; most notably, Latini, whom he never names. Yet in Gower's Dante episode, the implication is also that the poet—who presumably utters truths rather than falsehoods—has less control over the king than the flatterer. Gower, then, uses Dante to reflect on the limitations on his own role as poet and author of a mirror for princes. Gower's strong distrust of the king's advisors and his suspicion of rhetoric reflects back on himself. In Book VII of *Confessio*, Gower, speaking through the personae of Genius and Aristotle, sets himself up as an adviser to the king. The relationship between poet-counselor and king in what we might term the "outer" frame of *Confessio Amantis* parallels that between confessor and penitent in the "inner" frame. In both cases, we have the image of the older and more experienced man offering guidance to a more youthful figure. This pattern is, however, inverted in the case of Genius and Amans at the end of the Book VIII. At the same time, Gower strengthens his own identification with Aristotle in a way that does not show either man in a positive light. Aristotle appears in Book VIII amongst the company of Elde as a foolish lover who allowed himself to be bridled for the queen of Greece, "that in thilke time / Sche made him such as Silogime, / That he foryat al his logique" (VIII.2707–09). In depicting the by-now-fused figure of Amans/John Gower as a *senex amans*, the poet implies that he too has failed to follow the dictates of reason.

Gower problematizes his own position as a plain-speaking counselor. If Gower condemns verbal artifice as hypocritical and, by implication, effeminate and even sodomitical, at the end of *Confessio* he nonetheless makes the insincere (or at any rate rhetorical) claim, in the epilogue to the first recension, that he has used "no Rethoriqe" (*VIII.3064). In the revised poem he explains to the reader:

> And now to speke as in final,
> Touchende that y undirtok
> In englesch forto make a book
> Which stant betwene ernest and game,
> I have it maad as thilke same
> Which axe forto ben excusid,
> And that my bok be nought refusid
> Of lered men, whan thei it se,
> For lak of curiosite:
> For thilke scole of eloquence
> Belongith nought to my science,
> Uppon the forme of rethoriqe
> My wordis forto peinte and pike,
> As Tullius som tyme wrot.
> Bot this y knowe and this y wot,
> That y have do my trewe peyne
> With rude wordis and with pleyne,
> In al that evere y couthe and myghte
> This bok to write as y behighte,
> So as siknesse it soffre wolde;
> And also for my daies olde,
> That y am feble and impotent,
> I wot nought how the world ys went. (VIII.3106–3128)

In this passage, by specifying the vernacular status of *Confessio Amantis*, Gower distinguishes it from his earlier *Vox Clamantis*. Nevertheless, even if the language of his English text is far less elaborate than the Latin, the adjectives "rude" and "pleyne" are not entirely apposite. Gower cannot completely avoid the colors and conceits of rhetoric in *Confessio*

Amantis. Throughout the poem, Gower's Latin verses in particular display his virtuosity, but such demonstrations are not limited to them. Even as Gower claims that his book lacks "curiosite" or artful skill and denies that he can "peinte and pike" in the manner of Tullius Cicero, he demonstrates his ability to do so in English in an apology that is more than a mere humility topos.[63] What is more, we might well remember that at VII.1594 it was a style "plein withoute frounce" that Cicero was said to have advocated. Surely Gower's representation of his plain style, not as virile and the very opposite of effeminate, but as "impotent" and unmanly, should be read ironically rather than taken at face value.

Hostile critics might then find more reason to describe *Confessio*—a self-evidently eloquent and crafted work of literature—as made-up and effeminate rather than impotent. Writing in the sixteenth century, for example, Alexander Barclay dismissed it as a "thing wanton, not sad but insolent," that is, not serious but going beyond the bounds of propriety.[64] Barclay states (no doubt disingenuously) that his patron, Sir Giles Alington, had asked him to abridge *Confessio* and to modernize it in order to correct the "corrupte Englishe."[65] Barclay, however, claims that he refused on the grounds that "A man with hoare heres uncomely doth incline / To misframed fables or gesture feminine." This self-portrait of the aged translator, who knows better than to dabble in immature and womanly matters, is clearly intended as a criticism of the superannuated Gower, who (Barclay implies) has failed to learn from years of experience. Barclay's comments indicate that he took at face value Gower's depiction of himself in *Confessio.* Gower's narrator is indisputably not all that he seems. The marginal note at I.60 makes this manifest at the very start:

> Hic quasi in persona aliorum, quos amor alligat, fingens se auctor esse Amantem, varias eorum passiones variis huius libri distinccionibus per singula scribere proponit.

> (Here, as if in the person of others, whom love has fettered, the author represents himself as [*or* feigns himself to be] a lover, [and] he proposes to write, in the various parts of this book, [about] their various passions, one by one.)[66]

In my reading of this gloss, I take issue with Minnis's view that "the commentator on the *Confessio Amantis* was determined to prove that

Gower...was a good *auctor.*"[67] I would argue instead that the Latin gloss deliberately reveals the author-narrator's duplicity for ironic effect: disguised as the devoted lover he is falsifying his own appearance. And it is manifest throughout *Confessio* that Gower's double, Amans, is not exempt from charges of insincerity. Rather he might be included in the ranks of those lovers "that feignen hem an humble port, / And al is bot Ypocrisie" (I.674–75),[68] although for all his self-acclaimed skills in verbal masquerade, Amans is far less successful in love than he is at feigning penitence or at coloring his confession (to borrow a phrase from Quintilian).[69] By the end of the poem Amans has been exposed as a fraud when he beholds himself in the looking glass handed to him by Venus and sees his "colour fade" (VIII.2825). The transformation into both the likeness of the gray-headed author and the ridiculous *senex amans,* desirable to no one, is itself the distorted reflection of the deception carried out by those who adorn their own faces with cosmetics. Having associated false language with masquerade and effeminacy, and having attempted to distance his own plain style from such dishonest rhetoric, Gower and Amans find themselves implicated in these very vices.

To conclude this first section on language, let me link the discussion of Gower's anxiety of influence and concerns about literary inheritance to his own account of the origins of *Confessio Amantis.* The Prologue to *Confessio* begins with Gower's ruminations about textual survival, human mortality, and the legacy of knowledge. The poet declares:

> Of hem that writen ous tofore
> The bokes duelle, and we therfore
> Ben tawht of that was write tho:
> Forthi good is that we also
> In oure tyme among ous hiere
> Do wryte of newe som matiere,
> Essampled of these olde wyse
> So that it myhte in such a wyse,
> Whan we ben dede and elleswhere,
> Beleve to the worldes eere
> In tyme comende after this. (Prol.1–11)

Such a frank assertion of the didactic value of literature is perfectly in keeping with medieval theories about the function of poetry. Yet, these lines may well seem rather ominous when read in the context of Dante's *Inferno* XV, in which we learned the fate of that earlier writer and teacher who desired to see his work preserved for the benefit of future generations. The complexities of the genesis of Gower's poem become apparent when, in the first version of the Prologue, the author describes the moment of its inception. Here (in a scene passingly reminiscent of that in which Dante happened upon Latini by the embankment of the stygian brook), Gower relates how, rowing along the Thames one day, he by chance met with King Richard (*Prol.34–45). Having been invited to board the royal barge, Gower claims, in what is a subtype of modesty topos, that the monarch issued him a command to write "som newe thing" (*Prol.51).[70] Richard, in other words, is named as the father of Gower's text. This is of course a variation on the usual sort of anxiety of influence, which would refer to a literary authority or written source rather than a patron. The later elision of the dedicatory passage has been mentioned in the Introduction as possible evidence of Gower's political expediency. This elision may also reflect Gower's desire to distance himself from his former royal patron and from the accusations of incompetence and corruption made during his reign, and thus to preserve his book from moral taint. Indeed if we connect this elision to Gower's failure to name Latini as the main authority for Book VII, we might be tempted to conclude that the author specifically wanted to avoid the stain of sodomy.[71] At any rate, the Ricardian poet was aware that the writer, like the courtier, was as susceptible to charges of effeminacy and degeneracy as he was to those of flattery and hypocrisy, and that not only his success but also his masculinity was contingent on the reputation of his patron. Indeed, the decision on Gower's part to revise those parts of *Confessio* that praise the unpopular monarch is actually mirrored in Barclay's refusal to translate any part of it on the grounds that "to write, reade or commen of thing venerious" would be sufficient "to rayse bad name contagious."[72] Just as Gower did not want to be contaminated by Richard, so Barclay did not want to be infected by Gower.

My discussion of Gower's attitude to his craft has given primacy to the short section on rhetoric in Book VII of *Confessio*. The discussion of chastity that appears at the end of the same book indicates that it is not entirely divorced from the framing narrative of the confession and smooths the way for the return to the main theme of love. My argument in this chapter suggests that the section on rhetoric also connects with the matter of desire and the question of appropriate (male) conduct in a way not previously identified. Gower, like Dante before him and Barclay after, is preoccupied not only with literary genealogy and inheritance. He is concerned with his own reputation and the notoriety or eminence of his patron, forefathers, and other authorities, and also with the questions of whether writing is a legitimate and moral activity, what is the proper way to do it, and what are the difficulties in achieving a virile rhetorical style.

Part II

Sex

3

TRANSGRESSIVE GENDERS AND
SUBVERSIVE SEXUALITIES

❋

CONFESSIONAL SILENCES:
AMANS, CUPID, AND GENIUS

The relationship between confessional discourse, interiority or self-consciousness, and the regulation of sexuality is well established.[1] Yet, while in orthodox Christian thought the soul itself was held to be sexless, the penitential literature of the Middle Ages was gendered: it was written by and primarily for men. As Jacqueline Murray has explained, "confession and penance was in itself a singularly androcentric sacrament... whenever women enter the discussion it is as a marked category, a signal of difference, exception or emphasis."[2] Further, if, as Michel Foucault famously claimed, confession is "one of the West's most highly valued techniques for producing truth,"[3] the medieval church demanded that some truths—and specifically some *sexual* truths—should be produced only partially. As Allen J. Frantzen puts it, "confession was a site of contradictory demands and impulses."[4] Frantzen's comment refers specifically to sins that were considered to be contrary to nature, such as bestiality, self-abuse (or masturbation), and sodomy; all subjects that, within a confessional context, had to be broached indirectly, if they were to be broached at all. The fourteenth-century *Book of Vices and Virtues*, for example, demanded that unnatural vice should be confessed, but described it as "so foul þat it is abhomynacioun to speke it."[5] Sinful acts specific to sodomites as well as to women (and the two categories were not mutually exclusive in the Middle Ages)[6] remained unspoken or only partially articulated in the discourse of the medieval confessional.

Confessio Amantis clearly makes use of a penitential framework within a fictive and secular context. The unsuccessful lover, Amans, confesses his sins to Genius, the servant of Venus, while the priest elaborates his taxonomy of vices through a series of exemplary narratives.[7] As might be expected, this text is revealing about medieval notions of masculine heterosexuality, while its exploration of femininity seems somewhat superficial. In this chapter, however, it is my argument that within *Confessio* Gower is also concerned with the examination of other gendered identities—effeminacy and female masculinity in particular—that we might describe as "transgressive" because they cross over and obfuscate the divide between male and female. Furthermore, with its foregrounding of incest as the exemplary vice in Book VIII, *Confessio* is also a site for the exploration of what might be termed "subversive" sexualities, both male and female (subversive in the sense that they challenge societal norms and expose their inconsistencies).[8]

In the final chapter of her recent book, *Covert Operations*, Karma Lochrie stresses the importance of examining the intersection of gender ideology and sexual oppression. This, she argues, is necessary in order to counterbalance what she describes as "the dangerously narrow focus on sexuality in the Middle Ages that either excludes gender from its analysis or worse, posits gender as the conservative constraint that sexuality subverts."[9] In her analysis, sexuality (whether normative or otherwise) is actually *supported* by conservative gender ideology. Here I develop Lochrie's thesis in some directions, but come to rather different conclusions. According to Lochrie's reading of *Confessio*, Gower "fails to make clear distinctions between natural and unnatural forms of love, much less between heterosexuality and homosexuality."[10] She goes on to contend, however, that Gower adheres to a conservative gender ideology even as he reveals the inconsistencies, and she concludes that "for all its perversions, Gower's text is not finally subversive."[11] Lochrie's opinion that "John Gower is on the side of order, unity, and social hierarchy" is one with which I do not entirely concur.[12] In examining Gower's representation of gender, I am particularly fascinated by his portrayal of what Judith Halberstam refers to as "female masculinity," a category that she argues subverts binary divisions by offering another alternative to established norms.[13] Gower does not shy away from discussing some forms of gender transgression and sexual subversion; as will be seen, "unnatural" female desires are examined, or even countenanced within *Confessio*. Nonetheless, throughout the poem, male sodomy remains taboo.[14] In this chapter, I begin by examining the homosocial and potentially homoerotic relationships between Amans and Cupid and Amans and Genius, before focusing on three exemplary narratives embedded within the text of *Confessio* that are linked by the theme of cross-dressing.[15] In what follows, I suggest that these narratives reveal Gower's concerns about the unstable distinctions between the categories of male and female, masculine and feminine, manliness and effeminacy, ethical and unethical behavior, and natural and unnatural love. In the final section, I return to the frame narrative to examine the meaning of Genius's silence on the subject of sodomy between men.

Recent studies of sodomy in the Middle Ages have illustrated that it was widely viewed as a manifestation of feminine (and thus degenerate) and immature impulses, and thus not essentially different from immoderate and uncontrollable heterosexual desire.[16] From this perspective, Amans's excessive if frustrated longing might be seen to bear some similarity to medieval homosexuality. In addition, at the same time as the object of Amans's desire—the beloved lady—remains absent from *Confessio*, the frame narrative is dominated by the homosociality, or ho(m)mosexuality,[17] of the relationships between Amans and Cupid, and between Amans and Genius. Only one other figure makes a significant appearance in the frame narrative of *Confessio*: Venus. Gerald Kinneavy is of the view that, like the priest and the sinner, the goddess of love has a function within the poem's penitential structure.[18] He points out that proper penance demands cognizance of divine presence; the confessor only serves as an intermediary when the sinner bares his or her soul to the omniscient Creator. Kinneavy argues that in having Venus judge Amans and prescribe his penance at the end of the poem, "Gower employs a kind of *deus* (or *dea*) *ex machina*." Venus is privy to the truth of Amans's condition to an extent that Genius cannot be, since he relies entirely on what Amans chooses to tell him. Kinneavy fails, unfortunately, to acknowledge that Cupid's presence is more problematic.

Cupid's position is ambiguous; true, he relieves Amans's suffering, but he also is ultimately responsible for it. Cupid is, then, both tempter and redeemer, and his relationship with Amans is deeply homoerotic. At the start of the poem, Amans falls victim to Cupid's phallic arrow:

> Bot he that kyng with yhen wrothe
> His chiere aweiward fro me caste,
> And forth he passede ate laste.
> Bot natheles er he forthe wente
> A firy Dart me thoghte he hente
> And threw it thurgh myn herte rote. (I.140–45)[19]

Cupid's disdainful demeanor, while entirely conventional, anticipates that of the distant and dismissive lady to whom the lover devotes himself. This scene appears as the very striking third miniature in New York, Pierpont Morgan Library MS M.126 (fol. 8v; Figure 2). Here a crowned and gloriously robed god of love holds a scepter in one hand, and with the other thrusts the burning spear into the lover's exposed heart. Patricia Eberle observes that this miniature does not appear in other *Confessio* manuscripts and suggests that the illustrator(s) may have been inspired to include it by the example of *Roman de la Rose* manuscripts.[20] Nevertheless, Eberle acknowledges that in matters of detail it follows *Confessio Amantis,* for example, in depicting Cupid as armed with an *iaculum* rather than a bow and arrow. Equally significant, for my argument, is the positioning of Venus, who stands slightly behind the other two figures, balancing the scene, but otherwise almost incidental to it.[21] In the miniature, as in the poem, it is Cupid and Amans who hold centre stage.

In his supplication to Venus and Cupid in Book VIII, Amans compares his own powerlessness in the face of love to that of Pan, "which is the god of kinde" (VIII.2240), but who is, of course, also traditionally associated with Lechery.[22] Amans describes his inner conflict as a perpetual wrestling match that he can never win:

> For evere I wrastle and evere I am behinde,
> That I no strengthe in al min herte finde,
> Wherof that I mai stonden eny throwe;
> So fer mi wit with love is overthrowe. (VIII.2241–44)

This metaphor points toward the emotional, if not physical, encounters between men that are at the heart of *Confessio.* Some twenty-five lines further on, the lover reiterates that it is Venus's son rather than his lady who is responsible for his pain:

Figure 2. Amans, Cupid, and Venus. MS M.126, fol. 8v (detail).
Reprinted by permission of the Pierpont Morgan Library, New York.

> The which hath love under his governance,
> And in his hond with many a fyri lance
> He woundeth ofte, ther he wol noght hele;
> And that somdiel is cause of mi querele. (VIII.2269–72)[23]

Consequently, it is only Cupid who is finally able to release Amans from
his passion:

> This blinde god which mai noght se,
> Hath groped til that he me fond;
> And as he pitte forth his hond
> Upon my body, wher I lay,
> Me thoghte a fyri Lancegay,
> Which whilom thurgh myn herte he caste,
> He pulleth oute.... (VIII.2794–2800)

While Cupid's healing touch suggests that the old man's infatuation is a debilitating disease, comparable to the king's evil, the choice of language is noteworthy as "grope" clearly has erotic connotations that may extend in this context to "lancegay" (especially in the context of a gesture of withdrawal).[24] Indeed Rictor Norton has gone so far as to argue that Cupid, like the more familiar figure of Ganymede, is a coded trope within the homosexual tradition.[25]

The relationship between confessor and penitent is less sexualized than that between Cupid and Amans, but more fraught. Genius's fictive narratives are ostensibly used for exploring the lover's inner psyche and for bringing about his cure. Yet, as Genius himself is quite literally the first to admit, his own role is divided between that of servant to Venus and that of priest. Consequently he

> . . . mot algate and nedes wile
> Noght only make my spekynges
> Of love, bot of othre thinges,
> That touchen to the cause of vice. (I.238–41)[26]

As a result, there is often a marked disjunction between Amans's account of his unsuccessful love affair and Genius's exposition of the seven deadly sins. While Genius's discourse moves gradually if unevenly toward the instruction on ethics and self-government found in Book VII, Amans's own story fails to make any clear progress. His desire for guidance about how to achieve his love is frustrated and in the conclusion he is instead forced to abandon his pursuit. While he is made to admit his own inadequacies as a ridiculous *senex amans* and to give up his "unwise fantasie" (VIII.2866), Gower's impotent and increasingly isolated poetic persona continues to fall far short of Genius's ideal of the chaste and rational married man outlined in VII.4215–37.

Indeed, if it is at times tempting—although anachronistic—to think of the relationship between Genius and Amans not only as that of priest and penitent, but also as that of psychoanalyst and patient,[27] it is evident that the two often appear to be speaking at cross-purposes. Sometimes—most notably in Book VII where Genius directs his attention to the conduct of princes—it is not even clear that he is talking to Amans at all, except insofar as the monarch is intended to be read as a representative or everyman figure. Perhaps then, it should come as no surprise that the "talking cure" seems to fail in this instance. As I will explain toward the end of this chapter, it is in the context of this communication failure between Genius and Amans that Genius's silence on the subject of male sodomy can begin to be understood. First, however, I will look at some of the occasions in which Genius discusses other forms of effeminate and immature behavior and transgressive desire.

THE ETHICS OF CROSS-DRESSING: HERCULES, ACHILLES, AND IPHIS

In the course of the eight books of *Confessio Amantis,* the priest Genius relates to the penitent Amans three stories about transvestism, transgendering, and transsexuality: the Tales of Deianira and Nessus (II.2145–2307), Achilles and Deidamia (V.2961–3201), and Iphis and Ianthe (IV.451–505). Genius intends each of these narratives to exemplify a different vice or virtue. In none of them is the act of cross-dressing immediately relevant to the sin in question, nor, for that matter, to the lover's own transgressions. The story of Deianira and Nessus in Book II, for example, is narrated by Genius as a warning to Amans against the sin of "falssemblant," or false seeming. "Falssemblant" is a vice associated with masquerade and artful words; it is aligned with hypocrisy and, like hypocrisy, it is a form of Envy. Ostensibly, it is the giant Nessus who is guilty of this vice in his deception of Hercules and Deianira. He offers to carry both across a deep river but abandons the former and attempts to abduct the latter. But the story does not end here. Hercules both survives the river and shoots his foe with a poisoned arrow. Yet even as he is dying, Nessus continues to behave deceptively. He gives Deianira his bloody shirt, falsely promising that it will rekindle Hercules' love, should it ever fail.

The cross-dressing occurs in the continuation of the story, and it has the effect of undermining the moral. Suddenly Hercules is no longer an innocent victim. He abandons Deianira for another woman, Eolen, and his new love makes him so "nyce" or foolish, even delicate (II.2268) and "assote" or besotted (II.2269) that the adulterous couple take to dressing up in each other's clothing (II.2270–71).[28] At this point Deianira remembers Nessus's gift of the shirt and contrives to make Hercules wear it. However, this shirt, which metaphorically causes Deianira to burn with joy ("Hire thoghte hire herte was afyre": II.2256), is a pyrogen. Hercules' subsequent suffering drives him to such a state of madness that he destroys himself in a self-made fire. From this, it seems that Hercules' death is less the consequence of Nessus's deception and more the punishment for his own subsequent foolishness. Hercules' act of cross-dressing is itself a form of "falssemblant." The image of Hercules wearing a woman's coat is symbolic of his self-emasculation and loss of identity; as the narrator states: "thus fieblesce is set alofte, / And strengthe was put under fote" (II.2272–73).

This first cross-dressing narrative neatly illustrates the connection between cross-dressing and effeminacy. Effeminacy is condemned outright by Gower on a number of occasions. In *Vox Clamantis*, for example, the reader is warned that

> Demon femineos et molles diligit actus,
> Quando viri virtus omne virile negat

(Whenever a man's virtue will have no part in anything virile, the Devil highly favors his weak, womanly behavior.) (*Vox Clamantis*, III.1977–78)

In Book VII of *Confessio*, Genius begins to discuss love in terms of *kinde* or natural law. He asserts that "It sit a man be weie of kinde" to love, but "it is noght kinde," it is unnatural for a man to lose his wits for love (VII.4297–99). Such effeminate folly, which renders the strong feeble, is like frost in July, heat in December, or, significantly, in a sartorial context, the hose worn over the shoe (VII.4300–07).

The first of the "olde ensamples" Genius cites to illustrate the error of those who "for love hemself mislede, / Wherof manhode stod behinde" (VII.4310–12) is that of King Sardanapalus. Sardanapalus was so overcome by the fiery rage of love that he became "womannyssh" quite against "kinde," like a fish living on the land (VII.4321–23).[29] Shutting himself in his chamber in the company of women, he learned dainty sewing, how

> ...a Las to breide,
> And weve a Pours, and to enfile
> A Perle. (VII.4332–34)

When his enemy Barbarus discovered "hou this king in wommanhede / Was falle fro chivalerie" (VII.4336–37), he took his chance to invade his kingdom.[30] The moral of this exemplum, which occurs within a larger discussion about the importance of chastity, is unquestionably that *luxuria* (lust, or, in a broader sense, inordinate desire and intemperance) threatens masculinity. As is appropriate enough with the advice to princes' section of *Confessio*, Genius, as Gower's mouthpiece, directs his warning against effeminacy to the monarch, averring that the only solution is for a man to "love streite"(VII.4280) and then he will not be bound by women. "Streite" love in this context appears to mean moderate love.

Immoderate desire—or love that is not "streite"—is literalized by male cross-dressing; a travesty of masculinity, like all forms of effeminacy it is a symptom of ethical misgovernance. The conclusion of the Tale of Deianira and Nessus reveals that identity is known or constructed as much through knowing what one is not as through knowing what one is. Hercules—renowned for his physical prowess and courage—has undermined his greatness, his very selfhood, by donning the apparel of a weak woman. Seeming to be what he is not brings about an ontological crisis, which can only be resolved by self-destruction.[31]

The story of Hercules raises questions about gendered identity, which are explored elsewhere in *Confessio Amantis*. In Book V, in the Tale of Achilles and Deidamia, notions of masculinity are interrogated further. Once again there is a disjunction between the topic of discussion and the exemplary narrative. This exemplum is intended to illustrate the evils of "falswitnesse," a form of covetousness. "Falswitnesse" is a vice not dissimilar to "falssemblant" in that it too profits from lying and treachery: it is another form of verbal masquerade. In this case it is Thetis, goddess of the sea, who (indirectly) deceives another woman, Deidamia, daughter of King Lichomede. Thetis, in an attempt to prevent his going to Troy, disguises her son Achilles as a maiden and sends him to Lichomede's household, where he becomes Deidamia's bedfellow and then lover. According to Genius's earlier definition, "falswitnesse" in love is a form of secret procuration—not only in the sense of inducing or urging, but also in the sense of pimping (V.2903–13).[32] Thus, Thetis is, by implication, further guilty of "falswitnesse" insofar as she effectively procures Deidamia for her son by bringing it about that he sleeps in her bed.

And one might argue that just as Hercules is guilty of "falssemblant" in dressing up in his lover's clothes, so Achilles is guilty of "falswitnesse" in pretending to be a maid. Although not aware of his mother's motives, Achilles "buxomly" colludes with her plan (V.3030), smiling to himself at the success of his disguise (V.3012–13), or even, as Rosemary Woolf suggests, relishing "a moment of sexual indeterminacy."[33] As Woolf observes, at this point Gower adapts his source (Statius's *Achilleid*) in which Achilles is disgusted at having to dress as a woman and does so only with reluctance. However it should be noted that Gower may be influenced here by a version of the story found in Alain de Lille's *Anticlaudianus*, in which Achilles is censured as degenerate because he deliberately took upon himself the role of a woman.[34] At any rate, in Gower's version, Achilles reveals his duplicitous nature once and for all when he abandons his lover to join the Greek army.

Interestingly, the third figure in this story who might be accused of "falswitnesse" alongside Thetis and Achilles is Ulysses, who is sent with Agamemnon to seek out the hidden boy. Here eloquence reveals itself as a form of "falswitnesse," when Ulysses, "which hath facounde" (V.3126), greets Lichomede but disguises his true intent, choosing to discover the young hero's identity by trickery rather than exhortation. Ulysses' presence reinforces the link between gender transgression and ethical misgovernance, since elsewhere in *Confessio* this smooth-talking hero is revealed to be guilty of effeminacy. In Book IV, Ulysses is accused by Nauplus of dishonoring his reputation by feigning madness and staying at home with his wife rather than fighting like a man:

> "... that thou for Slouthe of eny love
> Schalt so thi lustes sette above
> And leve of armes the knyhthode,
> Which is the pris of thi manhode
> And oghte ferst to be desired." (IV.1877–81)

Genius then contrasts Ulysses with Protesilaus, who exemplified manly prowess, refusing to pay attention to the "wommannysshe drede" (IV.1924) of his spouse and embracing the prospect of losing his life in battle.

However, while still associated with effeminacy, Achilles' cross-dressing is also linked to immaturity. Whereas Hercules' death is vividly, if briefly, described, the story of Achilles breaks off at the point of his departure for the Siege of Troy. Unlike Hercules, Achilles is not punished for dressing as a woman. His sin of "falswitnesse" is apparently forgiven. One likely explanation for this seeming discrepancy is that

Achilles is not held culpable because his cross-dressing is engineered by his mother and because he indulges in it when he is not yet fully a man. Indeed, the narrator emphasizes that his appearance and manner are actually those of a child (V.3014–21).[35] Consequently, Achilles' masculinity, unlike that of Hercules, is never really in question. His feminine appearance or "wommannysshe chiere" is something that he quite consciously puts on, and his manliness is something that has to be restrained (V.3050–55). The subsequent adoption of his masculine identity is represented as maturation. This does not occur, as we might expect, when he sleeps with a woman, even though this is described in terms of Nature and "kinde" or natural law asserting themselves (V.3058–69). Rather, Achilles only fully assumes a traditional male identity when he is made to choose between women's dress and the trappings of chivalry (V.3152–67). In an episode derived from Statius *(Achilleid)* and Ovid *(Ars Amatoria)*,[36] but perhaps also reminiscent of the romance of Perceval,[37] Achilles is entranced by the shining gear and hastens to arm himself (V.3168–85). Achilles' female disguise signifies his childhood when he remains under the influence of his mother. His arming is a rite of passage. He forgets his promise to his mother and joins Ulysses and Diomedes. It is significant that it is at *this* stage in the narrative (and not earlier) that we are told that Deidamia is going to have his child (V.3194–95).

So far, these stories have focused on the effect of transvestism and transgendering on men. In the story of Hercules, the narrator did not comment on Eolen's cross-dressing: there was no suggestion that she was punished for putting on a man's clothing. This might indicate that women's cross-dressing has a meaning different from men's, a theory that is strengthened by Gower's Tale of Iphis and Ianthe. This narrative bears some resemblance to that of Achilles. Once again the mother plays a central role: on the instructions of the goddess Isis, Iphis's mother brings up her daughter as a boy, in this case to save her from her father who vowed that he would have the infant slain at birth if it were a girl. At the age of ten the child Iphis is wedded to a duke's daughter, Ianthe, and eventually the two girls become lovers, a union memorably described by Christopher Ricks as "'sche and sche': it is magnificent, but it is not marriage."[38]

The narrative of Iphis is far from straightforward and has resulted in some critical confusion. Whereas Woolf defines the relationship between Iphis and Ianthe as homosexual, Patrick J. Gallacher claims that "nature prohibits physical expression of their love."[39] Gallacher's read-ing of the narrative seems unlikely given that Gower adapts his source (Ovid's *Metamorphoses*, IX.666–797) so that the marriage has taken place *and* the sexual relationship has developed *before* the conflict sur-rounding Iphis's sex has been resolved. However a clue to Gallacher's reading lies in the Latin commentary. In the marginal gloss at IV.455 we are informed, "Set cum Yphis debitum sue coinage vnde soluere non habuit, deos in sui adiutorium interpellabat" (But when Iphis did not have it in her power to honor the debt owed to her spouse, she prayed to the gods in their oratories). This commentary is at odds with the English text, which does not mention Iphis's prayer and which seems to suggest that Iphis *does* have it in her power to honor her marriage debt. We are told that Iphis and Ianthe, lying side by side in bed, find themselves compelled not only by proximity but also by Nature (possibly meaning simply "sexual instinct" in this case) "so that thei use / Thing which to hem was al unknowe" (IV.486–87).

The discrepancy between the Latin and English verses is sympto-matic of the confusion that lies at the heart of Gower's telling of this story. Woolf argues that "Gower has obscured the moral issue... by some unclear generalizations."[40] Whereas in Ovid, Iphis laments that her desire for another woman is monstrous and unnatural, in Gower's Middle English version, she makes no such complaint, implying perhaps that neither she nor Genius views it as such. Nonetheless, in the next few lines, Cupid's intervention[41]—his decision to transform Iphis into a man—is described in terms of reasserting the supremacy of "kinde" and "kinde love" (IV.488–505). In other words, although driven by na-ture ("Nature... Constreigneth hem": IV.484–86), the love shared by Iphis and Ianthe is, paradoxically, now defined as an offense against nat-ural law:

> For love hateth nothing more
> Than thing which stant ayein the lore
> Of that nature in kinde hath sett. (IV.493–95)[42]

The resolution of the tale is indeed, as Genius asserts, a "wonder" in the sense of "a marvel" or "a miracle," but possibly also in the senses of a puzzle an "evil" or a "disaster" (IV.445).[43]

Genius's confusion reflects medieval attitudes to sex between women. Even though such sex came under the definition of sodomy, it seems to have been more or less invisible in Gower's own society: there is little or no surviving evidence in England or Wales of women being examined about sexual misconduct with women.[44] Despite his later assertion that the "madle" (male) is made for the "femele" (female) (VII.4215), Genius seems unwilling to condemn Iphis. The age of her betrothal (thirteen in Ovid) is changed to ten, and although it is suggested that time passes before the two women have sex (IV.481: "withinne time of yeeres"), Iphis would not have been considered old enough to bear criminal responsibility.[45] Furthermore, her innocence, or rather ignorance, is explicitly commented upon. As with the story of Achilles, childhood seems to be a space of legitimate transgression. Nonetheless, within a Christian moral framework neither Achilles nor Iphis would be *entirely* exonerated from blame, because from the age of seven (the age of reason) children were believed to be able to distinguish good from evil.[46] But if Gower is ambivalent about lesbian sex, he does not represent as problematic Iphis's transformation into a man (it is, in fact, anticipated by his, albeit inconsistent, use of masculine pronouns from the start of the story). One explanation for this is that according to certain theories of medicine, the one-sex model, the transformation from female to male was not in itself contrary to nature.[47] Indeed because women were perceived to be inferior to men, such a transformation could only be seen as an improvement, a change from an imperfect state to a perfect one; it could bestow on the woman a potency she would otherwise lack. It must be said that Iphis does not undergo any sort of identity crisis.

Whereas male cross-dressing poses a problem for Genius because, by implicating the heroes, Hercules and Achilles, in the sins of Nessus and Thetis, the morals of the exemplary narratives become confused as the boundary between ethical and unethical behavior is crossed, the same is not so true of female cross-dressing. Unlike Hercules, Iphis suffers no punishment for cross-dressing (quite the opposite, as she is rewarded for her perseverance as for a virtue), and unlike Achilles, she does not grow out of it. In fact, Iphis appears as one of the few desiring female subjects and *exemplary* female lovers in the text; exemplary, perhaps, because she exhibits virtues constructed as masculine rather than feminine. In her story, unlike those of Hercules or Achilles, cross-dressing is not intended to exemplify the evils of deception. Rather, the tale illustrates the vice of pusillanimity or Faint Heartedness, that lack of determination that is a form of Sloth. According to Genius, pusillanimity detracts from masculinity: the lover guilty of this vice "woll no manhed understonde, / For evere he hath drede upon honde" (IV.325–26). Later in the same book, Genius encourages Amans with the words

> Mi Sone, it is wel resonable,
> In place which is honorable
> If that a man his herte sette,
> That thanne he for no Slowthe lette
> To do what longeth to manhede. (IV.2029–33)

Iphis is apparently cited as the opposite of pusillanimity, as a *positive* example of the strength of character necessary to win love:

> And thus to take an evidence,
> It semeth love is welwillende
> To hem that ben continuende
> With besy herte to poursuie
> Thing which that is to love due. (IV.506–10)

Iphis can be usefully compared to the Amazon queen Penthesilea, who, inspired by the twinned chivalric ideals of love and honor in war, came to the rescue of Hercules in the siege of Troy (IV.2141–42). While Penthesilea's attire is not specifically mentioned, it can be assumed that she dons armor before entering battle.[48] Penthesilea's significance should not be underestimated. She is mentioned three times in all: here as an example of prowess (IV.2135–82), and again as an example of wealth (V.2547–51), and as a member of the company of lovers (VIII.2525–27). Penthesilea, then, can be cited as another example of a cross-dressing heroine who is intended as a positive role model for Amans, and as another woman who exemplifies masculine virtue.[49]

THE LACK OF SODOMY

In my analysis so far I have concentrated largely on issues of gender difference (specifically effeminacy and female masculinity), and the question of homosexuality or sodomy has been addressed only in relation to the Tale of Iphis and Ianthe. However, as I have already indicated, Gower's infamous preoccupation with incest suggests the centrality of sexuality—especially subversive sexuality—to the text as a whole. It is a significant point, then, that out of all of these cross-dressing narratives, which in their different ways explore the interconnection of transgressive gender and subversive sexuality, only one discusses a same-sex sexual relationship. And it is equally significant that the Tale of Iphis and Ianthe is one of only two stories retold by Gower out of the eight *Metamorphoses* that focus sympathetically on same-sex desire.[50] The other is the Tale of Narcissus (I.2275–2366).

Gower's treatment of this narrative draws our attention to what he is omitting. In Ovid's *Metamorphoses* (III.344–510), the proud and beautiful Narcissus, at the age of sixteen, is between boy and manhood. He is extremely attractive to both boys and girls, but only the nymph Echo dares approach him. After his rejection of Echo, he is punished for his selfish chastity by Nemesis who causes him to fall in love with his own reflection. As Narcissus comes to the realization that the boy whom he desires is his own image, he is consumed by an inner fire. Mark Jordan has argued that Alain de Lille adapted the story as an implicit condemnation of irregular sex, "to illustrate the danger of self-love, that is, the danger of the love of a body for another of the same kind."[51] From Genius's conclusion it might seem that Gower's English version has a similar moral: the flower that springs up on Narcissus's sepulcher and grows in winter

> . . . is contraire
> To kynde, and so was the folie
> Which fell of his Surquiderie. (I.2356–58)

Yet Gower's reshaping of the narrative removes the possibility of interpreting Narcissus's love as homosexual. We are told,

> He sih the like of his visage,
> And wende ther were an ymage
> Of such a Nimphe as tho was faie,
> Wherof that love his herte assaie
> Began, as it was after sene,
> Of his sotie and made him wene
> It were a womman that he syh. (I.2315–21)

The Latin gloss goes further still and identifies the image with Echo: "ipse faciem suam pulcherrimam in aqua percipiens, putabat se per hoc illam Nimpham, quam Poete Ekko vocant, in flumine coram suis oculis pocius conspexisse" (seeing his own very beautiful face in the water, he thought himself to be in the presence of that Nymph whom the poets call Echo, rather than gazing into his own eyes) (at I.2279).[52] Siân Echard suggests that this explanatory allusion to Echo "could be seen as an attempt to efface possible homoerotic implications in the original version of the tale."[53] If this was the case, it is lost in the attendant illustration in Pierpont Morgan MS M.126, which has a crowned Narcissus (the Latin commentary refers to him as "Principis filius") gazing longingly at what is unmistakably *his own* reflection.[54]

This is certainly not the only instance when Gower, or Genius, avoids the homosexual or homoerotic possibilities of his sources. For example, Genius does not make any allusion to Hercules' love for the youth Hylas,[55] or to Achilles' reputation as the friend and possibly lover of Patroclus (surely known to him through his reading of Benoît de Sainte-Maure, or perhaps even Alain de Lille).[56] Another example of Gower "straightening" his sources is his treatment of the story of Lot, discussed in Chapter 1 above. The nearest Genius comes to discussing the sin of sodomy is in the Tale of Hercules and Faunus in Book V (6807–6935). Here Genius returns to the affair between Hercules and Eolen, and on this occasion the exchange of clothing is described in almost loving detail with the former being represented as submitting to his woman's playful whims. Eolen dresses in her lover's lion skin, ties his mace to her belt, and winds a wimple around his face. In this instance, cross-dressing serves to protect the woman (although not the man) from sexual assault when the lustful Faunus mistakenly climbs on top of a sleeping Hercules. However, the homoerotic potential of this confusion is undeveloped, or at any rate displaced into virile physical aggression: Hercules wrestles Faunus to the floor and leaves him lying there humiliated.[57] This episode might be dismissed as a humorous interlude, but it gains significance from resonances elsewhere in the text. Faunus was often identified with Pan,[58] and, as we have already seen, Amans likens himself to Pan and considers himself doomed to fight a losing battle against love in an eternal wrestling match.

I suggested earlier that Genius's evasion of the subject of male sodomy relates in some way to the communication failure between

Genius and Amans. It is not simply that Genius is an inept confessor, whose choice of exempla sometimes appears bizarre, whose meaning is often unclear, and who frequently loses sight of the circumstances of his penitent.[59] The silence about male sodomy relates to a larger problem within penitential literature more generally. How can one be specific about sexual sins, without leading either the confessor or the penitent into a sin that they might not otherwise have imagined, or into a (sexual) relationship that would not otherwise have developed?[60] Near the start of Book I, Genius outlines to Amans his confessional procedure:

> Of my Presthode after the forme
> I wol thi schrifte so enforme,
> That ate leste thou schalt hiere
> The vices, and to thi matiere
> Of love I schal hem so remene,
> That thou schalt knowe what thei mene.
> For what a man schal axe or sein
> Touchende of schrifte, it mot be plein,
> It nedeth noght to make it quiente,
> For trowthe hise wordes wol noght peinte:
> That I wole axe of the forthi,
> My Sone, it schal be so pleinly,
> That thou schalt knowe and understonde
> The pointz of schrifte how that thei stonde. (I.275–88)

Genius asserts that, in confession, plain style is the order of the day and indirect or figurative language is to be avoided. But, as his own use of exemplary narratives illustrates, such an ideal cannot always be sustained; didacticism has to be clothed as entertainment, "lore" has to be dressed up in the language of "love."

In many instances, the indirect approach proves to be the most acceptable, if not the most effective. As I have already suggested, sodomy is one such instance. Chaucer's Parson referred to it as "thilke abhomynable synne, of which that no man unnethe oghte speke ne write" (the Parson's Tale, 909). Similarly, John Mirk instructed priests that they should not raise the issue of the "synne aȝeynes kynde" but only warn penitents indirectly that to "do hys kynde other way, / þat ys gret synne wyþowte nay."[61] When it came to sodomy—and sodomy committed by men in particular—priests could only "grope" in the dark, in the Middle

English sense of hearing confession or examining someone's conscience.[62] As a consequence, there was always the possibility that their warnings would go unheard, that their words would be misunderstood. This is what seems to happen in *Confessio*. Genius avoids the subject of sodomy in relation to the practices of men because it might prove too close to the bone. Because the masculine perspective limits this poem, like so many other confessional texts, the same difficulties do not apply to the sodomitical practices of women. But because Genius does ignore the subject of male sodomy, Amans has, quite simply, no idea that it might be an issue.

The conventions and regulations of the confessional have then their impact on this poem and what it discloses and does not disclose. A further factor contributing to Genius's failure to question Amans about sodomy, and about his relationship with Cupid in particular, relates to *Confessio*'s complex status as a mirror for princes and as a court poem that incorporates political commentary. In the Introduction, I commented on the connection between *The Legend of Good Women* and *Confessio Amantis,* and the likelihood that both poems are the product of an amicable rivalry between Chaucer and Gower. Hitherto, critics have overlooked the full implications of this probability, and consequently of the link between the works. As is immediately apparent, both poets frame their narratives with a polite but hostile encounter between the poet-narrator and Cupid and his lady (Alceste rather than Venus in Chaucer's *Legend*). A number of critics have argued that Chaucer's Cupid, a tyrannical male authority figure, stands for the imperious Richard II himself, with Alceste providing a fictional portrait of his conciliatory spouse, Anne of Bohemia.[63] The parallel might be extended to Gower's Cupid and Richard II; although it should be noted that Venus, eloquent, perceptive, and powerful though she is, would be an unlikely and not entirely flattering double of the queen consort.[64] The account, in the first version of *Confessio,* of Gower's encounter with the king, and of the king's personal commissioning of the poem, certainly invites the comparison of Cupid and Richard. And if the Richard II who charmingly and courteously invites the aged poet to join him aboard his barge in the original Prologue represents one aspect of this monarch's public persona, the angry and contemptuous pagan deity of Book I demonstrates another far more terrifying one. In later chapters, I will return to the question of Gower's fictional portrayal of his ruler in *Confessio;* suffice to say here that in both the Prologue and Book I, the poet/lover (Gower/Amans) is equally powerless to do anything more than submit. We saw in the previous chapters that sodomy casts its shadow over the relationship between author and reader, as well as over Gower's own rhetorical strategies and his anxieties about authorship. Gower as poet sees it appropriate in Book I to depict the conquest by Cupid/Richard of Amans in extremely sensual and suggestive imagery. Indeed, as Stephen Jaeger states, "the erotic has an important role to play both in political and personal relations that draw on the discourse of the king's love."[65] Nevertheless, it must surely come as no surprise that he refrains from representing male-male relationships in *explicitly* carnal terms, which could only be understood negatively.

In conclusion then, Genius's position on gender transgression and subversive sexuality is ambivalent: while he praises "honeste love" (marriage) and self-governance, he also explores transvestism, transgendering, and transsexuality, and even, at times, allows them to undermine norms of gender and sexuality. They are treated differently according to context, and according to the ethical issues raised. Hercules is viewed as effeminate because he is besotted with a woman and because, in dressing as a woman, he is guilty of "falssemblant". He can thus be compared to negative exemplary figures like Sardanapalus, or even Ulysses. Achilles' cross-dressing is legitimized by his youth and because his chivalric masculine identity asserts itself. It is not a form of "falswitnesse" insofar as he remains true to himself. Iphis, like Penthesilea, is taken as a positive "masculine" role model. These narratives destabilize not only male/female boundaries but also the oppositions of manliness and effeminacy, the ethical and the unethical, and the natural and the unnatural. *Confessio* presents the reader with a series of paradoxes. Nature can inspire unnatural desires and actions. It is possible, even desirable, for a woman to behave like or to turn into a man. The most manly of heroes can become effeminate. The most exemplary of figures can behave immorally, and vice versa. Sexual and ethical confusion are further indicators of the fallen world of which *Confessio* is a product. Yet, while neither female cross-dressing nor female homosexuality is condemned, male sodomy remains taboo. Although not divorced from other types of failure of self-governance or from other forms of excessive desire, male homosexuality is a topic that is not addressed in the mirror for princes and that is silenced within confessional discourse.

4

SEXUAL CHAOS AND SEXUAL SIN

❄

In the previous chapter, I challenged Karma Lochrie's conclusion that the gender ideology of *Confessio Amantis* is fundamentally conservative, in that Gower's narratives do not defy traditional gender hierarchies.[1] However, in many other respects, my reading is in accordance with that of Lochrie and supports her succinct summary of the relationship between sexual politics and sexual ethics in the text as a whole. According to Lochrie,

> What is useful is the way in which Genius's instruction exposes the perverse within the normative and the very instability of the normative itself. The violence against women, the selfishness, the feminization of men, the voraciousness of desire, the aberrant nature of sexuality, and the disorderliness of gender all speak through Genius's advocacy of an ordered, morally coherent guide for love.[2]

In the preceding chapters, I looked at some examples of effeminacy and of gender and sexual transgression or disorder in both the frame narrative and exemplary stories of *Confessio*. In what follows, I develop my analyses further by examining a selection of narratives about incest, rape, and seduction and sexual deception.

Critics focusing on Gower's treatment of incest in *Confessio* have hitherto tended to concentrate on his Tale of Canace and Machaire in Book III.143–336,[3] and on his Tale of Apollonius of Tyre in Book VIII.271–2008 (discussed in Chapter 6). I begin by considering Gower's oft-overlooked account of Venus's birth and of her relationship with her son Cupid. Although I suggest that Gower's Venus is a further example of the sort of sexual transgression examined in the last chapter, I am here less concerned with gender indeterminacy per se, than with the connection between gender and sin, and with the question of male and female accountability. Genius's even-handed treatment of Venus and Cupid is, as this chapter will demonstrate, entirely consistent with his emphasis on personal responsibility. Because *Confessio Amantis* contains such a large number of stories about violence against women and voracious masculine desire, I have chosen to focus in the discussion that follows on just one, representative, rape narrative: the story of Tereus. This, I argue, constitutes a damning critique of aggressive masculinity, which, from Gower's medieval perspective, is yet another example of sexual deviance and effeminacy. Here, I suggest that rape results in the dissolution rather than assertion of a stable masculine identity: Tereus loses not only his wife and son, but also his position within society and legacy for posterity. At the same time, Genius avoids placing the blame on female behavior, and (despite the atrocities the women go on to commit) sympathetically describes the effect of rape upon women. Rape is, it appears, caused by internal factors and the failure of self-government on the part of the rapist—will and desire overcoming reason—rather than by the woman who might otherwise be thought to have inspired it. Finally, in my analyses of the Tales of Mundus and Paulina and of Nectanabus, I address the vexed question of why some rapes are represented more positively by Genius, even inscribed with salvic qualities, and I relate this back to Genius's complex representation of Venus as sinner, temptress, and redeemer.

HERMAPHRODITIC MONSTERS: VENUS, SIN, AND SEX

In the middle of Book V occurs one of the many cruxes of *Confessio Amantis*. Genius, the priest of Venus, castigates the goddess and her son Cupid before Amans, their supplicant. When asked by Amans to explain the existence of these deities at the end of what appears to some critics to be a long and inopportune digression on the beliefs of the pagans (V.747–1597),[4] Genius admits to a sense of embarrassment about his own role as their servant:

> Mi Sone, I have it left for schame,
> Be cause I am here oghne Prest;
> Bot for thei stonden nyh thi brest
> Upon the schrifte of thi matiere,
> Thou schalt of hem the sothe hiere. (V.1382–86)

Yet even as Amans slowly explores and exposes to his confessor and to Gower's readers the "truth" of his own love affair, we might find ourselves questioning whether or not Venus and Cupid really are close to the hearts of either priest or penitent. At the beginning of the apparent departure on idolatry, Amans does, after all, align himself with Christianity, parroting as he does the first point of faith in asserting "For ther is bot o god of alle, / Which is the lord of hevene and helle" (V.732–33). Genius does not contradict this claim. Nevertheless, it is manifest from the way in which the narrative develops that both Genius and Amans are very much in the thrall of the very misbelief that the former proceeds to condemn so vituperatively. After all, in Book VIII, Amans only renounces his own idolatry *after* Venus and Cupid have chosen to relinquish their hold over him.[5] Genius's embarrassment about his position as priest of Venus is not simply caused by his awareness that his own faith, and that of his charge, is misplaced. Genius is, it transpires, fully aware of the absolute lawlessness of the edicts of love to which he and Amans are subject.

Genius's stated objections to Venus are fourfold. First, she is promiscuous: she "alle danger putte aweie / Of love, and fond to lust a weie" (V.1389–90). Second, she has committed incest, both with her brother Jupiter and with her son by that union, Cupid himself (V.1403–20). Third, to protect herself, she sanctions the licentiousness of the female sex generally (V.1421–29). Fourth, she encourages women to prostitute themselves (V.1430–31). As Theresa Tinkle explains, in her analysis of the poem's mythography, "The elaborate spectacle of [Venus's and Cupid's] incestuous, indiscriminate, commercial sexuality robs them of credibility and seemliness as sponsors of literary love."[6] Genius's rejection of Venus, whom (in Tinkle's words) he effectively demotes from a deity to "a degraded historical figure," is highly conventional. A wide range of texts, from the Bible to *De Planctu Naturae* and *Le Roman de la Rose,* place the blame for sin and diverse forms of sexual deviance at the doorstep of womankind and femininity; the latter two texts feature Venus herself.[7] Indeed, following St. Paul's teaching in Romans 1:26–27 ("For even their women did change the natural use into that which is against nature: And likewise also the men...."), the late-fourteenth-century English poem *Cleanness* implies that even the sexual practices of the men of Sodom and Gomorrah had their origins in the deviant desires of the womenfolk of the Cities of the Plain: "Uch male mas his mach a man as hymselven, / And fylter folyly in fere on femmales wyse."[8] *Confessio Amantis* seems then to fit firmly into a literary tradition that concerns itself with what are ultimately "*female* perversions*" (to borrow Lochrie's terminology).[9]

On the surface, Venus, as incestuous mother, does indeed appear to be little more than another Eve figure. The sexual chaos that she introduces into the world seems just another indication of "division," of humanity's postlapsarian state. According to Lochrie, Gower's portrayal of the goddess of love reveals that "the perverse" is at the heart of desire—whether "heterosexual" or "same-sex"—because, as she puts it, it is as "unstable, errant, and excessive" as Venus is herself. In other words, this portrait reflects what Lochrie goes on to characterize as "the pathologizing of all sexuality."[10] In some respects the story of Venus's relationship with her son has its ludic, carnivalesque qualities; as Georgiana Donavin explains, "Venus and Cupid are exposed as a gross parody of Mary and Jesus, their literal incest a perverted substitute for the spiritual relationship cultivated by the Christian Mother and Son."[11] In portraying Venus as having sex with the child born from a union with her own brother, Jupiter, Gower also implicitly compares her to Sin in his earlier Anglo-Norman work, *Mirour de l'Omme*. Here, in an anticipation of Milton's *Paradise Lost*, Book II, *Pecché* (Sin) is seduced by her father, *Le deble* (the Devil), and sleeps with her son and brother, *Mort* (Death).[12] The devil rejoices in his children and encourages their union:

> Car tout quidoit par leur enhort
> De l'ome avoir sa volenté;
> Car quant ils deux sont d'un acort,
> Tout quanque vient a leur resort
> Le deble tient enherité.

(for by their persuasion he expected to have his will with man; for whenever both of them are in agreement, whatever comes in their power the devil has inherited.) (*Mirour de l'Omme*, 224–28)

In Gower's *Mirour,* the alliance of *Pecché* and *Mort* results in seven off-spring: the deadly sins of *Orguil* (Pride), *Envye* (Envy), *Ire* (Anger), *Avarice* (Avarice), *Accide* (Sloth), *Glotonie* (Gluttony), and one "que se porte / Sur toutes autres la plus nice" (who bears herself the most attractively of all) (*Mirour de l'Omme,* 263–64): *Leccherie* (Lechery). The parallels between the *Mirour* and *Confessio Amantis* are found not only in the representation of incest, but also in the structural organization according to the deadly sins. Taken together, they may lead us to the conclusion that the seven transgressions in love described by Genius are themselves the natural children of the union of Venus and Cupid, with the final unexpected sin of incest seeming the most alluring and irresistible.

In (albeit indirectly) likening Venus to Sin, or vice versa, Genius might then be suggesting that sin is essentially feminine. Yet this explanation is too simple. To understand the complexity of Genius's representation of Venus, we have to consider her birth, an event to which Genius alludes at V.1388, where we are told that "Venus Saturnes dowhter was." Here Genius refers back to the story of Venus's birth related at the very start of the digression, a narrative that Sarah Kay has described as "a *topos* of medieval mythography,"[13] but that Tinkle overlooks in her fine analysis of *Confessio*.[14] At this earlier point Genius relates the tale of the overthrow of Saturn, the patriarch of the gods, who, in a futile attempt to preserve his own position of power, tore to pieces and ate all of his own children, with one notable exception:

> Bot Jupiter, which was his Sone
> And of full age, his fader bond
> And kutte of with his oghne hond
> Hise genitals, whiche als so faste
> Into the depe See he caste;
> Wherof the Greks afferme and seie,
> Thus whan thei were caste aweie,
> Cam Venus forth be weie of kinde. (V.852–59)

According to tradition (though Gower does not make this point), the castration and exile of Saturn marked the end of the Golden Age. Kay, in her compelling analysis of the account of the birth of Venus in *Le Roman de la Rose,* argues that these events are analogous to the Fall of

Humankind, and reiterates the idea that Venus herself, associated as she is with uncontrolled sexuality, stands for Original Sin.[15] Here again, we may look for a parallel in *Mirour de l'Omme*, in which Gower describes how, after Lucifer's rebellion against God, the devil mirrored God's own act of autogenesis in creating Adam:

> Ly deable, qui tous mals soubtile
> Et trestous biens hiet et revile,
> De sa malice concevoit
> Et puis enfantoit une file,
> Q'ert tresmalvoise, laide et vile,
> La quelle Pecché noun avoit.
> Il mesmes sa norrice estoit,
> Et la gardoit et doctrinoit
> De sa plus tricherouse guile;
> Par quoy la file en son endroit
> Si violente devenoit,
> Que riens ne touche que n'avile.

(The devil, who contrives all evils and who hates and reviles all good, in his malice conceived and gave birth to a daughter, who was very evil, ugly and vile, who had the name of Sin. He himself was her nurse, looked after her and indoctrinated her in his most treacherous guile; whereby the girl in turn became so fierce that she touched nothing without vilifying it.) (*Mirour de l'Omme*, 205–16)

Here, of course, Lucifer's rebellion and the birth of Sin bring about the expulsion from Eden (although Gower blurs the chronology, perhaps in an attempt to evade directly engaging with issues of free will and determination). But if, in Gower's works, Venus is implicitly likened to Sin, for Kay, in the *Roman*, Venus quite literally has her redeeming side. Kay persuasively suggests that the myth of Venus is, in a sense, anti-oedipal. It uncannily resembles the oedipal story in both its classical and Freudian forms (the conflict between father and son; the importance of actual or symbolic castration, the elements of incest). At the same time, the myth of Venus's birth inverts and adapts it: the father is castrated by the son, rather than vice versa; the woman sleeps with her brother as well as her son; the narrative moves from order to disorder instead of the other way round. And, crucially, the myth of Venus is anti-oedipal because the woman is given an active role.[16]

The importance of the Oedipus myth, or its medieval recycling in the Tale of Apollonius, to Gower's *Confessio Amantis*, will be discussed in Chapter 6. Here I am interested in the way the Venus legend retold at the very heart of the *Confessio*—a legend that, like that of Oedipus, reveals the generational tensions in patriarchal society—challenges the hierarchy of gender and undermines our assumptions about the sinfulness of (transgressive) sexualities. Venus's existence, which in *Confessio* exposes the limitations, inadequacies, and failures in this postlapsarian world of the "rule of reason over sexuality,"[17] is a by-product of the conflict between Saturn and Jupiter (just as Sin is born out of the conflict between God and Lucifer). According to Donavin, "Venus derives her very being from Jupiter's usurpation of the throne; her existence thus depends upon social disorder."[18] Kay expresses the same idea slightly differently, arguing that Venus in the *Roman*, who is born as a consequence of the overthrow of Saturn by his son, "is not the object of patriarchal wrangles but the result of the way these wrangles weaken male control."[19] What is more, because of the sheer energy she exudes, the Venus of the *Roman* can, in Kay's words, "be read as a positively valued and powerful force in a world of fragmentation and loss."[20] Similarly, in *Confessio*, Jupiter has to take the blame for the events that culminate in the birth of his sister. And, unlike Gower's Sin in the *Mirour*, his Venus is much more than simply the instrument of her father; she has both independence and authority.

At the same time, Venus points to the sort of indeterminacy of gender seen in the previous chapter. She is in fact more (or less) than a woman, in that she is born exclusively from her father's sexual organs. She thus crosses the boundaries of sexual difference, spanning the categories of male and female; she is in a sense hermaphroditic. Recalling the *Mirour* once more, we might note that there Gower tells us that the sins that he describes, although superficially female, are in fact "mostre hermafodrite / ... / Femelle et madle ..." (hermaphroditic monsters ... female and male ...) (1026–29). Kay concludes that the story of Venus's birth "erases the very boundaries that confer stability on such concepts as 'sex' or 'knowledge.'"[21] In Gower's version, our attention is drawn to this erasure by the sheer illogicality of the narrator's claims about her birth. Looking again at the passage quoted above, describing Venus's birth, we might wonder what sort of "kinde" (Nature or Natural Law) produces a female child out of the body parts of her father.[22] Is not male autogenesis itself "unnatural"? The birth of Venus, like so many other narratives in *Confessio*, forces us to rethink what is "natural" and to reassess our assumptions about the differences between male and female, masculine and feminine. It also makes us rethink whether sin and perversion can in fact be equated with the feminine. In what follows we will see that Genius often ascribes male weakness to effeminacy: when men sin sexually, they too undermine gender boundaries, in a sense become hermaphrodites.[23] This is not to say that Genius is consistent, that all those who blur or transgress gender categories are by definition culpable. As we saw in the last chapter in the cases of Iphis and Penthesilea, masculine women in particular can be taken as positive models of ethical behavior. Yet such internal contradictions are typical of Gower, and these may be exceptions that prove the rule: as I argued in Chapter 1, sexual transgression underlies all other forms of division (linguistic, ethical, even political), and division itself is at the heart of humankind's postlapsarian experience.

Returning to Gower's—or Genius's—analysis of Venus, and thus also of sexuality and sin, we can find further evidence that it may not be as straightforwardly misogynist as it seems on first analysis. Crucially, in describing the relationship between Venus and her son, Gower shares the culpability in a fairly even-handed manner, and if anything shows greater sympathy for the mother than for the son:

> And thilke Sone upon a tyde,
> Whan he was come unto his Age,
> He hadde a wonder fair visage,
> And fond his Moder amourous,
> And he was also lecherous:
> So whan thei weren bothe al one,
> As he which yhen hadde none
> To se reson, his Moder kiste;
> And sche also, that nothing wiste
> Bot that which unto lust belongeth,
> To ben hire love him underfongeth.
> Thus was he blind, and sche unwys:

> Bot natheles this cause it is,
> Why Cupide is the god of love,
> For he his moder dorste love. (V.1406–20)

Cupid, not Venus, is made the active protagonist in this adventure. The allusion to Cupid's maturity reinforces the impression that he initiates the affair; at the very least it excludes Venus from the charge of seducing a minor. Cupid's blindness is symbolic rather than literal (indeed, as we saw in the previous chapter, Cupid is portrayed in Book I.140 as having "yhen wrothe"). It signifies his own guilt, revealing him to be as blind as Amans in his pursuit of his always distant and remote object of desire, and indeed as sightless as those who idolize himself and his mother. Furthermore, it signals the defeat of reason by will or desire that is so much a leitmotif of *Confessio Amantis*. Venus, in contrast, because she "nothing wiste" and is "unwys," is characterized as imprudent, if not exactly innocent. Tinkle is certainly correct to suggest that the centrality of Venus and Cupid to the text draws our attention to the theme of incest that is woven through it. Their presence makes us aware of "the immanence of sexual desire, from which almost no human relationship is immune, no private space exempt."[24] The relationship between Venus and her son picks up on themes introduced earlier in the famous Tale of Canace and Machaire, in which Genius condemns the violent anger of a father who discovers the sexual relationship between his daughter and son. These themes are revisited later in the Tale of Apollonius that occupies most of Book VIII. In *Confessio,* incest is metonymic of sexuality, which is simultaneously perverse and natural, and sexuality itself is metonymic of humanity's fallen, sinful state. Nonetheless, and this is a point I want to emphasize, while Genius does not let her off completely, he stops short of making Venus solely responsible for sexual sin; instead Cupid is made to share the blame.

TYRANNOUS MASCULINITY, MUTILATED AND MONSTROUS FEMININITY

Book V, the book devoted to the sin of Avarice, includes the highest number of rape narratives in *Confessio.* Genius chooses to discuss rape under headings such as "ravine" (literally "robbery" or *rapina*),[25] and

"robberie" (V.5505–6074 and V.6075–6358). The Latin verses that introduce the former section state that innocent women are the victims:
"Viribus ex clara res tollit luce Rapina, / Floris et inuita virgine mella
capit" (Rapine seizes in broad day by force / The blossom's honey from
unwilling maids) (V.5504a–b). However, Genius states that it is men
who lose out: "Ravine of othre mennes folde / Makth his larder and pai-
eth noght" (5512–13). These very forms of classification illustrate the extent to which women are seen as commodities, objects of patriarchal
exchange.[26] In this taxonomy, rape is figured as a crime not simply, or
even primarily, against women, but as an offense against those who hold
property, men. In an important essay, "Rivalry, Rape and Manhood: Gower
and Chaucer," Carolyn Dinshaw points out that rape, one of the most
violent manifestations of antifeminism, is associated with intense homosociality. As she phrases it, "at the moments when ... men seem most
explicitly preoccupied with each other, they are most fundamentally
misogynist."[27] The opposite is equally true: when men are most fundamentally misogynist they are most preoccupied with themselves and
with one another. Dinshaw cites the Tale of Geta and Amphytrion, in
Book II.2459–95, as an example of a narrative that focuses on the competition between two men, at the expense of the woman who is deceived
and tricked into bed.[28] Nevertheless, in his Tale of Tereus, Genius cri-
tiques the notion that rape, like male sodomy, is fundamentally a crime
against men and the whole structure of patriarchy. In this retelling, I
argue, Genius goes to some lengths to reinstate women as the real victims of rape, and to counter the misogyny so common in this sort of
narrative. The reading I offer here is indebted to, but also revises and
develops Dinshaw's own analysis of the tale that appears in the essay
just cited.[29] The moral that this narrative points toward (if not the moral
that Genius himself draws) is that rape, which is both a crime and sexual sin, inverts the "natural" order of things because it disrupts rather
than reinforces gender categories.

In the Tale of Tereus (V.5551–6052), Genius initially appears to give
us a somewhat sympathetic representation of Tereus, for whom the
sight of Philomela's beauty alone proves enough for him to "sette his
oghne herte on fyre" (V.5622). The emotional response of the would-be
rapist is comparable to that of the traditional love-sick youth, pierced
through the heart by the "firy Dart / Of love" described in Book I (I.322–
33). Yet while Genius's narrative may rationalize rape as an extreme

example of will overcoming reason, it does not, as it progresses, represent the rapist in a positive light. In this context, the question of agency is once again crucial. Claire Fanger has argued that in Gower's *Confessio* "rape is never the woman's fault."[30] Her contention is supported here: Genius's careful phrasing makes it clear that it is Tereus who sets himself on fire and cannot prevent himself from being devoured by the flames. Philomela is not responsible for what has happened. Her innocence is indisputable. Tereus on the other hand has allowed his sexual desire to preside over his reason. Rape turns a king, husband, and father into a "tirant raviner" (V.5627; the concepts of "tirant" and "tirannye" are reiterated in the tale at lines 5646 and 5921), but it also results in the dissolution (rather than assertion) of a stable masculine identity. Rape is about an unconstrained lust, and, as we have seen in the previous chapter, such lust (which is contrary to reason) unmans or renders effeminate the individual who allows himself to experience it. Elsewhere in Book V the positive examples Genius chooses to illustrate his discourse on the blessed state of virginity are all male: "Noght onliche of the wommen tho, / Bot of the chaste men also / It [virginity] was commended overal" (V.6367–69). Virginity and chastity are important to the construction of masculinity as well as femininity in the medieval period.[31] Tereus's incontinence compromises his manliness as well as his honor. Furthermore, in committing rape and also incest (because he sleeps with his sister-in-law), Tereus offends not only against women and against himself but also against the patriarchal society that he represents. As a result, the consequences he has to face are all the greater. When his wife and Philomela's sister, Procne, discovers his crime, she murders their son Itys, serving him to Tereus for dinner. The narrator states categorically that the punishment fits the crime. Tereus devours his own flesh and blood "ayein kinde, / As he that was tofore unkinde" (V.5905–06). His own unnatural and consuming passion is countered by infanticide (in its way another form of incest, as will been seen in Chapter 6) and by cannabalism, a form of unnatural consumption. The torn maidenhead of the victim (Procne's sister) is answered by the severed head of the son, placed between the dishes upon the table (V.5910–13). Of course, within a patriarchal society, the loss of son also means the loss of the heir and all that the heir stands for, both legally and psychologically. Thus, as Dinshaw observes, "when Tereus is made to eat [Itys] . . . he destroys his own legitimate chance at life beyond his own decay."[32] In effect, Tereus loses that sign of his own masculinity that guarantees not only that his wealth will be inherited by his direct descendant but that his name will be passed on to posterity.

Particularly striking about Gower's retelling of this story, and indeed about virtually all of the narratives of rape, seduction, or abandonment found in *Confessio,* is the lengths to which Genius goes to represent not only the perspective of the aggressor, but also the point of view of the victim. Tereus is compared to a wolf taking his prey (V.5633), or a goshawk seizing a bird (V.5644–45). The latter simile may well remind us—as Dinshaw has suggested—of the dream of Chaucer's Criseyde before her ill-fated submission to Pandarus's relentless importuning on behalf of Troilus; or, alternatively, of the representation of the tercel birds of prey in *The Parliament of Fowls.*[33] Philomela cries out for the help of her mother and father, but to no avail, and yet even after the rape has been committed she refuses to remain silent. She determines "That I schal telle out al mi fille, / And with mi speche I schal fulfille / The wyde world in brede and lengthe" (V.5659–61). Our response to Tereus's tearing out of her tongue is more horrified than our reaction to the rape only because the account is more vivid and grotesque:

> And he than as a Lyon wod
> With hise unhappi handes stronge
> Hire cauhte be the tresses longe,
> With whiche he bond ther bothe hire armes,
> That was a fieble dede of armes,
> And to the grounde anon hire caste,
> And out he clippeth also faste
> Hire tunge with a peire scheres.
> So what with blod and what with teres
> Out of hire yhe and of hir mouth,
> He made hire faire face uncouth. (V.5684–94)

Gower tones down his Ovidian source, omitting the description of the severed tongue writhing like a snake on the ground and the "detail" that even after this act Tereus continues to force himself upon Philomela (*Metamorphoses,* VI.557–62). Yet Genius does not need these grotesque particulars to make his point. As if the rape were not enough, Tereus sets out to render Philomela the more impotent by denying her the only power that remains to her—the power of speech—in what amounts to no less than symbolic castration. The narrator makes it clear that rape represents what Dinshaw terms the rejection of female autonomy,[34] and also that it results in the destruction of her sense of her own self-worth. We are told that after her transformation into a nightingale Philomela hides away from humankind for shame at the loss of her "maidenhiede," her thoughts constantly returning to her former "wommanhiede," the rhyming couplet drawing our attention to the necessity of the one to the maintenance of the second (V.5955–56). Philomela's Ovidian mutation is simply the literal manifestation of the aftereffects of her double defilement (the tearing of the tongue as well as the hymen).[35]

This tale illustrates the extent to which rape threatens the stable gendered identity of not only the aggressor but also the victim. At the same time, Genius's retelling counters the dominance of bonds between men, so characteristic of the sort of patriarchal society that fosters rape by fostering male rivalry, with bonds between women of equivalent or even greater strength. In Genius's version of the tale, the only male casualties are the aggressor himself and his son. This is because Tereus's victim, Philomela, is unmarried, and at the time when the rape is committed she has been separated from her parents (Tereus has taken her on a journey by sea to visit Procne). Thus, unlike the Ovidian source, *Metamorphoses,* VI.424–674 (and unlike the tales of the rapes of Lucrece and Virginia discussed in the following chapter), we never see the suffering of the father. Significantly, what ultimately seems to provoke Tereus's further act of atrocity (the mutilation) is Philomela's reflection on how her sister might respond to discovering the truth of her husband's untruth. At no point does Philomela doubt that Procne will believe her (cf. V.5759–68). This is perhaps somewhat surprising given the number of narratives in *Confessio* to feature women's betrayal of, or vengeance upon, other women. Examples of this include Deianira and Eolen, Thetis and Deidamia (discussed above in Chapter 3), and, in the Tale of Jason and Medea (V.3247–4225), Medea's punishment of Creusa. Indeed on the two occasions in Book V in which the narrator uses the word "sosterhode," he does so ironically. The word is applied to the relationship between Medea and Creusa (V.4205), where Medea exploits the relation-

ship to trick the woman who has supplanted her. It is also applied to
that between Fedra and Ariadne (V.5398), where the former's joy at
her sister's marriage is clearly soon forgotten when Fedra goes off with
Ariadne's husband. If, in context, unexpected, Philomela's absolute
faith in her sister is nonetheless well founded. Immediately Procne receives the white silk handkerchief woven with "lettres and ymagerie"
(V.5771) Philomela sends her from her prison (Tereus has locked her up
and told Procne she is dead), Procne understands the symbolism and
the message. Indeed, the embroidered cloth may be taken to represent a
form of female discourse beyond the control of men.[36]

Genius's choice of this narrative enables him to document the impact of rape, not on men as fathers and husbands, nor even solely on the
rapist and his victim, but on the betrayed wife as well. Procne reacts by
swearing she will wreak revenge upon her husband. She is so affected
by her husband's betrayal that she loses those very qualities (compas-
sion and fear) that define her role and her sex: she "Withoute insihte of
moderhede / Foryat pite and loste drede" (V.5893–94). Dinshaw contends
that what she calls Procne's critique "is not allowed too much force in
the narrative."[37] After all, Procne's power and autonomy only emerge in
reaction to male tyranny, and her trauma is foreclosed by her subsequent metamorphosis. Furthermore, Dinshaw argues that, after her metamorphosis, Philomela's song converts rape and sexual violence into
"that exquisite pain called 'love,'" thus normalizing it and effectively re-
ducing its significance.[38] Yet, Tereus's betrayal of his wife and her sister
is just the latest of a whole series of stories of male infidelity to be told
in Book V (earlier examples include Achilles and Deidamia, Jason and
Medea, and Theseus and Ariadne). Consequently our sympathy for Procne
as well as her sister may be the greater, not only because of the greater
horror of the events, but also because of the pattern that has emerged.
Men, it seems, simply cannot be trusted with a woman's heart, her maidenhead, or even her tongue. In Book VIII, Amans encounters Procne
and Philomela amongst the company of lovers, joining their voices together in a complaint against the one who "of his untrouthe / Undede
hem bothe" (2585–86). The punishment of Tereus parallels that of Jason. The wives of both men chose to get their revenge by slaying their
male offspring. But, whereas Jason's sons are dispatched in a mere seven
lines (V.4210–16; compare the ten lines devoted to the revenge upon

Creusa at V.4200–09), the horror of Procne's murder of Itys—what Dinshaw refers to as the sisters' "culinary vengeance"[39]—is starkly but vividly described. The narrator explains how Procne coldly calculates what act will cause Tereus the greatest grief and then describes the subsequent events with grave concision.

> And in hir chambre prively
> This child withouten noise or cry
> Sche slou, and hieu him al to pieces:
> And after with diverse spieces
> The fleissh, whan it was so toheewe,
> She takth, and makth therof a sewe,
> With which the fader at his mete
> Was served, til he hadde him ete;
> . . .
> And thanne, er that he were arise,
> For that he scholde ben agrise,
> To schewen him the child was ded,
> This Philomela tok the hed
> Betwen tuo disshes, and al wrothe
> Tho comen forth the Sostres bothe,
> And setten it upon the bord. (V.5895–5913)

Gower omits some of circumstantial material found in Ovid's account (for example, the fact that the reunion of the sisters and the murder of Tereus's son take place during a Bacchic festival: *Metamorphoses*, VI.587–646). Even some of its finer points are left out (such as Procne's cold observation concerning the resemblance between her son and his father: *Metamorphoses* VI.621–22).[40] However, the starkness of this description of violence draws our attention to its position as the last in the triptych: the murder of Itys parallels the earlier descriptions of both the rape and the mutilation of Philomela. The innocent victim is quite literally torn apart by the cruel figure who steals into his chamber under the cover of the night (in Ovid, the mother drags the child into the forest to kill him). Interestingly, it is the mutilation of Philomela and the revenge of Procne that are combined in the illustration to the tale in New York, Pierpont Morgan Library MS M.126 (fol. 122r; Figure 3). While Tereus rips out his victim's tongue in the foreground, he is shown, crowned and having

Figure 3. Tereus, Philomela, and Procne. MS M.126, fol. 122r (detail).
Reprinted by permission of the Pierpont Morgan Library, New York.

completed his banquet in the middle of the picture. As he starts up from
the table in horror, Procne is in the process of explaining to him what he
has just eaten. The sequence indicates the cause and effect relationship
between the two principal events being depicted, while the bloody knife
and the overturned goblets on the table fuse them into one moment of
crisis. The three birds swooping above the figures in the central tableau
signal the conclusion of the narrative. In both the original text and this
illustrated miniature, the most memorable picture we are given of
Philomela is that of a victim of rape and torture, and our enduring image
of Procne is of a monster created by the deeds of a man.

RAPE, SEDUCTION, AND REDEMPTION

To complete this discussion of sex in *Confessio Amantis,* I would now like to turn to two tales of seduction and sexual deception, the first of which is the Tale of Mundus and Paulina in Book I (761–1076). This story forms part of Genius's exposition on the hypocrisy of lovers. Although it illustrates further a number of the points I have already made, its conclusion betrays a fundamental inconsistency in the poem's ethics. This inconsistency stands out the more when the tale is read alongside its framing narrative. The discussion of Pride (of which hypocrisy is the first point) is preceded by a section on the five senses, in which Genius emphasizes the importance of self-control as a defense against love. Given that the fateful encounter with Cupid and Venus has already taken place, Genius rather belatedly warns Amans against

> thilke firy Dart
> Of love which that evere brenneth,
> Thurgh him into the herte renneth:
> And thus a mannes yhe ferst
> Himselve grieveth alther werst,
> And many a time that he knoweth
> Unto his oghne harm it groweth. (I.322–28)

It is the eye—evocatively described as "a thief / To love" (I.319–20)—that is responsible for letting desire enter the heart.[41] The stories that follow—the Tales of Acteon, Medusa, the Sirens—place the blame firmly on the failures of men to protect themselves from the wrath of the goddess Diana, or from the seductive powers of the monsters. Genius then prefaces the Tale of Mundus and Paulina by reinforcing the point that love can prove irresistible and "makth the hertes yhen blinde, / Wher no reson mai be comuned" (I.774–75). Nonetheless, in keeping with his treatment of the topic elsewhere, he stresses that the responsibility cannot fall onto the woman, who "may noght lette the corage / Of him that wole on hire assote" (I.780–81).

   Despite this enlightened introduction to the tale, a number of critics, most notably Rosemary Woolf, have commented upon, and, in the case of Hugh White, centered an argument around, Gower's/Genius's allegedly "sympathetic" portrayal of the rapist, Mundus.[42] In support of their views, it might be noted that the narrator more or less condones

Mundus's emotional state; his passion is uncontrollable and he loves "malgre wher he wole or no" (I.789). Indeed, in offering us a description of Paulina's appearance, "which in hire lustes grene / Was fair and freissh and tendre of age" (I.778–79), Genius encourages the reader to view the victim from the perspective of the seducer.[43] Some readers assume that Paulina actually collaborates in her own downfall, in that she allows herself to succumb to Mundus's flattery.[44] Furthermore, in the conclusion to the tale, the narrator deflects the blame away from Mundus and onto his two accomplices on the extenuating grounds that "Love put reson aweie / And can noght se the rihte weie" (I.1051–52). Consequently, Mundus is exiled rather than condemned to death. Meanwhile the corrupt priests in his employ, who have hypocritically betrayed a woman's trust, are damned by the "lawe resonable" and the "wise jugges" (I.1031–32).[45] Yet, despite all this, Mundus hardly cuts a sympathetic figure as we watch him conspire to trick a devout young noblewoman into sleeping with him. Indeed, he is soon reduced to little more than a personification of stealth and deceit as he lurks (like *Mort* or Death in *Le Mirour,* discussed in Chapter 1, above) hidden "in a closet faste by" awaiting to seize his prey (I.897). He is, we are told, an "ypocrite of his queintise" (I.906), the very opposite of the disingenious and pious Paulina. And whereas she "which alle trowthe weneth" (I.925) is oblivious to what is happening, Mundus, "that alle untrowthe meneth" (I.926) uses lying tales and feigned speech to get what he wants. Paulina, on discovering the truth, certainly lays the blame firmly on Mundus's doorstep when she cries, "'O derke ypocrisie, / Thurgh whos dissimilacion / Of fals ymaginacion / I am thus wickedly deceived!'" (I.956–59).

The unsatisfactory resolution to this narrative, which allows Mundus, despite all his plotting, to escape with his life, undercuts Genius's own stated belief that the individuals have to take responsibility for their actions. The religious elements in the narrative widen the gap between crime and punishment, moral and exemplar. In the Tale of Mundus and Paulina, the plot against Paulina involves Mundus impersonating the Egyptian god Anubis, with the collaboration of the priests of the temple of Isis. Gower retells the story as a ludic parody of the Annunciation: Paulina's "holinesse" and "simplesse" (I.831–32) render her a second Virgin Mary; the deception of her husband makes him a comic cuckold, a second Joseph. Mundus's initial approach echoes that of the angel Gabriel:

Bot he with softe wordes milde
Conforteth hire and seith, with childe
He wolde hire make in such a kynde
That al the world schal have in mynde
The worschipe of that ilke Sone;
For he schal with the goddes wone,
And ben himself a godd also. (I.915–21)[46]

Genius's stance on offenses against the gods is far from consistent in *Confessio*. Elsewhere, it should be noted, Genius attacks, on the grounds of sacrilege, the abduction of Helen by Paris in Book V.7195–7590 (Helen is taken from the Temple of Venus), and Troilus's passion for Criseide in Book V.7597–7602 (Troilus falls in love with Criseide when he sees her in church). Here, in what can only be described as a glorious inconsistency, Genius does not condemn Mundus's behavior as sacrilegious, even though he is only a mere mortal impersonating a higher power, and even though the seduction occurs in a holy place.

James Simpson argues in *Sciences and the Self* that the inconsistencies in Genius's moralizing can be explained by the fact that examples such as the narrative of Mundus and Paulina occur early on in *Confessio*. He suggests that the progression of the poem reflects the learning curve of Genius as well as Amans,[47] but I would argue that such inconsistencies are found at the end of *Confessio* as well as the beginning. The Tale of Mundus and Paulina is, in fact, only one of a whole series of rape or seduction narratives in *Confession* to play with Annunciation symbols and metaphors.[48] The Tale of Leuchothe is just one other example, although here it is at least a pagan deity (Phoebus) who steals into the enclosed space to ravish an innocent virgin (V.6712–95). The closest parallel to the story of Mundus and Paulina is Nectanabus's seduction of Olympia in Book VI.1789–2366 (this event is also anticipated at V.6671 in Amans's daydreaming). Overcome by the beauty of this queen, the sinister figure of Nectanabus uses not only feigned words, but also necromancy or magic to trick the woman into sleeping with him. Once again the success of the plot depends upon the seducer disguising himself as a god—in this case, Amos of Lybia[49]—who wishes to conceive a child with a mortal woman. Nectanabus, like Mundus, takes the role of the angel Gabriel, announcing the event that is to take place. The piety and humility of Olympia's response is comparable to that of Paulina

"with that word sche wax al mylde, / And somdel red becam for schame"
(VI.1918–19), although Olympia is no doubt implicated in her own deception just as Paulina is.[50] Genius seems to relish in describing "the
deceipte and nigromance" (VI.2179), lavishing on his accounts of Nectanabus's various astrological predictions and metamorphoses some of
the care he had previously devoted to the conjuring and spell-casting of
Medea (V.3957–4174).[51] Nectanabus is, of course, eventually punished
for misusing his "craft" (VI.2343) for his own erotic gain. His ability to
see into the future does not correspond to complete knowledge, or self-
knowledge, and thus he cannot prevent his own son from killing him.
Fanger is no doubt correct when, in her analysis of Gower's Tale of Circe
and Ulysses, she draws parallels between the male protagonist of that
narrative and Nectanabus, characterizing both as "learned men shown
to be guilty of misusing the powers granted by their knowledge."[52] Certainly, even if Nectanabus succeeds in hiding his deceit (in contrast to
Mundus, who effectively boasts to his victim about how he has tricked
her [I.940–51]), there is a sense of poetic justice in what happens later.
In order to disprove Nectanabus's oedipal prophecy that he will die at
the hands of his own son, that very son—ignorant of the identity of his
father, whom he refers to disparagingly as "this olde dotard"—throws
him over a cliff (VI.2298–2316). Unlike Mundus, Nectanabus loses his
life as a result of his crime, albeit indirectly.

Nevertheless, in the course of retelling the latter's story, Genius emphasizes that some good does come from this act of sorcery, deception,
and impersonation. The child born from the union, conceived through
deception, is Alexander the Great, the conqueror and flower of chivalry:
"So that thurgh guile and Sorcerie / Ther was that noble knyht begunne, /
Which al the world hath after wunne" (VI.2090–92). The birth of Alexander anticipates the birth of the Son of God himself, and also his death
(see Matthew 27:45–54):

> Ther felle wondres many on
> Of terremote universiel:
> The Sonne tok colour of stiel
> And loste his lyht, the wyndes blewe,
> And manye strenghtes overthrewe;
> The See his propre kinde changeth,
> And al the world his forme strangeth;

The thonder with his fyri levene
So cruel was upon the hevene,
That every erthli creature
Tho thoghte his lif in aventure. (VI.2260–70)[53]

Nectanabus is of course Satan-like in his usurpation of the power of the Creator (see VI.2344–50). Yet, in taking upon himself the power and authority of the Almighty, in behaving like God, he has created in his own son a Christ figure. Gallacher believes that the tale illustrates the *felix culpa* or "fortunate fall"; sin and seduction result in a "redemptive antithesis, albeit in a somewhat secularized form."[54] As we will see in the next chapter, Alexander is not an unambiguous model of kingship but a tyrant with some very human failings, who nonetheless has something of the divine about him. Like the Tale of Mundus and Paulina, the Tale of Nectanabus resists easy moralization. Unlike the Tale of Mundus and Paulina, however, the sympathetic portrayal of the seducer in the Tale of Nectanabus can be explained, at least in part. From its conclusion, it seems that the act of seduction or rape—the indulging of uncontrolled desires at the expense of the wishes of another—should not always be condemned out of hand, because it can result in some at least partial good for humankind as a whole. In fact, the parodic and ludic annunciation scenes in the Tales of Mundus and Paulina and Nectanabus might remind us of the divided role of Genius himself. As servant to Venus, Genius is implicated in the idolatrous and sacrilegious errors of both the hypocritical lover and the exploitative magician, but as confessor to Amans he aims to bring the penitent to a point of self-knowledge within some sort of semi-Christian ethical framework.

The very real contradictions written into the Tales of Mundus and Paulina and Nectanabus point to the meaning of *Confessio* as a whole. To understand the ambiguities and discontinuities in and between these narratives we have to recognize Gower's ambivalence about the nature of sin and loss of self-control. Gower, the controlling principal behind this narrative and behind the whole work, wishes to acknowledge that it is our capacity to err, our fallen state, that makes us human. I would strongly oppose Dinshaw's dismissal of Gower's poem as "a conservative social vision ... a text that nostalgically yearns for proper Christian hierarchy and social order."[55] Quite the opposite, in fact, as it seems to me that in exploring, sympathetically, our fallen condition, Gower finds himself reenacting the state of "division" in his fiction. And because good can come out of evil, Genius, as Gower's spokesperson, does not invariably condemn sin per se, and especially not sexual desire and transgression. Certainly in telling stories about seduction, rape, and incest, he stresses the need for self-restraint. Yet even as he vividly portrays abuse of power and its damning consequences, Genius also draws us into imaginatively identifying with the sins he portrays, and into understanding that they can serve some positive functions. We can see this more clearly if we look once again at Venus's presence in *Confessio*. While Venus may represent the sort of uncontrolled desires and dark instinctual urges associated with postlapsarian chaos itself, she also has, as Kay insists, salvic properties.[56] Thus according to Kay, in *Le Roman de la Rose*, Genius asserts in his sermon that sex will have its spiritual rewards (see especially 20369–659). Likewise, at the very end of *Confessio*, the by-now fused persona of Gower/Amans turns from earthly to heavenly love. It is surely apparent that it is not simply (as Tinkle seems to suggest) "the psychological effects of old age"[57] that have brought him to this point of understanding, any more than it is simply the victory of reason over passion. More important surely to his spiritual reconciliation is the grace of Venus and Cupid (albeit a grace expressed through rejection rather than acceptance).[58] After his all-too-brief moment of enlightenment, as he sets off homeward with "a softe pas" (VIII.2967), Gower/Amans does not so much transcend sexual love and reject sin, as simply and rather sadly leave them behind. Sin and sex are the inescapable parts of the human experience that Gower chooses to explore in *Confessio*. The disunities within Gower's text reflect the complexities of his subject, the human condition; thus the reader, like Amans, continually (re)encounters contradictions that are not and can never be fully resolved.

PART III

POLITICS

5

Tyranny, Reform, and Self-Government

Apocalypse Now: Nebuchadnezzar's Dream

In the Prologue to *Confessio Amantis,* Gower's integration of estates satire and biblical prophecy is reminiscent of his earlier Anglo-Norman and French works, *Mirour de l'Omme* and *Vox Clamantis.* The Prologue to *Confessio Amantis* begins, as we saw in Chapter 1, with an account of the poem's origin, and of its intentions. This is followed by a discussion of the decline of the world, which focuses on the corruption of each of the estates in turn: those who govern, the church, and the commons. Explaining that this corruption comes not from God, nor even from Fortune or the stars, but from ourselves ("For man is cause of that schal falle": Prol.528), Gower introduces the story of Nebuchadnezzar's dream in order to illustrate his point that the world itself is founded upon division.

Gower bases this account on Daniel 2. In line with his main theme, and reminiscent of Daniel 2:20–22, he stresses the opposition between God's "almyhti pourveance" (Prol.585) and the precariousness of the world, which will continue to "torne and wende" before its inevitable ending (Prol.591–92). In relating Nebuchadnezzar's dream, Gower makes a number of significant changes to the biblical narrative. The most immediately apparent of these is the change of perspective. In the Bible account, it is the prophet Daniel who describes the vision Nebuchadnezzar saw in his sleep, before he goes on to give his explanation of it. In Gower's version, it is the king of Babylon who relates the dream to his interpreter (Prol.602–24). The effect of the switch in narrator is to place the king and the statue or idol rather than the prophet at the center of a *theatrum mundi*.[1] Gower also introduces a stage on which the statue is standing (referring to it again at Prol.651). The third alteration to the biblical story is that no mention is made of the mountain that grew from the boulder and filled the whole earth (Daniel 2:35). These changes can begin to be explained if we look at Gower's versions of the interpretation offered by Daniel to the king, versions characterized by James M. Dean as "moral-historical" and "political."[2] The first (Prol.625–62), the moral-historical explanation, is derived not from the Bible narrative itself, but from medieval interpretations of it, and is influenced by Ovid's account of the four ages (*Metamorphoses*, I.89–150). In *Confessio*, the statue stands for the spiritual state of humanity. The "figure strange" (Prol.627) represents the steady decline of the world from a worthy and noble place to one that is divided and full of woe. The stone that pulverizes the statue represents the might of God, which will "whan men wene most upryht / To stonde" (Prol.656–57) eventually overthrow them, and begin a new world that will last endlessly. The conventional Christian understanding of this dream and its interpretation, which derives from the exegesis offered by St. Jerome, is that the boulder refers to Christ's first Advent, and the mountain stands for the church.[3] Gower in contrast reads the dream as an eschatological prophecy, concerned with the end of the world (especially Prol.881–85). The stone stands for the Second Coming of Christ.[4] The tone is reminiscent of Revelation 21:1 ("for the first heaven and the first earth were passed away"). With no mention of the mountain, the emphasis in this narrative is on judgment (as at Prol.1032–44) rather than redemption, on the passing of the old world rather than the arrival of the new.

Gower then goes on to explain the dream a second time in familiar political and teleological terms (Prol.663–909): the head and neck, the breast, shoulders, and arms, the belly, guts, and thighs, and the legs represent succeeding civilizations. This is closer to the actual interpretation offered in the Book of Daniel, although in accordance with medieval tradition it is fully developed to explain the unfolding of history, from the fall of Babylon into Christian times. Thus, rather than simply allude in general terms to the decline of the kingdoms that follow Nebuchadnezzar's own, it specifies, amongst others, the reigns of Alexander, Julius Caesar, Charlemagne, and the Lombards and German princes. As Russell Peck notes, this scheme undergoes a process of updating, bringing the reader to the start of the 1390s, the present day.[5] The feet represent the last and current age, which "now is old and fieble and vil, / Full of meschief and of peril" (Prol.887–88), as is evidenced by the fragmentation of the empire, the corruption of the church, and the prevalence of war amongst Christians. The interpretation of this dream prefaces the important account of division and sin and the reference to the Tower of Babel, which I discussed in Chapter 1. As I have already explained, this account may also have topical significance, relating to anxieties about the dissolution of the social hierarchy and to contemporary debates about the dangers of vernacular texts.

The importance of this dream to *Confessio Amantis* as a whole is indicated by the fact that in the illuminated manuscripts of the poem, this dream is most frequently taken as the subject of illustration, alongside that of the confessor and the penitent.[6] As Richard K. Emmerson states, this dream miniature emphasizes the macrocosmic concerns of the poem; "the passing of kingdoms and vicissitudes of world history."[7] As noted in the Introduction, these dream illustrations can be classified according to two types.[8] The first shows the king dreaming in his bed, alongside the statue. This miniature tends to appear as a frontispiece at the start of *Confessio Amantis*. It is mainly found in manuscripts dating from the reign of Richard II, for example, Oxford, Bodleian Library MS Fairfax 3 (fol. 2r; Figure 4). The second shows only the statue. It usually appears within the text column, introducing the English narrative account of the dream. This miniature is typical of later manuscripts, dating from the reign of Henry IV. Joel Fredell argues that the shift between the two types of illustration may have been politically motivated. He observes that Nebuchadnezzar was often represented in the Middle Ages as a tyrannical ruler, or sometimes even as the Antichrist, and Fredell notes similarities with Gower's own (albeit much later) characterization of Richard II in *Cronica Tripertita*.[9] Illustrations such as that in the Fairfax manuscript make explicit the parallel between the destruction of the statue and the future fate of the Babylonian king, transforming the latter into a figure of *de casibus* tragedy.[10] Fredell concludes that retrospectively, in the period after the deposition of Richard II, illustrations such as that found in the Fairfax manuscript would have had uncomfortable implications for members of the Lancastrian court, thus the preference in fifteenth-century manuscripts of the poem for the statue solus.[11] In the description of the dream in *Confessio Amantis*, the emphasis placed on the king, as narrator of his own dream, and the elevation of the statue on a stage or platform reinforce the argument that this narrative offers more than an explanation of world history. The statue represents the corrupt body politic, but it can also be read in terms of the king's two bodies, the godhead and manhood, the mystical body and the human body, which should be at one in the person of the king, but which are here fissured and decaying.[12] In Gower's poem, Nebuchadnezzar's dream articulates a warning about the consequences of failures of government, self-government, and self-regulation, and also about the fragility of the monarch's position; a message equally applicable to the past, present, and future. That Gower wants his readers to make the connection between his version of Nebuchadnezzar's dream and the *fürstenspiegel* of Book VII of *Confessio* is indicated by the fact that he anticipates the discussion of the statue in his earlier analysis of the mutual responsibilities of the body politic (Prol.151–56). That Gower himself does not at this point intend to make this admonishment any more direct or threatening to his own monarch, Richard II, is suggested by the fact that in describing the world's mutability at the start of the dream, Gower chooses not to cite Daniel 2:21: "And he changeth the times and the seasons: he removeth kings, and setteth up kings...."

Gower's apocalyptic retelling of Nebuchadnezzar's dream of the statue in *Confessio Amantis* has already been anticipated in *Vox Clamantis*. In the first Prologue of *Vox Clamantis*, Gower cites the biblical examples of Daniel and Joseph as evidence that dreams can be meaningful (*Vox Clamantis*, I.7–8), and animal imagery and Ovidian metaphors of degeneration pervade Book I. However, it is only in the final book that Nebuchadnezzar's statue makes its monstrous appearance.

> Nunc caput a statua Nabugod prescinditur auri,
> Fictilis et ferri stant duo iamque pedes:
> Nobilis a mundo nunc desinit aurea proles,
> Pauperies ferri nascitur atque sibi.

> (The golden head of Nebuchadnezzar's statue has now been cut off, yet the two feet of iron and clay still stand. The noble, golden race of men has departed from the world and a poor one of iron has sprung from it.) (*Vox Clamantis*, VII.5–8)

Figure 4. Nebuchadnezzar's dream. MS Fairfax 3, fol. 2r (detail).
Reprinted by permission of the Bodleian Library, University of Oxford.

What first distinguishes Gower's use of the image of the statue in *Confessio Amantis* and his use of it in *Vox Clamantis* is that in the latter the statue is not explained in the context of a retelling and analysis of the entire dream sequence of Daniel 2. But even more strikingly, in *Vox Clamantis* the statue is not shattered but decapitated, and the feet remain. Indeed, in *Vox Clamantis,* it is only the head and feet of the statue that are dwelt upon; the shoulders, arms, breast, belly, and legs are omitted altogether. If in *Vox Clamantis* the biblical narrative context of the statue is never expounded, its political significance *is* made explicit. Here, as in *Confessio Amantis,* the feet of alloy represent the present time, a world in which avarice and carnal lust corrupt the world, an age of death and judgment, and the end of an era. Eve Salisbury contends that Gower holds the young King Richard II responsible for this world turned up-side down: "The evocation of the Babylonian tyrant and the period in biblical history when the prophet Daniel lived in captivity resonates in the events of contemporary England and Richard's oppression of his own subjects. The king as the 'ranting Prince of hell' [as he is described in the *Cronica Tripertita*] cuts himself off from the concerns of his people as the decapitated head of the statue seems to proclaim...."[13] Certainly the king is not excluded from opprobrium, even in the early versions of *Vox Clamantis*, but it is clear from the wider context of Book VII that the statue in *Vox* represents nothing more specific than the monstrous body politic of late-fourteenth-century England. As Gower explains:

> Torpescunt proceres, clerus dissoluitur, vrbes
> Discordant, leges sunt sine iure graues:
> Murmurat indomitus vulgus, concrescit abvsus
> Peccati solitus; sic dolet ominis humus.
> Hinc puto quod seuit pes terreus in caput auri....

(The nobles grow indolent, the clergy are dissolute, the cities are quarreling, and the laws are unjustly severe. The untamed rabble are grumbling, the customary sinful abuses are on the increase. Thus the whole country is suffering. It is for this rea-son I think that the earthen foot rages against the head of gold...)
(*Vox Clamantis*, VII.1375–79)

Blame for this chaos is placed not on the individual shoulders of the monarch, but on the corruption and contention amongst nobles, clergy, and laymen, the powerful and the powerless. In what may be a post-1381 revision to this section of the poem, the decapitated head and corrupt feet also seem to represent the recent temporary inversion of the politi-cal hierarchy. In a possible allusion to John Ball, one the leaders of the mob during the Peasants' Revolt, Gower tells us that the disorder of En-glish society is signaled by the fact that the rabble now preach as if they were members of the clergy (*Vox Clamantis*, VII.233–34).[14]

Gower makes rather different political use of the dream of Neb-uchadnezzar in his major Latin and English poems. In both the statue represents history, in which, as Eve Salisbury puts it, "the 'here' and 'now' of Gower's historical moment [is] severed so violently from its

Golden Age past."[15] Yet, whereas *Vox Clamantis* adopts the statue image as a symbol for the turmoil that resulted in the crisis of 1381, *Confessio* uses the whole dream sequence to give advice about government and rule. Gower's contrasting employment of the statue image in *Vox* and *Confessio* reflects the less overtly political and satirical nature of his vernacular work. At the same time, in the context of a discussion of good kingship, the image of the beheaded statue may have had rather more ominous implications. This would be the case even in the relatively peaceful years of the early 1390s, following Richard's contest with the Lords Appellant, and assertion of his majority. Consequently it should come as no surprise that Gower did not find it appropriate for his English poem.

    Confessio Amantis clearly shares some of the apocalyptic feel of *Vox Clamantis,* especially at its beginning. (This is seen, for example, in the description of the wars and other portents of the End at Prol.1032–36, or in the references to Joachim of Fiore at II.3056–65 and the Latin commentary at II.3056).[16] Nevertheless, when viewed as an entirety, *Confessio Amantis* (in both its versions) can be distinguished from *Vox Clamantis* by what Peck characterizes as its movement from apocalypse to confession, from judgment to penance.[17] This movement is mirrored in the transition from the Prologue and its biblical-political content to the main body of the poem with its framework of the lover's confession, and the erotic narrative embodied therein. Indicative of this change in direction is Gower's integration into Book I of *Confessio* of another narrative centering on Nebuchadnezzar: the story of his transformation into a beast (Daniel 4). Again the poetic personae blur as Genius tells Amans that the king is one "of whom that I spak hier tofore" (I.2787); it was of course the voice of the author himself, not that of Genius, that spoke in the Prologue. The exemplum appears in Genius's discussion of the sin of Pride and the virtue of Humility. The penitential story of the fallen king illustrates vividly the proverb "pride will have a fall"[18] and demonstrates in very literal terms that false glory is little more than bestiality. Nebuchadnezzar appears here in his more familiar medieval role as a type of the sinner who repents and is redeemed. Daniel interprets the king's dream of the great tree that shall be hewn down to the root, and he admonishes Nebuchadnezzar in Christian terms: "Amende thee . . . / Yif and departe thin almesse, / Do mercy forth with rihtwisnesse, / Besech and prei the hihe grace . . ." (I.2934–37; cf. Daniel 4:27). Eventually, after living seven years as a beast, Nebuchadnezzar responds accordingly with a confession of the greatness of God, a prayer for mercy mingled with justice, and a promise of reformation.[19] This Nebuchadnezzar is quite different from the one encountered in the Prologue. He is here less of an Antichrist and more a figure of Christ himself: he is one who has suffered in the wilderness, and who ultimately resolves to follow the divine will. In contrast to the earlier account of Nebuchadnezzar's dream (with its omission of the mountain that would rise up to replace the shattered statue) it offers a promise of restoration and recovery, of the reintegration of the monarch's divine and human aspects. If Richard II is supposed to identify with Nebuchadnezzar, the tyrant king of Babylon, then taken together these exemplary narratives suggest that there remains hope that all will come good in the end. However, Gower's message to England and its ruler becomes more ominous in his depiction of Alexander the Great.

ALEXANDER'S FEET OF CLAY

Alexander the Great is discussed, or at least mentioned, in the Prologue and five of the eight books of *Confessio* (II, III, V, VI, and VII).[20] In the Prologue, in the account of the history of the world, we are told that the Age of Brass represents the reign of Alexander and the supremacy of the Greeks (Prol.692–700). Book III includes three Alexander legends: the Tale of Diogenes and Alexander (III.1201–1330); the Tale of Alexander and the Pirate (III.2363–2437); and the account of the Wars and Death of Alexander (III.2438–80). Together, these narratives illustrate the evils of discord and war; the last leads into a discussion of the legality of the crusades. In Book V, in a condemnation of Greek idolatry that occurs in Genius's discussion of the religions of the world, Alexander is named twice. Once he is mentioned in the context of his exchange of letters with Dindimus, king of the Brahmins (V.1453–59), and once in the context of a legend concerning his worship of idols (V.1559–90). Book VI includes the retelling of the Tale of Nectanabus and the story of Alexander's birth, leading into the account of Nectanabus's death at Alexander's hand (VI.1789–2366), already analyzed in the previous chapter. Book VII, of course, which is based on the Pseudo-Aristotelian *Secretum Secretorum, De Regimine Principium* of Giles of Rome, and the *Livres dou Trésor* of Brunetto Latini,[21] documents Alexander's education under Aristotle. Also embedded within Book VII in some manuscripts is a story about Alexander and a worthy knight (*VII.3168–79).

Gower's Alexander is a complex figure, and his representation visibly shifts in the course of *Confessio Amantis*. The first three tales of Alexander—those that appear in the third book—offer a fairly coherent depiction of a willful king and aggressive warrior. In the Tale of Diogenes and Alexander, the wise philosopher who spends his time in solitary contemplation of the firmament convincingly argues the case for his own superiority. Diogenes is governed only by his reason, whereas the mighty ruler, engaged in continuous and ultimately fruitless warfare, is subject to his will. As Diogenes states, "Will is my man and my servant, / And evere hath ben and evere schal. / And thi will is thi principal" (III.1280–82).[22] The Tale of Alexander and the Pirate and the Wars and Death of Alexander are also concerned with the will/reason opposition (III.2428–37 and 2442–46). In the former episode, the pirate, an infamous robber and murderer, convinces Alexander that the only real difference between the two of them is that he (the pirate) is poor, while Alexander is rich. The pirate shows himself to be the alter ego of the rapacious conqueror, a point that is pictorially developed in the manuscript miniatures that illustrate this tale (Oxford, New College MS c.266, and New York, Pierpont Morgan Library MS M.126).[23] Tellingly, in the tale both Alexander and the pirate use the phrase "Mi will is" to describe their ambitions and intentions (III.2383 and 2408). The subsequent account of Alexander's death by poisoning, after his return home from victorious battle, exposes the futility of all of his achievements: "And as he hath the world mistimed / Noght as he scholde with his wit, / Noght as he wolde it was aquit" (III.2458–60).

Alexander's appearances in Book V are, if anything, even more negative. Dindimus's letters to Alexander condemn the Greeks because "thei for every membre hadden / A sondri god" (V.1457–58). The conqueror's own idol worship results from a deception comparable to that enacted by Mundus on Paulina, or by Nectanabus on Olympia: Candace's son, Candalus, lures Alexander into a cave where, "thurgh the fendes sleihte" (V.1582), he is tricked into believing he has heard the gods speak. However, in Book VII, in the context of the account of his education, the portrayal of Alexander changes markedly. Here, in the story of the knight who was wrongly judged, Alexander demonstrates qualities that appear almost divine, tempering wrath with pity and granting grace to the man who has offended him (*VII.3175–79). Elizabeth Porter notes that Gower here adapts his sources (in which Alexander condemned the knight when drunk and forgave him when sober), in order to make "the nature of Alexander's response the consequence of an appeal to his ethical self-governance."[24] Following on as it does from the retelling of his education, we seem to be presented with a king who has grown considerably in moral stature. Grady also argues that, in the penultimate book of *Confessio*, Gower's Alexander appears as a positive model of good government aimed at his patrons (Richard II in the first instance) and at least part of his target audience: "What aristocratic or royal reader of the *Confessio* could object to an implicit comparison to Alexander the Great?"[25]

There are, nevertheless, some very real problems with reading even the Alexander of Book VII as a positive model of kingship and ethical self-governance. In retelling the legends of Alexander, Gower and Genius disrupt the chronology of Alexander's life. Most significantly, the events surrounding Alexander's death are related long before those resulting in his birth. In the Prologue to *Confessio*, Gower describes the decline of Alexander's realm following his demise as a result of his decision to divide it up between his knights (Prol.701–13), and in Book II, the fall of Macedonia is mentioned albeit in passing (II.1840–42). The full account of Alexander's death is given, as we have seen, in Book V. The effect of this ordering of materials is to draw attention to the transitory nature of Alexander's achievements, and to make the decline of his realm appear fated. By the time we encounter the story of Alexander's miraculous birth, and begin to see him in God-like terms, we have already witnessed the frailty of his human nature.

Likewise, the education of Alexander is shown to be insufficient and ineffectual even before it is described with so much respect in Book VII. Whereas in Book VI, Alexander's first tutor, Nectanabus, misused his lore and magical powers for his own ends, here Aristotle provides Alexander with the sort of scientific learning (cosmology, politics, and ethics) that will result in self-knowledge. Aristotle appears as a good teacher, or, in James Simpson's terms, "the anti-type" of Nectanabus and "a positive pedagogic model."[26] Yet, Aristotle is also an ambivalent master for Alexander, and (as the conclusion of the poem will reveal) for Amans, because according to medieval tradition, and even *Confessio* itself, he is a *senex amans*, one who fails to practice what he preaches (VIII.2705–13).[27] The effectiveness of the teaching embodied in Book

VII is deliberately brought into question. For example, the section on "Theorique," the first part of philosophy, in Book VII includes a long discourse on astronomy and astrology (the last of the four types of mathematics): the planets, signs, stars, and authorities in these sciences (VII.633–1506).[28] Yet, as the Tale of Diogenes and Alexander makes clear, this knowledge has had little real impact. While Diogenes spends his time in a tun revolving on an axle, observing the movements of the heavenly bodies, Alexander, in his ignorance, only succeeds in obstructing him by standing in his light (III.1307–11). And as Simpson observes, "Diogenes is said to have 'enformed' Alexander (III.1313 [and cf. also the Latin gloss at III.1204]), but the fact that Alexander needs information implies that Aristotle had failed."[29] Simpson also suggests that the fact that the Tale of Alexander and the Pirate comes after the Tale of Diogenes and Alexander is further evidence of Alexander's intellectual and ethical stagnation

Similarly, at the end of Book VII, Genius develops his analysis of chastity by explaining that Aristotle taught Alexander how to control his lusts (VII.4235–37). In his account of Aristotle's teaching of Alexander, once again Genius emphasizes that it is not women who beguile men, but men who beguile themselves (VII.4265–75). Alexander is here cited as "an essamplaire, / His bodi so to guide and reule" (VII.4262–63); at the end of the book, he is mentioned again as a king who has been successfully instructed in chastity and honesty (VII.5384–88). In the light of the revelation that Aristotle, as *senex amans,* does not live up to the standards he sets, is such a positive reading of his pupil really plausible? In Book VII of *Confessio,* Alexander is contrasted with Solomon, a promiscuous and idolatrous king, whose sins resulted in the collapse of his realm (VII.4469–4568). Yet Alexander and Solomon are more alike than they are different. Alexander is himself guilty of idol worship, and with his death his kingdom is divided and goes into decline. Furthermore, the tradition of Alexander as courtly lover, suitor of Candace, flourished in the later Middle Ages (following Quintus Curtius Rufus, Petrarch in his *De Viris Illustribus* represents Alexander as lascivious, susceptible to beautiful men as well as women).[30] Gower himself alludes twice to Alexander's relationship with Candace (V.1571 and V.2543–46). Once again the implications are that the teaching relayed in Book VII, no matter how sound in its own right, does not necessarily work, and that even ideal kings are flawed.

A further weakness with reading the legends of Alexander as retold in *Confessio* as a narrative of progress, a medieval bildungsroman, is that even within the individual tales there are contradictions in the depiction of Alexander. The merciful king of Book VII is also a rash tyrant who has condemned a knight "of sodein wraththe and nought of right" (*VII.3170). While the arrogant and misguided assertion "'Non is above me'" (*VII.3173) cannot be countered while Alexander is alive, the reader already knows that it will be with his death. In the Tale of Alexander and the Pirate, Alexander responds to the pirate's request that he should "let rihtwisnesse / Be peised evene in the balance" (III.2402–03), by releasing the pirate from prison and taking him into his own service. In so doing, he overlooks the ominous implications of the pirate's claims that "Oure dedes ben of o colour / And in effect of o decerte" (III.2394–95) and that wealth as well as poverty is transient. Sure enough, Alexander's fortune is reversed when he least expects it. The conqueror who had killed men like beasts dies like a beast (III.2468–77).[31] Like Nebuchadnezzar, he has become a figure of *de casibus* tragedy. What is more, the punishment he receives for his sins is eternal: "And in such wise as he hath wroght / In destorbance of worldes pes, / His werre he fond thanne endeles..." (III.2464–66). In contrast, in the Tale of Diogenes and Alexander, Alexander demonstrates his sagacity and self-restraint in treating the old philosopher with courtesy and respect (III.1263–64) and refusing to be angered by his blunt rebukes. But even though he praises the man's "hihe wisdom" and "goodly wordes" (III.1295–96), Alexander still fails to understand that, unlike the pirate, the philosopher does not desire and has no use for worldly rewards. Simpson states that Gower represents Alexander as a king "whose first class education produced a rotten apple."[32] Certainly, as Grady notes, Alexander "had a double exemplary meaning for the medieval imagination, 'rapacious ambitious conqueror' and 'philosophically adept prince,'" which Gower exploits in *Confessio*.[33] Gower's depiction of Alexander mirrors the representation of Nebuchadnezzar's statue: like that idol, Alexander may have a head of gold, but his legs are alloy and his feet are clay. It is plausible to assume that Gower's representation of Alexander reveals something of his anxieties concerning Richard as king and man. But what of Gower's actual politics? To get an insight into these, it is necessary to look at Book VII.

Book VII and the Politics of Chastity

Interspersed amongst these legends and anecdotes is a series of allusions to Alexander, all spoken by Amans, that draw comparisons between the state of the unsuccessful lover and that of the mighty conqueror. In Book II, for example, Amans tells Genius that, even if he
were as strong as Alexander, he would be unable to supplant his rivals
for fear of slander (II.2412–20). In Book V, he asserts first that it does
not matter to him whether his beloved be as poor as Medea or as rich as
Candace, who gave presents to Alexander in order to woo him (V.2534–
46). He then claims that even if he himself had the authority of Pompey
or Alexander, he would never commit such a terrible crime as "ravine"
or rape (V.5531–37). In the Tale of Diogenes and Alexander, Amans himself anticipates the philosopher's condemnation of Alexander when he
describes his own inner conflict between reason and will (III.1179–84).
Individually, these passing references seem incidental, but taken together
they indicate a close connection between Alexander the Great and the
figure of Amans. It is, nevertheless, Book VII that provides the crucial
link between king and subject, state and citizen, rule and self-rule,
counsel and confession, the ethical and political and the erotic. The representation of kingship and the advice offered here is characterized by
political moderation. To demonstrate this, I will concentrate on two narratives embedded within the exploration of chastity (VII.4215–5397), the
fifth and final point in the discussion of policy.

Although the preponderance of rape narratives appears in Book V, it
is not until Book VII that two of the most famous medieval legends concerning rape and violence against women are told: the Tales of Lucrece
(VII.4754–5130) and Virginia (VII.5131–5306). The former, of course, is
retold in Chaucer's *Legend of Good Women* (F.1680–1885); the latter became the subject of the Physician's Tale in *The Canterbury Tales* (1–286).
Unlike the narratives examined in Chapter 4, the women *as women* are
marginalized in the Tale of Lucrece and in the Tale of Virginia. At the
same time, the connection between rape and tyranny, which was certainly anticipated in earlier rape narratives such as the Tale of Tereus, is
particularly foregrounded in these two stories. Genius consistently cou-
ples uncontrollable or uncontrolled desire with corrupt rule. In the Tale
of Tarquin and Arrons, which introduces the Tale of Lucrece, the words

"tirannyssh" and "tirannie" both occur (VII.4594 and 4601). In the Tale of Lucrece, "tirannysshe," "tirannie," and "tirant" appear four times (VII.4889, 4899, 5118, and 4959), and in the Tale of Virginia, twice (VII.5235 and 5285). Gower pairs "tirannie" with "tresoun" (VII.4601) or with its rhymes "tricherie" (VII.4900 and 5287) or "lecherie" (VII.5119, 5236, and 5288). Indeed in the Tale of Virginia, rape is a metonym of failure in government (no other evidence of tyrannical behavior is given).

The Tale of Lucrece is prefaced at length with the account of the deceitful plotting of tyrant Tarquin and his son, here named Arrons, against the Gabiens (VII.4593–4753), a story that is incidental to the main theme, chastity. Genius attempts to establish a connection between the two, stating of both father and son that "al that evere was plesance / Unto the fleisshes lust thei toke" (VIII.4606–07). Yet the link is a tenuous one. Indeed, the irrelevance of sexual desire to the Tale of Tarquin and Arrons serves to draw the reader's attention to the political content of the Tale of Lucrece. In introducing the story of Lucrece with this matter, Gower follows the classical rather than the medieval versions of the story (e.g., Le Roman de la Rose, 8608–50, and Giovanni Boccaccio's De Claris Mulieribus, XLVI).[34] In so doing he renders the story of Lucrece's rape subservient to a larger narrative about the political community, a community in which women do not figure. As in Gower's sources, Lucrece is represented as a pawn passed between men. The rape is immediately precipitated by Arrons, the son of Tarquin, who, after a night of feasting, drinking, and boasting in the company of "a part of the chivalerie" (VII.4765), instigates a "strif" (VII.4772) amongst his men over the question of whose wife is the most worthy. The harsh reality is that the rape of Lucrece is brought about directly as the result of a bet. Her husband, Collatin, uses her as a counter in a game played only by men, and as a result unwittingly places her in jeopardy. Arrons, needless to say, takes the bet further than Collatin intends: whereas Collatin gambles on her fidelity, Arrons determines to win much more than he admits. The attack on Lucrece is represented as something other than an attack on a woman: it is a form of "slih tresoun" (VII.4936) that takes place within Collatin's own household, and that directly parallels the treacherous penetration of the nation of the Gabiens. Just as Arrons used underhand means to gain the trust of the Gabiens and bring about their downfall, so he tricks his way into Lucrece's chamber. Gower has Arrons force Lucrece into submission by threatening to kill her and her people (VII.4978–81). This is an adaptation of the major sources (Ovid's *Fasti* and Livy's *History of Rome*), in which the rapist threatens to kill his victim and make it look as if she has been caught in the act of adultery.[35] In Craig Bertolet's words, Gower's Lucrece "submits to save her family."[36] In this way, the rape in Gower's version is very much figured as a crime against society rather than a women, her chastity, and her reputation.

Following Ovid rather than Livy, Gower represents Lucrece as effectively silenced by the rape. She immediately sends for her patriarchal guardians—her husband and her father—but she is only able to relay what has occurred after a number of false starts (VII.5040–44), and her words are reported in the third person. By denying Lucrece a voice in the second half of the narrative, Gower moves her from center stage. Bertolet argues that Lucrece is thus reduced to a "political sacrifice."[37] Unusually, Lucrece does not herself desire vengeance,[38] and neither religious piety nor pride motivates her suicide; her main concern seems to be that she should not find herself reproved by the world (VII.5063–64). It is up to Brutus (described here as Lucrece's cousin), who has already sworn revenge against the atrocities of the Romans (VII.4735–45), to take the initiative. He is elevated to the position of hero.[39] Brutus emerges as the opposite of Arrons, restoring unity and stability where Arrons brought division and chaos (first to the Gabiens and then to Collatin's household). Whereas Arrons, rendered effeminate by his uncontrollable desire for Lucrece (see VII.4847–57 and 4868–88), hypocritically disguised his heinous intentions with "tales feigned" (VII.4929) and "frendly speches" (VII.4943), Brutus, with "manlich herte" (VII.5093),[40] turns private grief into public oration (VII.5101–19). The rape and suicide of Lucrece become the catalysts for public action. The message of *Confessio Amantis* Book VII ("Awey, awey the tirannie / Of lecherie and covoitise!") is placed in the mouths of the Roman people (VII.5118–19). The tyrannical deeds of Tarquin and his son are finally overcome by council and decisions made by the commonality, both greater and lesser.

Genius depicts the overthrow of father and son as a revolution without bloodshed, with Tarquin and Arrons driven into exile (VII.5121–22). According to Livy, Brutus and Collatinus were then chosen as consuls of the newly established Roman Republic, but as Larry Scanlon points out Genius "neglects the transition from the Old Roman kingdom into the Republic."[41] The effect of this change is, however, to make the story more rather than less applicable to the situation in Gower's England, since the

overthrow of the monarchy as a political institution would be unthink-
able in the late fourteenth century. Genius ends the narrative abruptly
but appropriately, simply stating that the people have "taken betre governance" (VII.5123). Bertolet is no doubt justified in viewing Gower's
Brutus as a reformer,[42] but is surely mistaken to read the tale's conclusion as an "unveiled message to the king to be aware that popular revolt
similar to what had happened in the early 1380s could again occur."[43]
Gower's Roman citizens bear no resemblance to the rabble of 1381, as
described in Vox Clamantis Book I. Brutus—also a member of the House
of Tarquin, although Gower does not acknowledge this—has stronger
affinities with England's own magnates, many of whom were Richard
II's own kinsmen, than with its peasantry. Yet even if Brutus does have a
greater resemblance to Henry of Derby (who had joined the Appellants
in their attempt to regulate Richard's rule) or to his father John of Gaunt
(who returned to England from Spain in 1389) than to John Ball or Jack
Straw, the significance of this is still limited. Gower's Tale of Lucrece
clearly cannot and does not go so far as to envisage a future in which
"Richard would follow the fate of Arrons, with Bolingbroke playing the
part of Brutus."[44]

The themes emphasized in the story of Lucrece's rape are reiterated in the immediately ensuing narrative, the Tale of Virginia, another
Roman legend derived from Livy's History of Rome.[45] Once again Gower
deviates from other medieval renderings of the classical narrative (e.g.,
Le Roman de la Rose, 5589–5658) in order to preserve its political dimensions.[46] A number of other changes Gower makes to the story of Virginia
serve to reinforce its congruence with the previous narrative.[47] Again, it
is the reputation of the woman (the daughter of Livius Virginius, here a
knight rather than a plebian)—this time for beauty—that serves as the
gauntlet for the villain of the piece, Apius Claudius, the city's governor.
As with most of the previous rape narratives, the innocence of the female victim is stressed, and it is Claudius's own evil "thoght" that is
responsible for igniting the fire of lust (VII.5140–147). Claudius, like
Arrons and also like Tereus in Book V (and the evil Antiochus in Book
VIII), is entirely subject to "the blinde lustes of his wille" (VII.5147).
Unlike Lucrece, who is muted only after her rape, Virginia has no voice
of her own from the very beginning. She is simply a fair young maiden
on the verge of marriage to a worthy and well-born man in a match that
has the full approval of her father, a military leader. When Claudius falsely

asserts his prior claim on her (in the absence of her father who is on a military campaign), the narrative turns on issues of rights and owner-ship. The friends of Virginius petition the king, arguing that it is unjust that a man should suffer such a wrong when the reason he cannot de-fend himself is that he is occupied in defending his country. Virginia's death at the hands of her father (he chooses to kill her himself rather than to see her defiled) is horrifyingly brutal, but it also echoes Lucrece's suicide. The implication is that death is the fate that the daughter would have chosen for herself had she been offered the opportunity to speak or to act.[48] There are some unexpected aspects to this story, especially given Gower's earlier treatment of the topic of rape and his previous sensitiv-ity to the plights of its female victim. For example, Gower's Virginius concentrates on his daughter's shame should she be defiled (VII.5247–52), whereas Livy's father also presents her as an individual who has lost her freedom.[49] Indeed, as in the Tale of Lucrece, Gower's Tale of Vir-ginia effectively glosses over the sacrifice of the woman.

The Tale of Virginia, like the Tale of Lucrece, focuses on a male rather than female principal. In this case it is the father who is the leading fig-ure (in Livy's version the prospective son-in-law also has a more signifi-cant role, and her great-uncle or grandfather is also involved). Virginius, however, emerges as a more ambiguous protagonist than the heroic Bru-tus in the Tale of Lucrece does. As María Bullón-Fernández observes, Virginius's behavior comes across as shockingly self-centered.[50] He is concerned with his own name and reputation rather than with what his daughter may be suffering. Indeed his action in stabbing his daughter is clearly symbolic: if Virginius cannot control to whom he gives his daugh-ter's virginity he will take it himself. Again, critics have looked for and found political meaning in this narrative. For Bullón-Fernández, the father-daughter relationships in Gower stands for the responsibilities a monarch has for the state. Yet if we pursue Bullón-Fernández's argu-ment—that Virginius is just as much a tyrant in the private sphere as Claudius is in the public one—to its logical conclusion, it is difficult to see how it can read as a coherent comment upon Richard II's reign. What solutions or alternatives are actually being offered? Claudius may eventually be punished but Virginius is praised for comparable actions. (We will see in Chapter 6 that similar problems emerge in reading the Tale of Apollonius of Tyre politically, since Apollonius seems to share in the crimes of the evil Antiochus.) What is more, there is a switch in direction toward the end of the narrative, when it turns away from Virginius and his murder of his daughter and back to Apius Claudius. It is not Virginius or Virginia's intended husband, Ilicius, or any other kinsman (in the Tale of Lucrece, Brutus *was* at least a kinsman) who heads the revolt against this tyrant, but the Roman people acting, in this case, on their own initiative.

In the opinion of Bullón-Fernández, "such a change in focus suggests that in this story Genius is more interested in showing the power of the common will against the tyranny of kings than in Virginius's plight."[51] Although Gower's Tale of Virginia lacks the public oratory of his Tale of Lucrece, the poem does have some relevance to contemporary politics. Gower adapts his main source to render Claudius not a *decemvir* (one of Rome's ten rulers) but a king, and as Judith Ferster points out, Gower's story turns on questions of good and bad advice. Unlike Tereus or Arrons, Claudius does not act alone but with the connivance of his brother, another "of such riote" as himself (VII.5168).[52] The language here is again loaded: the plotting of these two villains is referred to as "conseil" (VII.5171), but it is of course an evil counsel, which results in the inverse of natural law when the king "The lawe torneth out of kinde" (VII.5220). Fortunately, however, this evil counsel is balanced by the "comun conseil" (VII.5294) of the people of Rome, who, if somewhat belatedly, decide to act to prevent further tyrannical atrocities. The terminology is crucial here as Claudius is actually said to have been "deposed" (VII.5295), and as Ferster explains, the phrase "comun conseil" is "an important idiom in late fourteenth-century England, used in chronicles and parliamentary records, in Magna Carta and the notices of Edward II's deposition."[53] Ferster asserts that, "in case that does not thrust the story into the fourteenth century, with the deposition of Edward II and the threats of deposition against Edward III, and most immediately Richard II . . . in VII.5302–03 [Gower] pointedly applies it to his own time to warn modern kings 'That scholden afterward governe.'"[54] Once again, however, we have to be cautious in how we interpret the political message of this tale. Genius finishes with the anodyne advice that one should learn from it "How it is good a king eschuie / The lust of vice and vertu suie" (VII.5305–06). The lengthy account in Livy of the revolt of the plebians and the troops is omitted. Equally tellingly, Genius does not mention the exile, imprisonment, or eventual death of Claudius, or the election of Virginius as plebian tribune. Like the Tale of Lucrece, the

Tale of Virginia in *Confessio Amantis* is about the overthrow of a tyrant but not about a revolution, about deposition but not about republicanism. Scanlon's argument that these narratives are concerned with condemning the excesses and uncontrolled appetites of individual monarchs but only as part of the larger scheme of royal *self*-regulation advocated in Book VII (rather than from, say, a constitutionalist perspective) is convincing.[55] According to Scanlon, Gower presents us in Book VII with a model of a successful monarchy that depends upon the *"voluntary* restraint of [the king's] awesome, potentially absolute power [my emphasis]."[56] Beyond this, no practical suggestions for political change are offered. Even if we believe that Gower here signals that monarchies can fail, that such power sometimes goes unrestrained, this is hardly a radical message. Gower's *Confessio Amantis,* with its criticisms of not only unjust kings but also their advisers, is neither so contentious nor so risky as Ferster's analysis assumes.[57] Even in a period such as the late fourteenth century when advice was a topical, even urgent, issue, there is certainly nothing inherently subversive or dangerous about advocating good counsel and pointing out the vulnerability of those monarchs who choose to ignore it. In fact, Ferster herself acknowledges that Gower's criticisms of Richard II are far less "insolent" in *Confessio Amantis* than in his 1393 revisions to *Vox Clamantis,* and suggests that in the former poem he is constrained by the fact that he is writing in English rather than Latin.[58] These are sound observations, although as a final caveat it is worth remembering that Latinate readers of *Confessio,* versed in the writing of Ovid and Livy, would have been aware of what Scanlon calls "the repression of republicanism" in the Lucrece and Virginia narratives.[59] Such readers would have been free to make what they would of these omissions.

To conclude this chapter, I would argue that *Confessio Amantis* is a poem with a shifting political perspective. This is manifested most clearly in the poem's revised dedications, but it is also evidenced within the poem itself, in those sections that do not change with Gower's revisions. The contrasting depictions of Nebuchadnezzar in the Prologue and in Book I offer us images of a king who is corrupt and about to face Judgment, but there are no threats here of the king's overthrow, and the possibility of personal reformation remains. Like Nebuchadnezzar, Alexander the Great is a complex figure of tyranny and wisdom, sin and redemption. This portrayal expresses only indirectly and equivocally Gower's

concerns about the failures of his own monarch, Richard II, and some
hope remains for the future. With Book VII, this diminishes. In Book
VII, the Tales of Lucrece and Virginia take on an allegorical significance
not found in the earlier rape narratives. Gower is less interested here in
questions of male and female culpability and innocence than in the implications that his exploration of gender politics has for the government
of the realm. The domestic sphere is almost crudely reduced to a metaphor for the body politic. The rapists and their avengers stand for tyrants
and their opponents, and the female victims in their innocence come to
represent the king's subjects, with whom the poet and his narrator identify. In both the Tale of Lucrece and the Tale of Virginia, Gower adapts a
classical story to make comments about the current political situation,
but does so only with considerable caution and some ambivalence. These
narratives warn that tyrannous kings may be overthrown, but do so in a
context of advocating greater self-government on the part of the monarch
rather than structural political change. However, the full implications of
the Tales of Lucrece and Virginia can only be comprehended when read
alongside the Tale of Apollonius in Book VIII.

6

OEDIPUS, APOLLONIUS, AND
RICHARD II

Near the end of *Confessio Amantis*, the poet famously inscribes his own name into his vernacular poem. When Venus, the goddess of love, asks her supplicant, Amans, to identify himself, he replies, "John Gower" (VIII.2322). This revelation is startling for two reasons. First, both reader and lover are shocked by the recognition of what the latter is, or at any rate what he has become. Like the poet, Amans is now old, decrepit, and almost blind. Shortly afterwards, Venus holds up a mirror to his face (VIII.2820–23). In this reversal of the Lacanian mirror stage, the viewer does not misrecognize himself as unified and whole, but has his identity exposed as fragmented, divided, and duplicitous. Second, the reader is confronted with the question of why the author chooses to publish his own name in this way. In attempting to answer this, we might be reminded of the Derridean notion that the inscription of the proper name is driven by two desires. One is oedipal ("to preserve one's proper name, to see it as the analogon of the *name* of the father"), the other narcissistic ("to make one's own 'proper' name 'common,' to make it enter, and be at one with the body of the mother-tongue").[1] According to Anne Middleton, internal self-naming performs a specific "grammatical and ontological" function in medieval poetry.[2] However, in such texts, authorial signatures are not ostensibly egotistical. Rather, they serve to ground the text ethically in the lived experience of a posited historical individual. As Middleton explains (borrowing Johan Huizinga's words), "to signify historically or literally" in this way is "to 'choose the text for the sermon of one's life.'"[3] Yet, as we have seen, in signing his name to *Confessio*

Amantis, Gower chooses a very odd kind of sermon, one that takes as its exempla tales of oedipal urges and narcissistic longings and stories of repression and impotence. Nowhere is this more manifest than in the final book, with its focus on the sin of incest.

In the frame narrative of Book VIII, Gower's alter ego, Amans, repeatedly insists that the subject Genius has chosen to complete the confessional narrative is irrelevant to his situation. While usually willing to admit that he is subject to "loves Rage" (VIII.150), Amans denies that he is so "wylde" as to seduce either kinswomen or nuns (VIII.171–75). In so doing, he anticipates an epithet later applied to the evil incestuous King Antiochus in the Tale of Apollonius. Amans also reiterates his innocence after the tale is done (VIII.2204). Genius acknowledges that Amans is not guilty of this particular sin (VIII.184–89), yet pushes on regardless with his examples of lust that "excedeth lawe" (VIII.263). But in a sense Amans *is* guilty of incest insofar as he seems to be engaged in an oedipal struggle with his own incestuous parents: Venus and Cupid, the queen and king of love.[4] Genius, as the priest of love, has already condemned these two deities (V.1406–20), yet, as we saw in Chapter 4, both he and Amans continue to worship them until Amans's own aged image is revealed and he is dismissed from their court. It is only with this dismissal that Amans is finally freed from his bonds of unnatural love. This chapter attempts to explain why Gower decided to end *Confessio* with an exploration of the topic of incest, and why he might have wanted to put his name to these particular narratives. In so doing, it focuses on the representation of oedipal and narcissistic desire in the Tale of Apollonius, the main exemplary narrative in Book VIII, and the longest tale in the whole of *Confessio Amantis.*

Significantly, the story of Oedipus, which since Freud has been so central to any analysis of gendered and sexual identity, and indeed to many analyses of language and narrative, did not often appear in the literature of the Middle Ages.[5] But amongst the other tales of murder, incest, and self-destruction that were hugely popular, it was perhaps that of Apollonius of Tyre that most captured the medieval imagination (despite its confusing and highly repetitive plot, the story of Apollonius achieved wide circulation in Latin).[6] In an important essay on Gower, Larry Scanlon uses the insights of psychoanalysis to explicate the Apollonius narrative, and the riddle at its heart, while arguing that the narrative itself exposes the limitations of psychoanalysis in relation to father-daughter incest and other social and historical factors.[7] My own reading of Gower is greatly indebted to Scanlon's, although in offering my interpretation, I not only examine the parallels between Oedipus's story and that of Apollonius, but also look at Gower's divergences from his immediate sources and analogues. In approaching the story (its riddle and its characters), if only in part, from a psychoanalytical perspective, I am, like Scanlon, aware of its blind spots. In this analysis, I place greater emphasis than traditional psychoanalysis would allow on the role of women and on the importance of female sexuality, while at the same time exploring the hitherto ignored subject of homosociality and the feminization of the hero. Psychoanalysis is simply one of a number of analytical tools to inform my central argument that there exists a connection between the construction of gender and sexuality in this tale and the political concerns and historical context of *Confessio* as a whole.

FATHER-DAUGHTER INCEST AND THE ABSENT MOTHER

There are clear similarities between the plots of Sophocles' *Oedipus* and both the Latin *Historia Apollonii* and Gower's Tale of Apollonius. In addition to the focus on incest and its ruinous consequences, all involve familial recognition scenes, and in all of them the hero solves a riddle either before or near the beginning of the narrative.[8] Gower's tale is typical of the histories of Apollonius in that it begins with the story of Antiochus, king of Antioch, who, after the death of his wife, rapes his only child. The centrality of Antiochus's crime to Gower's version of the story, and thus the importance of the riddle that both hides and betrays it, is revealed by the Latin gloss. The story is a "mirabile exemplum de magno Rege Antiocho" (extraordinary exemplum of the great King Antiochus) (at VIII.271). In order to keep his daughter for his own use, Antiochus devises the riddle for her suitors to solve and then executes those who are unable to provide the correct answer. As the bodies pile up, the number of suitors soon diminishes. When Apollonius, the high-spirited and hot-blooded young prince of Tyre, hears news of the beautiful princess and the seemingly impossible task, he resolves to undertake the quest and sets sail from Tyre. On his arrival in Antiochus's court, the king explains the terms of the agreement, and repeats the riddle:

"With felonie I am upbore,
I ete and have it noght forbore
Mi modres fleissh, whos housebonde
Mi fader forto seche I fonde,
Which is the Sone ek of my wif." (VIII.405–09)

This riddle has vexed critics for the last hundred years and more.[9] The closer one looks at it, the more elusive its meaning becomes. Inconsistencies in punctuation in the manuscripts of the text, or its complete omission, render any attempt at translating such grammatically ambiguous verses at best only provisional. Gower's inclusion at this point in the narrative of a Latin gloss does little to help with the rendering into Modern English. The gloss reads "Scelere vehor, materna carne vescor, quero patrem meum, matris mee virum, vxoris mee filium" (I am carried along by my crime, I feed on my mother's flesh, I seek my father, my mother's husband, my wife's son) (at VIII.405). In fact, the ambiguity of the riddle is in itself a clue to its meaning. We have already seen that Gower links grammatical indeterminacy to sexual and moral confusion. The riddle reveals itself to be concerned with something that is perverse and unethical.

Gower's riddle can only be further explained when seen in context; it is impossible to attempt to solve it by looking at it in isolation. No direct answer is given in the story itself. Apollonius replies, "'The question which thou hast spoke, / If thou wolt that it be unloke, / It toucheth al the privete / Betwen thin oghne child and thee, / And stant al hol upon you tuo'"(VIII. 423–27). Apollonius does not identify the speaker of the riddle, but he does reveal that its answer lies in the relationship between father and daughter and is not only private, but also secret and of a sexual nature.[10] But how does he know this? Broken down into its constituent parts, the riddle itself, in the English and Latin versions, offers three further pointers to facilitate interpretation. The first is that the speaker—who would seem most obviously to be Antiochus himself—has committed a crime. The second is that the speaker is governed by a monstrous appetite and has even consumed his own mother. The third is that the object of the speaker's quest is his mother's husband, his own father, who is paradoxically also his wife's (and thus, logically, also his own) son. These clues direct the reader to the surrounding narrative. The reference to "felonie" or crime points toward Antiochus's rape of his daughter (incest is a crime as well as a sin), and the metaphor of monstrous appetite directs us to the same event. It has already been anticipated in the text: first at VIII.309–10: "The wylde fader thus devoureth / His oghne fleissh . . ." and again at VIII.312 in the reference to "this unkinde fare" in which *unkinde* means "unnatural" and *fare* may mean "feasting" as well as "business."[11] Much later, and in a quite different context, the quest for the father is echoed by the daughter of Apollonius when she complains, "'Mi fader eke / I not wher that I scholde him seke'" (VIII.1721–22). How these allusions fit together, and how they relate to the consuming of the mother's flesh and the search for the mother's husband/father/son, can only be begun to be understood when considered in relation to the tale as a whole.

Scanlon and other recent critics such as Georgiana Donavin argue that the riddle lends itself to Freudian interpretations.[12] Certainly, psychoanalysis can explain the figuring of incest as monstrous appetite in Antiochus's riddle and in the account of his rape of his daughter. Antiochus's riddle with its references to the devouring of the mother's flesh expresses the speaker's repressed desire to devour or to marry/to sleep with his own mother, a desire that resurfaces in later life in the seduction or rape of the daughter. Yet, an understanding of psychoanalysis can only take us so far in solving Antiochus's riddle (in Gower's version of the story at least). This is because the role of the mother—as an active rather than passive figure—appears to reach further than an oedipal interpretation would suggest. The history of Apollonius is littered with absent and often nameless women. The events at the beginning of Gower's version of the tale (although not of *Historia Apollonii*) are precipitated by the loss of Antiochus's wife. We are told: "Bot such fortune cam to honde, / That deth, which no king mai withstonde, / Bot every lif it mote obeie, / This worthi queene tok aweie" (VIII.279–82). The demise of Antiochus's wife is not related in order to explain the events that follow (although the king's isolation and the proximity as well as beauty of his daughter— she is living in his chamber—are stressed), but to draw the reader's attention to the vulnerability of his daughter. We are told that the king "caste al his hole entente / His oghne doghter forto spille" (VIII.296–97); in other words he has decided to *destroy* his daughter. The king has strength and opportunity on his side, and, unlike the Latin source, he has no scruples of conscience.[13] The daughter is defenseless: "For thei that scholde hir bodi kepe / Of wommen were absent as thanne"

(VIII.306–07). We are not told why the women are not present (in *Historia Apollonii* the servants are sent away by the king).[14] But the subsequent reappearance of the nurse, who has looked after Antiochus's daughter since her childhood, and who has in a sense taken the place of her mother, reveals the full extent of her vulnerability. On hearing what has happened, this woman offers no protection but only empty words of consolation: "In confortinge of hire ansuerde, / To lette hire fadres fol desir / Sche wiste no recoverir: / Whan thing is do, ther is no bote, / So suffren thei that suffre mote" (VIII.336–40). In effect, the nurse, in remaining silent, colludes with the king. Antiochus's daughter is indeed one whom "non socoureth" (VIII.310).

Later in the text, aspects of the suffering of Antiochus's daughter are repeated in the anguish of Apollonius's daughter, Thaise. Although Apollonius's wife does not die, she falls into a death-like state, giving birth on board ship during a storm, and is placed in a coffin and thrown overboard. Apollonius then leaves his daughter in the care of the burgess of Tharse, Strangulio, and his wife, Dionise. Initially, this does not seem an unfortunate act of entrustment—although the sheer length of Apollonius's absence (at least fourteen years) might imply a degree of paternal neglect—but the cancerous hatred of Thaise's foster-mother, jealous on her daughter's behalf, makes the situation a dangerous one. The parallel between Thaise's situation and that of Antiochus's daughter is made explicit when we are told of the death of Thaise's nurse, Lychoride, who, unlike the nurse of Antiochus's daughter, is a "trewe" servant (VIII.1350), although even she cannot protect her ward beyond the grave.[15] Once again, the absence, and in this case also the cruelty, of the maternal figures, combined with the sexual incontinence or, as here, the neglect of the father imperils the daughter's chastity. Thaise finds herself threatened with murder, captured by pirates, and eventually sold to the keeper of a brothel. Thaise's own mother does not reappear in the narrative until after Thaise's marriage to Athenagoras.

In *Historia Apollonii*, the daughters of Antiochus and Apollonius are also doubled in the unnamed figure of Apollonius's wife: the daughter of Archistrates, king of Pentapolis in Cyrene. One significant change Gower makes to his sources is to give Archistrates (Artestrathes) a wife. Although this queen does not figure largely in the narrative, she is mentioned three times at VIII.659, VIII.721, and, most significantly, VIII.930–37. It is this third mention that reveals her importance as wife and mother. Artestrathes seeks her approval for their daughter's marriage: "And forthe withal the king als swithe, / For he wol have hire good assent, / Hath for the queene hir moder sent" (VIII.930–32). The crucial point to note here is that Artestrathes' daughter is the one daughter in the narrative who is not vulnerable to assault, and she is the one daughter whose mother is present.

The importance of the mother figure may also be linked to the metaphors of monstrous appetite mentioned above. Incest is likened elsewhere in Gower's text to poisoned food. In the frame narrative, Genius warns Amans: "For al such time of love is lore, / And lich unto the bittersweete; / For thogh it thenke a man ferst swete, / He schal wel fielen ate laste / That it is sour and may noght laste. / For as a morsell envenimed, / So hath such love his lust mistimed" (VIII.190–96). Incest may be sweet to the taste, but its aftereffects are unpleasant, and seemingly even deadly. Even though Genius does not make the connection, the first three examples he gives of incest—Caligula, Amnon, and Lot—are all linked to feasting and drinking. In Suetonius, Caligula seats his sisters below him at a banquet. In 2 Samuel 13, Amnon has Tamar prepare his food with her own hand and instructs her to feed it to him. In Genesis 19, Lot's daughters intoxicate him with wine before sleeping with him.[16] It is something of a commonplace to remark on the close association of women and food in the Middle Ages. Nonetheless it is the case that food was an important, and sometimes scarce, commodity, and that, within the household, women, as wives and mothers, were largely responsible for providing safe and nutritious sustenance.[17] Such women, as it were, figuratively and sometimes literally offer their own bodies to supply the needs and wants of their husbands and children. In Gower's Tale of Constance, the heroine is represented as the perfect, self-sacrificing mother, who forces herself to provide her infant child with sustenance even when, isolated and quite literally at sea, she feels overwhelmed with despair at her situation (II.1068–83).

Women are likewise responsible for controlling the intake of tempting but potentially illness-inducing foodstuffs. The message of the Tale of Apollonious seems to be that without their wives to check their unhealthy desires, men are irresistibly drawn to such comestibles. Like Antiochus, who indirectly confesses his desire to cannibalize his own mother and looks to satisfy his lust in his daughter, such men indulge their "likinge and concupiscence" (VIII.293). At the same time, women

like Dionise, who reject the nurturing role, clearly take the part of the ar-
chetypal antimother, the wicked stepmother from fairy tale. Dionise's
role in the Tale of Apollonius bears a close relationship to the parts played
by the Sultan's mother and Domilde in the Tale of Constance (II.587–
1612). Both evil mothers-in-law plot to overthrow the wife of their sons
(the former, like Dionise, is driven by jealousy, the latter has no stated
motive). The Sultan's mother actually plans a feast (II.677–92) at which
she can slay her son and his advisers. The murder of the child is itself,
metaphorically, an incestuous act, as the mother devours her offspring
rather than offers it sustenance. As a consequence of their crimes,
Dionise and her husband, as well as Antiochus and his daughter, have to
suffer death.

The Search for the Father and the Desire for the Son

In Gower's tale, then, the role of women as wives and mothers is crucial
to the proper functioning of the household. Nonetheless the father figures continue to dominate the story. Gower's version of Antiochus's riddle is derived from a corruption of the medieval Latin prose romance. In
Historia Apollonii the riddle reads "Scelere vehor, maternam carnem vescor,
quaero fratrem meum, meae matris virum, uxoris meae filium: non invenio" (I am borne on crime; I eat my mother's flesh; I seek my brother,
my mother's husband, my wife's son; I do not find him).[18] Gower's
Latin and English versions, and/or the version of the text that Gower
used as his source, make two transformations to the original: "*patrem*"
and "father" replace "*fratrem*," and "non invenio" is dropped. (In Gower's
Middle-English version of the riddle "I fonde" should possibly be translated as "I try"—thus "I try to seek"—rather than "I found.")[19] Rather
than, as one critic contends, "being guilty of translating what he did not
properly understand,"[20] Gower exploits the ambiguities that he has inherited. These "corruptions," which change the whole meaning of the
riddle in Latin and English, can be read as examples of parapraxes (the
so-called Freudian slips); that is, they have a meaning beyond that intended by the speaker/translator. In these corruptions, repressed material,
in this case an oedipal search for the father, forces its way to the surface
of the reader's consciousness.[21] The parapraxes in Gower's versions of

the riddle draw our attention to the importance of the mother's husband, who is also the father, and to the equivalence of these terms to the wife's son. Furthermore, they suggest that this search is not fruitless.

Once again, Scanlon looks to psychoanalysis for an explanation. For Antiochus, as an abusive patriarch who has defied the paternal prohibitions on incest, and whose Oedipus Complex has been repressed rather than destroyed, the significance of the father is critical. His riddle not only exposes the desire for his mother/daughter but also reveals that he is obsessed with his father. According to Scanlon, what Antiochus is lacking, what he simultaneously desires and fears, is not his actual father but, in Lacanian terms, the Name of the Father, or paternal and patriarchal authority.[22] What this reading does not acknowledge is the sexual dimension to such a quest. Ultimately, in sleeping with his daughter and desiring his mother, Antiochus represses the longing for his actual father.[23] Just as the infantile desire for the mother is displaced onto the daughter, so the fixation on the father reemerges in a search for the son. Antiochus redirects his longing from his father onto, not his actual son (since he has none), but his son-in-law presumptive, Apollonius.[24] In Gower's version, Antiochus's tone is certainly paternalistic when he warns Apollonius: "'Forthi my Sone ... / Be wel avised of this thing, / Which hath thi lif in jeupartie'" (VIII.415–17; cf. also 432–39).

Antiochus's riddle draws our attention to the homosociality, or what Luce Irigaray calls the hom(m)o-sexuality, of patriarchal society.[25] María Bullón-Fernández observes that Lévi-Strauss's theories about the relationship between the incest taboo and the patriarchal order are based on the assumption "that there is a sexuality prior to the incest taboo, that men and women have a 'natural' desire for the opposite sex."[26] She goes on to explain that the taboo actually "establishes heterosexuality as the only legitimate form" at the same time as it regulates it.[27] The incest taboo coincides with and is dependent upon a taboo against homosexuality. Irigaray states that the traffic in women, which relies upon the incest prohibition, takes the form of transactions exclusively between men.[28] This is an economy based on a symbolic form of homosexuality. Actual male homosexuality is prohibited, however, "because the 'incest' involved in homosexuality has to remain in the realm of the pretence."[29] Antiochus's longing for the father/husband/son challenges the structure of society, and the law of patriarchy, just as much as does his rape of his daughter. Paradoxically, in trying to hide his deed, Antiochus articulates it, acknowledging it to be a crime ("felonie") and also to be interconnected with homosocial desire or homoeroticism.

Antiochus—referred to by the narrator of Gower's tale as a "tirant of his felonie" (VIII.463)—is described as determined to "grieve [the] bodi" of the prince of Tyre (VIII.465),[30] but his behavior is, in fact, somewhat unpredictable. Fearing for his own reputation, Antiochus pretends that Apollonius has given a wrong response to the riddle, but (in Gower's narrative, although not in the sources) allows Apollonius thirty days' respite. Antiochus seems to be driven by conflicting desires: simultaneously he wants to catch and to kill Apollonius and to let him escape and live. The implication may be that Antiochus has actually found what he was looking for: his lost son. Or perhaps Antiochus sees himself in Apollonius and, recognizing him as the harbinger of his own death, is paralyzed by his appearance.[31] Whatever the explanation for the delay, Apollonius distrusts Antiochus and decides to flee, only to discover that he is being pursued. Yet, whereas in the sources Apollonius escapes a second time, and Antiochus orders a major search, in Gower's narrative Antiochus simply gives up on him (VIII.533–36). George Macaulay observes, "The change made by Gower is not a happy one, for it takes away the motive for the flight from Tarsus."[32] Thus it is not only Antiochus's behavior that appears erratic, but also Apollonius's, since he keeps on fleeing after the hunt has ceased. Apollonius by this stage displays some signs of paranoia, a disorder tied in with what Freud calls ruler taboos. It is Freud's view that "when a paranoiac names a person of his acquaintance as his 'persecutor,' he thereby elevates him to the paternal succession and brings him under conditions which enable him to make him responsible for all the misfortune which he experiences."[33] Like Antiochus, Apollonius has become obsessed with the father figure.

Father fixations can, according to Freud, result in the feminization of the son.[34] At the start of Gower's tale, we are told that Apollonius is both learned and a gifted speaker (indeed Apollonius clearly shares the intelligence traditionally attributed to Oedipus), and this is manifested in his ability to solve the riddle. As he stands in the presence of the king and his daughter, the narrator briefly interrupts the story in order to tell us that "Of every naturel science, / Which eny clerk him couthe teche, / He couthe ynowh, and in his speche / Of wordes he was eloquent" (VIII.390–93). Yet this eloquence may actually threaten his masculinity, since the use and abuse of rhetoric is associated with femininity and ef-

feminacy. The feminization of Apollonius is also manifested in his failure to kill Antiochus on discovering his crime (given that Antiochus is
not his father, such an act would be both legal and laudable),[35] and in
the passive role he plays in the relationship with his future wife. It is the
princess of Pentapolis who experiences the fire of love, and the loss of
appetite and sleeplessness attendant on it (VIII.834–65), and it is the
princess who makes known her desire for the impoverished young hero.
Apollonius's feminization does not run so deep that he cannot recipro-
cate the woman's desire, but after the loss of his wife, he returns to his
former quiescent state. Subject to the vacillations of Fortune, he is also
the victim of the maliciousness of others, more acted upon than acting.
Whereas in the Latin prose narratives, after the loss of his wife, Apollonius travels because he has become a merchant,[36] Gower does not include this detail, and as a consequence Apollonius's constant flight appears even more motiveless and random.

     It is in the context of Apollonius's relationship with Antiochus and
of his feminization that Gower's treatment of the homosociality evident
in his sources has to be understood. Gower's account of Apollonius's
trip to Pentapolis is particularly revealing. In Pentapolis, Apollonius first
comes to the attention of the king, Artestrathes, rather than to that of
his daughter. It is as if the father figure has been split into two in Apollonius's story.[37] Artestrathes is the counterpart to Antiochus: he plays
the good father to the latter's bad one. Artestrathes and Apollonius bond
in a way in which Antiochus and Apollonius failed to. This can be seen
in the account of the game in which Apollonius takes part and wins. The
preparation for the game is described thus:

> Thei made hem naked as thei scholde,
> for so that ilke game wolde,
> As it was tho custume and us,
> Amonges hem was no refus:
> The flour of al the toun was there
> And of the court also ther were,
> And that was in a large place
> Riht evene afore the kinges face.... (VIII.683–90)

What is remarkable about this passage is the emphasis that it places
on the nakedness of the young men, at the expense of describing the

nature or the rules of the sport. Yet, if there is a suggestion of male homoeroticism in Gower's text, it is carefully controlled.[38] In the original
text the homoerotic elements are far more explicit: the sport occurs at
the gymnasium, and the king recognizes Apollonius as a worthy opponent in the game of ball, and then massages him with oil in the baths
afterward.[39] Gower does, however, keep the notion of Artestrathes as
spectator/voyeur, whose gaze lingers on the naked body of this athletic
young man: "Was non so semlich of persone, / Of visage and of limes
bothe, / If that he hadde what to clothe" (VIII.708–10). Indeed, the king
not only rewards Apollonius but wants to keep him in the royal line of
vision: "And he, which hath his pris deserved / After the kinges oghne
word, / Was mad beginne a Middel Bord, / That bothe king and queene
him sihe"(VIII.718–21). Gower's rendering of the games episode is in
keeping with changes he makes elsewhere.[40] He also excludes a comparison between Apollonius and Orpheus found in the text that Gower
(misleadingly) claims is his main source, Godfrey of Viterbo's *Pan-
theon*.[41] Orpheus was, of course, one of the most famous lovers of men
in classical literature.[42] The main focus of Gower's account of the games
is on the men rather than the women, but the world represented is primarily an economic rather than a sexual one, a world of male exchange
and bonding. Indeed, later in the narrative the relationship between
Apollonius and Artestrathes is reinforced rather than undermined when
the latter's daughter expresses her desire for the former. The father
finds himself in a position to present his daughter as a gift to the young
man, thus forging the bond that Antiochus may have desired at some
level, but was unable to offer. The interconnection of the themes of
homosociality and patrilineage becomes manifest when, at the end,
Apollonius succeeds the king of Pentapolis.

The final point to make about Apollonius in this context is that he
plays along with the conspiracy of silence surrounding Antiochus's
crime. He certainly does not threaten to expose Antiochus or his daughter. Nor, as we have seen, does he threaten to kill Antiochus. In solving
the riddle and then fleeing, Apollonius uses the knowledge with which
he has been blessed selfishly to save his own skin, rather than for the
common good. It is possible that, like Shakespeare's Hamlet, he is
unable to kill because he recognizes that in some way he shares in the
crime.[43] In this respect he resembles previous authority figures in *Confessio* such as the learned Alexander whose education is the subject of

Book VII, or the magicians Nectanabus and Ulysses.[44] Scanlon contends that, in Gower's text, Apollonius is effectively punished—he is forced to flee his homeland, and he loses his wife and his daughter—because as a patriarchal figure he shares in the guilt of incest.[45] Certainly, Apollonius, like Antiochus, is afflicted by the loss of his wife, but Gower makes it clear that he has no conscious incestuous intentions toward his daughter and clearly intends to find her a husband. (On leaving her in Tharse, he announces that he will not shave his beard until he has arranged her marriage: VIII.1301–06). Nonetheless it is clear that he does become implicated in Antiochus's sin. As Apollonius, isolating himself in his cabin aboard ship, withdraws into his own world of grief and melancholy, the parallels between his situation and state of mind and those of Antiochus at the start of the narrative become apparent. By chance, after his boat has been driven by storms to Mitelene, Thaise is brought before Apollonius to entertain him and thus to draw him out of his misery, but neither recognizes the other, and the atmosphere is fraught. Thaise offers Apollonius exactly the sort of comfort and consolation her own mother was instructed to offer him when he arrived, shipwrecked, in Pentapolis. After her questions and riddles fail to evoke a response, Thaise reaches out in the dark cabin to touch Apollonius, and he responds with anger, striking her with his hand (VIII.1691–94). Her response, "'Avoi, mi lord, I am a Maide'" (VIII.1697), suggests that he has taken her to be a prostitute and interpreted her gesture as a sexual advance. The explanation of the intimacy that exists between the father and daughter (an explanation original to Gower) adds to the tension: "And yit the fader ate laste / His herte upon this maide caste, / That he hire loveth kindely, / And yet he wiste nevere why" (VIII.1705–08).[46]

Gower actually adapts his sources to make the resemblance between Apollonius and Antiochus the more marked. In the *Historia Apollonii*, the relationship between Antiochus and his motherless daughter is not only mirrored in that between Apollonius and Thaise, but also in that between Archistrates and his daughter. With the appearance of the queen of Pentapolis, this last parallel is undercut in Gower's tale. Furthermore, in the *Historia Apollonii*, the incest theme is again reiterated when we are told that Athenagoras is restrained from raping Thaise in the brothel because he is reminded of his own motherless child.[47] Gower's Athenagoras is, in contrast, childless and spotless (he does not even visit the brothel). Scanlon believes, however, that Apollonius is punished less for any actual desire to possess the daughter, than for a more abstract, paternal desire to protect and thus also to dominate her.[48] As a result, Scanlon argues, Apollonius has to suffer abjection in order to atone for Antiochus's sins as much as his own.[49] This is, after all, a tale in which even those who have unwillingly or unknowingly been involved in a crime (most obviously Antiochus's daughter, but also Dionise's husband, Strangulio) have to take the consequences. But, in Gower's narrative, Apollonius also suffers for another sin in which he is implicated and that both he and the narrator have failed to acknowledge: the desire for the father. Apollonius is thus doubly implicated in the tyranny of Antiochus.

THE RIDDLE OF FEMALE DESIRE

Teresa de Lauretis argues that the appearance of the Sphinx in the story of Oedipus draws attention to the elusive nature of female desire in the narrative.[50] As de Lauretis notes, the Sphinx, which, like Medusa and other monsters, is inscribed in a hero narrative, is recognizably female.[51] The Sphinx is not only monstrous but destructive as well: she kills men and devours them too. Michel Zink suggests that the riddle in *Historia Apollonii* is derived from the Sphinx's riddle in the legend of Oedipus.[52] If we accept this, then Antiochus's daughter takes the role of the Sphinx herself. In the Latin prose narrative, the king sets the riddle, and the princess remains silent, as is appropriate in a patriarchal state. This is also the case in Gower's narrative. However, the association between the riddle and the princess is preserved in the one surviving manuscript illustration to the story, which is found in New York, Pierpont Morgan Library MS M.126 (fol. 187v; Figure 5).[53] This illustration shows Antiochus face-to-face with his daughter and with Apollonius, who is evidently offering his answer to the riddle.[54] Patricia Eberle, in her analysis of this miniature, draws our attention to Apollonius's horrified expression and to the exchange of glances between Antiochus and his daughter. These, she suggests, reveal that the couple share a terrible secret ("privete" [VIII.425]). Eberle also comments on the barren landscape in the foreground, which may reflect the unnatural, unfruitful, savage, and self-consuming passion of the king.[55] Equally striking is the depiction of the two decapitated suitors, who are lying at the princess's feet, their limbs and bodies entangled behind her skirts, and their heads rolling ominously in

Figure 5. Apollonius, Antiochus, and Antiochus's daughter. MS M.126, fol. 187v (detail). Reprinted by permission of the Pierpont Morgan Library, New York.

Apollonius's direction. The artist has here deviated from the attendant narrative in leaving the heads of the suitors to Antiochus's daughter rolling around in the mud, rather than, as Gower has it (VIII.369), placed on the gate of the city (visible in the background). The effect is to foreground the woman's role in the drama and to expose her guilt. She is represented as monstrous as well as cruel (the hero does not meet her gaze). The woman's guilt is made explicit in other retellings of the story: there exists an Anglo-Saxon version of the riddle in which the speaker changes halfway through, and in Shakespeare's *Pericles,* the speaker is Antiochus's daughter throughout.[56]

In Freud's analysis of Sophocles, and in his concept of the Oedipus Complex, the focus is inevitably on men. Female desire is a riddle and a mystery and associated by implication with the Sphinx (and thus dangerous and potentially monstrous).[57] As de Lauretis points out, we do not know the Sphinx's story: why, like Oedipus's mother Jocasta, does she kill herself?[58] Gower, in contrast, uses the Apollonius story to examine and to attempt to unravel female sexuality and desire. In other words, at least to some extent, Gower allows the Sphinx to tell her own story. If according to Vladimir Propp's analysis of Sophocles' play, the Sphinx takes on the roles of the princess and the dragon of traditional folklore,[59] Antiochus's daughter assimilates those of the Sphinx and Jocasta from Sophocles' play, and like them, she has to die. Remarkably, however, at the very start of the tale, Gower does depict the rape from the victim's as well as the aggressor's point of view, and thus gives a voice to her suffering. For example, after Antiochus has committed this dreadful crime, and left the chamber, the focus switches exclusively to his daughter, who "lay stille, and of this thing, / Withinne hirself such sorghe made, / Ther was no wiht that mihte hire glade, / For feere of thilke horrible vice" (VIII.314–17). After her nurse says she is unable to help her, Antiochus's daughter has no apparent choice but to give in to her father's will, and with the words "sche dorste him nothing withseie" (VIII.347) the narrator also abandons her. Thereafter, Antiochus's daughter is dropped from the narrative and only mentioned again in the brief report of her death. Gower emphasizes that both father and daughter suffer equivalent fates: "Antiochus, as men mai wite, / With thondre and lyhthnynge is forsmite; / His doghter hath the same chaunce, / So be thei bothe in o balance" (VIII.999–1002). The Latin *Historia Apollonii* takes this further and has them struck down while they are in bed together.[60] It would appear from her end that Antiochus's daughter is, after all, stained by sin and deserving of a similar fate to that of the truly monstrous Dionise, whose execution for treason threatens to dominate the conclusion of the story (VIII.1936–62).

However, soon after he has finished describing the events surrounding the rape of Antiochus's daughter, Gower's narrator returns to the question of female sexuality. It is evident in the text that the situation in which Antiochus's daughter finds herself is reflected in the experiences of Apollonius's wife and daughter. Just as Apollonius journeys from Tyre to Antioch and places himself amongst the potential suitors of the king's daughter and heir, so he travels from Tyre to Pentapolis and finds himself in competition with the suitors of the daughter of Artestrathes. And in both cases the father expresses his power through the possession of his anonymous daughter's "privete," or her secrets, to Apollonius. Antiochus simultaneously hides and exposes his crime through the riddle; the king of Pentapolis exposes his daughter's "secret" desire through a private letter. In the final movement of the narrative, the situation is more complex: Apollonius again finds himself in the presence of a young woman but in this case she is his own child, and here it is Apollonius who has to give away his daughter and heir in marriage to another. In *Historia Apollonii,* the connection between the daughters of Antiochus and of Apollonius is made explicit when the latter tries to awaken her father's interest by repeating a series of riddles.[61] Gower, however, plays down this element of the story although he does not remove it completely (cf. VIII.1675–77 and 1681–83). These plot parallels serve to emphasize the social issues behind the prohibition on incest and to focus on the traffic in women that is crucial to the patriarchal economy. Antiochus's relationship with his daughter is represented as "unkinde" or "unnatural," the father-daughter relationships of Artestrathes and Apollonius are "kinde" or "natural." The unnatural relationship manifests itself in a refusal to traffic in women; the natural relationships involve a recognition of the importance of exogamy.

The idea, central to the economy of exogamy, that woman is a commodity is made explicit in Gower's tale at two separate points. The first of these occurs after the "death" of Thaise's mother, when Apollonius wraps his wife's body in gold cloth and encloses it in a coffin filled with enough treasure to pay for a fitting burial (VIII.1112–30). The second occurs when Thaise is quite literally sold by pirates to Leonin, the keeper of a brothel (VIII.1406–15), who in turn offers her virginity to whoever will pay for it with gold (VIII.1416–20). In contrast to the daughters of Antiochus and Artestrathes who are wooed by royal suitors, Thaise can, in theory at least, be purchased by anyone who has enough money. And whereas Artestrathes can command his daughter to offer comfort and entertainment to his guest because she is a princess, Athenagoras and his advisors send Thaise to offer solace to Apollonius because her position is only just above that of a common whore. Gower, however, stops short of including a scene found in *Historia Apollonii,* in which the young woman's pimp makes her kneel before a golden statue of Priapus.[62] Nonetheless, Thaise, like all women, is clearly subject to patriarchy in Gower's narrative. It is noteworthy that in this version, unlike the Latin prose source (in which the pimp is burned alive and his wealth is given to the prostitutes who are then freed), Apollonius does not wreak vengeance on the brothel keeper, any more than he did on Antiochus.[63]

Despite the fact that Antiochus's daughter and Apollonius's wife and daughter find themselves in similar situations and are all to a greater

or lesser extent represented as chattels, there are marked differences between them. Most obviously, whereas Antiochus's daughter expresses
no desire and can only lament the loss of her virginity (VIII.327–31),
Artestrathes' daughter feels the full force of overwhelming passion for
Apollonius. She is able to express to her father her wishes in the strongest
possible terms, insisting in her letter: "Bot if I have Appolinus, / Of al
this world, what so betyde, / I wol non other man abide" (VIII.898–
900). Yet Artestrathes' daughter still has to live by the rules of the patriarchal society in which she lives: she is still concerned for her good
name and fears for her womanly reputation (VIII.854–55), and she real-
izes that she cannot pursue Apollonius without her father's approval
and connivance. Furthermore, Apollonius's wife cannot really be seen
as a desiring female subject because, as de Lauretis would have it, in
this oedipal narrative her desire can only be congruent to that of the
hero.[64] Even as she seems to be expressing her own desires, she is con-
senting to those of Apollonius and enabling him to fulfill his destiny.
Thus, even when Gower appears to be sympathetically describing female
sexuality, to be suggesting that it is not necessarily Sphinx-like and monstrous, he represents it as something that has to be restrained by the
rules of traditional courtship and marriage that keep men in the position of power.

After her marriage, Artestrathes' daughter becomes subject to her
husband. When she is then separated from him, she enters a deathlike
state, coming to life only with the help of the doctor who is effectively
Apollonius's agent. The doctor demonstrates a knowledge of the natural
sciences that he shares with Apollonius, and later on, he is even taken
into his employ (VIII.1876–83). Apollonius's wife subsequently withdraws from the world of men, entering the temple of Diana (the goddess
of women and virginity) in Ephesus. Thaise resembles her father in
many ways, including her travels and afflictions. But she also seeks to
protect her virginity at all costs (even "converting" the men who fre-
quent the brothel and try to deflower her), and, like her mother, retreats
from society, in this case setting up a school for gentlewomen. It is only
in the final major sequence of the narrative that the status quo is restored.
Normative male control of female desire is fully reestablished when
Athenagoras falls in love with Thaise (his love longing is passingly reminiscent of that of Thaise's mother) and she agrees, with her father's approval, to become his wife. If, as Scanlon suggests, the suffering that

Thaise and her mother have to endure is an extension of that of Apollonius, it may also be an extension of that of Antiochus's daughter.[65] Whereas Antiochus's daughter loses her honor and dies, Apollonius's wife and daughter preserve their chastity and evade death. Both Thaise and her mother are recovered from the sea and miraculously resurrected (in Apollonius's mind at least); the latter almost literally when the physician awakes her from her deathlike coma. The resurrections of Thaise and her mother mark the posthumous redemption of Antiochus's daughter.

READING POLITICALLY

In the light of this reading of the Tale of Apollonius, it is fascinating that in a mid-twentieth-century psycho-biography of Richard II, we find him portrayed as a physical weakling and tortured neurotic. According to Anthony Steele, Richard was a king who failed to live up to the standards of leadership and chivalry set by his father, the Black Prince.[66] Although Richard's devotion to his mother, Joan, princess of Wales, was not unhealthy, his father's influence may have been more "abnormal."[67] Although Steele avoids the Freudian terminology, he implies that Richard never succeeded in resolving his Oedipus Complex, and that his entire life was dominated by his obsession with his father. The possibility of connecting Richard, the Oedipus of psychoanalysis (if not of classical myth), and Gower's Apollonius is tempting, if risky. Steele's analysis is a controversial one, and the story he tells about the king should not be afforded much weight.[68] Nevertheless, some credence can be given to more balanced historical analyses that also explain the failures of Richard's reign, at least in part, in terms of the monarch's personality. Nigel Saul, for example, claims that as a result of his "essentially narcissistic" disposition he craved public recognition and was unable to forgive those who challenged his self-image.[69] This portrait of Richard II as narcissistic as well as tyrannical has its origins in early, if biased, accounts of his reign, such as Thomas Walsingham's *Chronicle*.[70] It is a portrait that is, I would suggest, to some extent confirmed by Gower's complex representations of kingship in the Tale of Apollonius.

    The argument that Gower is offering a commentary upon Richard II's reign in the Tale of Apollonius is not a new one. Elizabeth Porter, for example, suggests that the character of Apollonius himself "is an image of that doctrine of personal kingship within the ethical microcosm which ... offer[s] the way to personal peace of mind and harmony within the body politic."[71] According to this analysis, Apollonius is "the final model" in a whole series of characters—Alexander the Great, discussed in Chapter 5 above, is another example—who are intended to offer instruction about private and public life to both the monarch and the common man.[72] As Genius observes at the conclusion of the narrative, "And every man for his partie / A kingdom hath to justefie" (VIII.2111–12). The view that Apollonius stands for good kingship as well as ethical self-governance is influential and it has been reiterated by other critics, including Russell Peck, as well as Bullón-Fernández.[73] But is it reliable? Porter herself illustrates that Confessio offers negative as well as positive examples to the king, admitting that Alexander plays both roles.[74] In a later reading of Confessio, and of the Alexander narratives within it, Simpson concurs with Porter and concludes that in this poem Gower "foresees failure" for the king, and in effect prophesies his downfall.[75] To conclude this chapter, I argue that in his Tale of Apollonius, Gower once again betrays his cynicism about Richard II's conduct and rule.

Elizabeth Archibald observes that in incest narratives such as this one, the moral status of patriarchal figures is measured as much by their treatment of their daughters in private as by their public behavior; the former is an index of the latter.[76] In the Tale of Apollonius, Antiochus's abuse of his daughter impacts upon his standing in the outside world. Bullón-Fernández takes this further and places it in a political context. Because Antiochus is a monarch as well as a patriarch, he not only abuses paternal authority but also royal authority: he is an absolutist king who "uses the law according to his own will and regardless of the will and interest of his country."[77] Bullón-Fernández stops short of identifying Antiochus with Richard II himself because, as she observes, the first accusations of tyranny were only made in the final years of his reign.[78] Nevertheless, Richard II had faced a series of crises in the period 1382–88 and had suffered a number of rebukes about his personal conduct and mode of government. Antiochus's narcissistic defiance of the law (both his rape of his daughter and his repressed homosexuality) may therefore be intended as a warning to Richard II against arrogant behavior and arbitrary rule.

Evidence to support this argument is found in the representation of other figures in the narrative. Most obviously, juxtaposed to the tyrant Antiochus, who is isolated in his court, subject only to his own will, and whose crimes are not checked, is the good king Artestrathes, who does not compromise his authority, nor does he act rashly and without due consultation. The implicit praise of Artestrathes's wife, who, while always remaining in the background, offers her husband counsel and support, might be read as a celebration of the mediatory role of Anne of Bohemia.[79] (Anne died in 1394, four years after Gower had completed the first recension of *Confessio*; and her famous intercession in Richard's quarrel with London occurred two years before she passed away.) Or, Artestrathes's wife may have a more abstract significance. As David Wallace has recently shown, the relationship between a king and his subjects is often figured as that between a husband and wife.[80] In VIII.2106–10, Genius advises Amans that good counsel is an absolute prerequisite for the man who wants to be a king; earlier he recommended marriage to the man who would conduct himself well.[81] Gower may be suggesting to Richard that he should be open to advice (a recurring theme in Gower's earlier Latin work *Vox Clamantis*). Certainly, complaints that Richard failed to listen to good counsel recurred throughout his reign and were forcefully expressed during the Appellant crisis, as well as at the time of his deposition.[82] Just as a political significance can be read into the role of Artestrathes's wife, so too can it be seen in that of Antiochus's daughter. Scanlon sees the daughter's suffering and death as revealing the injustice of the patriarchal law, while he considers Thaise's role to reflect the transcendent moral force of the church.[83] Again, a more immediate reading is possible. In the aftermath of the Appellant crisis, the resurrections of Apollonius's wife and daughter may also mark the (albeit temporary) restoration of the power of the councils to curb the king's will. It might then seem that the mothers and daughters in the Tale of Apollonius—as women and as representatives of the king's subjects or his country—are given a degree of independence and autonomy that challenges both patriarchal authority and the supremacy of the crown. The recontainment of female sexuality suggests, however, that female empowerment can only be countenanced within severely prescribed limits, and moreover that Gower's political vision is ultimately a limited and conventional one. Whatever his views of Richard II's government, he certainly does not, at this stage, seem to be advocating the overthrow of the king.[84]

This reading offers no new historical perspective on Richard's reign, but it does force us to reconsider what Apollonius stands for in Gower's poem. If Gower had his own sovereign in mind when he translated the Apollonius story, it is evident that his message was not straightforward. As I have already noted, Bullón-Fernández follows Porter in adopting the view that Apollonius is an ideal monarch, who is instructed by the negative example of Antiochus and the positive example of Artestrathes.[85] My interpretation indicates that this view is untenable. Although the ending of the story is a happy one, and Apollonius regains his wife and daughter, he has been shown to share the sins of Antiochus. What is more, it is far from clear that he has learned much along the way.[86] If Apollonius *is* intended as a double of Richard II, he is not, after all, a particularly impressive model of kingship. Gower's representation of Apollonius is as ambivalent as his attitude toward his monarch. In directing this book to Richard II, Gower may be offering advice, even a warning; he is not necessarily offering praise. This brings me back to the dual figures of Gower/Amans, with whom I began. Porter argues that, like Apollonius, Amans represents yet another model for Richard II.[87] If this is the case, or if there is at least some congruence between them, then what does Amans's fate tell us about Gower's view of his monarch's prospects? Like that of Apollonius, the example Amans offers is that of one who does not necessarily learn from experience. But unlike Apollonius he does not see the fulfillment of his desires either. We saw in the previous chapter that, when forced to renounce his quest at the conclusion of the final book, he does so with sadness, regret, and resignation, rather than determination and zeal. In the final analysis, Amans's misdirected desire reflects the king's unchecked will and it is perhaps his failure in love that looks most like a prognostication of the usurpation of Richard II's throne. At the same time, Gower's decision, not only to sign his own narrative, but to identify himself with Amans, and thus implicitly with Richard himself, may indicate his personal frustration with and sense of failure about his role, not as poet of love, but as political advisor. Gower's signature points to the author's perception of limitations of his own major vernacular work.[88]

EPILOGUE

ETHICAL GOWER

GOWER'S LITERARY PROJECT

Confessio Amantis concludes with a long colophon, which provides a summary of Gower's three major works: *Mirour de l'Omme, Vox Clamantis*, and, of course, *Confessio*.[1] This colophon, like the *Confessio* itself, went through a series of revisions (some after Henry IV's accession), and according to Derek Pearsall, represents "his final statement concerning the content and purpose of his three major works."[2] It gives us a sense of what Gower intended to achieve by composing these "tres libros doctrine" (three books of instructive material) (Col.5). We are told that the *Mirour*, referred to here as *Speculum hominis/Speculum Meditantis*, was written for the reformation of the sinner and that *Vox* set out to give an account of the Peasants' Revolt of 1381.[3] *Confessio* is described as a treatise about Daniel's prophecy concerning the mutability of earthly kingdoms, the ages in world history, and Alexander's training, but also, and principally, about love and the "infatuatas amantum passiones" (foolish passions of lovers), or, in the earlier version, merely the "condiciones" (conditions) of lovers (Col.28).[4]

For Pearsall, this colophon is evidence that Gower "spent his last years almost obsessively putting his house in order."[5] He views the colophon as being of a kind with the Latin apparatus of which it is part, as well as the other material often appended to it (which Pearsall summarizes succinctly as "a series of Latin poems of moral exhortation, political criticism and self advertisement").[6] Pearsall's Gower intended, with the help of his Latin chapter headings, verses, and academic-style glosses in *Confessio* and the summary of his major works in the colophons, to limit the meaning of his poems. The fact that we can even now re-construct the revisions (politically motivated and otherwise) that Gower made to *Vox Clamantis* and *Confessio* reveals that, like William Langland and his various versions of *Piers Plowman*, he was concerned with re-viewing what he had already written in the light of events unfolding around him.[7] At the same time this scheme of revisions and corrections provides evidence that he supervised the copying of his works. Indeed, as we saw in the Introduction, there is a whole school of Gower criti-cism that argues that Gower carefully controlled the appearance and production of his manuscripts, even down to the finest points of detail.[8] Even if we do not accept this proposition wholesale, there can be no dis-pute that the state of completion and quality of most manuscripts of Gower's *Confessio* is much greater and better than that of the majority of manuscripts of Chaucer's *Canterbury Tales*. Gower's literary bequest cer-tainly is very much at odds with Chaucer's "foul papers" and more in line with the production of the works of his successor John Lydgate.[9]

A common view, which was originally put forward by John Fisher, is that Gower saw his major works as part of a single project.[10] Pearsall, for one, is convinced of Gower's "sense of his responsibility to posterity... [his] solicitude for the accuracy of his text and the integrity of his canon."[11] Nevertheless, Pearsall describes the summary of *Confessio* in the Latin colophon as a "misrepresentation" of the poem.[12] The central problem is that in the synopsis of *Confessio* that Gower provides here, he chooses to place the political before the erotic, even as he admits that the theme of love is the main subject of the work as a whole. Thus, emphasis is put on the Prologue and Book VII of *Confessio* over Books I–VI and Book VIII, but without establishing any ethical connection between the two (something Gower does at least attempt to do in the poem itself). Pearsall is puzzled as to why the narratives of love are so summarily dismissed, especially in the revised form. Pearsall goes on to state that

> An author is surely entitled to misappropriate his own work: what we have to do is to recognise the act of misappropriation, and regard it with proper curiosity; what we have not to do is to give authority to it as explication of text.[13]

This conclusion is rather odd, to say the least. On the one hand, Pearsall would have it that Gower used the colophon to help establish his authority of his poetry, on the other, he warns us against accepting its claims as authoritative. Pearsall's problem with Gower's colophon is that he wants to represent Gower as striving "to establish his reputation as a serious writer," as one who sought to present "a coherent body of writing" and "to confirm and complete [its] moral message."[14] Yet here, at the heart of the colophon, is what Wolfgang Iser has called a "blank" or a gap that requires the reader to use the imagination in order to fill it in.[15] The problem vanishes, however, if we approach Gower and his literary project from a different angle. There is no problem if we challenge Gower's supposedly inherently conventionalist and inflexible nature and suggest that he actually combined a conservatizing mode of production with a destabilizing hermeneutic. The colophon makes more sense if we do not assume that Gower was trying to resolve the disunities of his major English work.

Amongst the miscellaneous material that sometimes appears at the end of *Confessio* manuscripts, in this case Oxford, Bodleian Library MS Fairfax 3, we find two poems praising Gower's poetic achievement. They are ascribed to an anonymous philosopher, tentatively identified by George Macaulay as Ralph Strode, friend to both Gower and Chaucer.[16] The longer of the two poems contains the following lines.

> Eneidos Bucolis que Georgica metra perhennis
> Virgilio laudis serta dedere scolis;
> Hiis tribus ille libris prefertur honore poetis,
> Romaque precipuis laudibus instat eis.

(You take the metres of the *Aeneid*, the *Bucolics [Eclogues]*, and *Georgics* seeking to achieve the wreaths of praise surrendered by Virgil; for these three books the honor of poetry is awarded you, and Rome presses special praises upon them.) (1–4)[17]

Pearsall has suggested that Gower himself may even have written these poems. He is of the opinion that they "represent the English poet in an extraordinary light, not merely kissing the steps on which the classical poets stand, which is what Chaucer modestly advises his book of *Troilus* to do, but clambering up them."[18] The question of the authorship of these poems cannot be resolved, although, given the fact that Gower does appear to have glossed his own text, it is not unreasonable to suppose that he also commented on his own literary feat. Furthermore, we should keep in mind that in *Vox Clamantis* the author repeatedly asserts that the narrative voice is his own; for example, one headnote states that the text is written "quasi in propria persona" (as if in his own person) (headnote to Book I, chapter 16). Nevertheless, in the title, he does not hesitate to liken himself to John the Baptist, "the voice of one crying in the wilderness" (Matthew 3.3; Isaiah 40.3). At the end of the Prologue to *Vox* he also identifies with John of the Apocalypse: "Insula quem Pathmos suscepit in Apocalipsi, / Cuius ego nomen gesto, gubernet opus" (May the one whom the Isle of Patmos received in the Apocalypse, and whose name I bear, guide this work) (Prol.57–58). In *Vox*, then, Gower asserts that the didactic and public voice with which he speaks was his own, and that it follows in the tradition of the great biblical prophets and visionaries. Gower may well have believed his vernacular poetry kept equally exalted company.

Should we then read the Latin poem, with its allusions to Virgil, as Pearsall does? The comparison Pearsall draws with Chaucer is an apposite one. Chaucer's famous stanza in which he evokes the reputations of Virgil, Homer, Lucan, and Statius begins, "Go, litel bok, go, litel myn tragedye" (*Troilus and Criseyde*, V.1786), while the final line of the final Latin verse of *Confessio Amantis* proper begins "Vade liber purus ..." (Go book, unstained and free) (at VIII.3172). And if this address to the book is itself conventional,[19] the preceding lines that express the hope that it will receive praise rather than censure from its readers suggest that Gower experienced similar anxieties to Chaucer's concerning the possibility of misinterpretation of his works and his intentions. A closer look at *Confessio* itself reveals that Gower's concerns extended from the reception of his work to his self-representation as a poet. Even if Gower *is* responsible for making the comparison between his own works and those of Virgil, it may well be a loaded one. We might remember that in *Confessio* VIII.2714, Virgil appeared alongside David, Solomon, Sampson, Aristotle, Socrates, Plato, and Ovid, not as a figures of great authority, but as a member of the company of aged—and foolish—lovers, who let themselves be led by their emotions. Certainly, by the end of *Confessio*, when Venus commands Amans to abandon his desire, when Genius gives up on seeing him settled in marriage, and when Gower's muse advises him that he should "nomore of love make" (VIII.3143), the poet distances himself from his own project.

Authorial Self-Representation

Paul Strohm has argued that, for the reader of *Confessio*, there are three Gowers: the historical John Gower, Gower as poet or *auctor*, and Gower as Amans.[20] In the Introduction, I addressed the first of these Gowers (the historical, or social Gower). Here I want to look at Gower as poet and Gower as Amans. Like Pearsall, Alastair Minnis has argued that Gower, with his elaborate system of prologues (Minnis distinguishes both extrinsic and intrinsic prologues) and self-commentary, is concerned in *Confessio* to represent himself as *auctor*, a figure of authority, and *sapiens*.[21] This is in line with Gower's representation of himself, in Book VII of *Confessio* and also elsewhere, as an adviser to princes and to the common man.[22] I interpret Gower's self-portrayal rather differently from Minnis. While I agree that Gower does establish authoritative voices within the poem, I also believe that he deliberately undermines these by an alternative, ludic, self-portrayal. This is evidenced most obviously in the erotic sections, which are characterized by what Simpson calls "Ovidian disunity,"[23] and this portrayal has, I suggest, an equivalent status within the poem to the other forms of authorial self-representation. Furthermore, Gower does not in fact maintain the distinctions between the multiple voices of his poem.[24]

In the prologue of *Confessio*, Gower certainly, as Minnis suggests, seems to be adopting an authoritative poetic voice to comment on the ills of society. Indeed, as Strohm has observed, with the revision to a Latin gloss at Prol.22, which represents Gower as a "composer" rather than as mere "compiler," Gower moves "away from self-depreciation and toward authorial pride."[25] Near the start of the first book, Gower appears to draw a clear distinction between this voice and the poem's protagonist.

> Hic quasi in persona aliorum, quos amor alligat, fingens se auctor esse Amantem, varias eorum passiones variis huius libri distinccionibus per singula scibere proponit.

> (Here, as if in the person of others, whom love has fettered, the author represents himself as (*or* feigns himself to be) a lover, (and) he proposes to write, in the various parts of this book (about) their various passions, one by one.) (at I.61)[26]

Earlier, in Chapter 2, I looked at the problematics concerning "feigning" in these lines (which has far more negative implications than simply creating a character). Here I want to suggest—*pace* Minnis—that the distinction between Gower and Amans, between author and character, established so carefully in this gloss, is not in fact maintained in the course of the poem.[27] Right at the start of the poem, the English verses equate Gower's narratorial voice with the figure of the lover when he states, "I am miselven on of tho [improper lovers]" (I.62). This confusion of authorial and poetic voices is developed at the conclusion to the poem, when Venus asks Amans to identify himself and, when he replies "John Gower" (VIII.2322), she holds up a mirror to reveal his "true" appearance (VIII.2820–23). In Chapter 6, I looked briefly at this episode from an ethical-political perspective and suggested that the failure of Amans/Gower reflects the poet's own sense of his deficiency as an adviser to the prince (this itself mirrors the undermining of Aristotle's instruction to Alexander, discussed in Chapter 5). This episode forces the reader to reconsider what both Amans and Gower represent. As Strohm expresses it, "The would-be Lover sees himself dwindle to the physical person of the aged Poet, with dimming eyes and thinning cheeks and wrinkling countenance and graying hair."[28] James M. Dean's commentary, in his study *The World Grown Old,* is useful here: "this naming of the *senex amans* seems to be an elaborate and sophisticated joke, at the author's expense, with the poet's well-documented physical incapacities as referent and occasion."[29] This is not simply a *coterie* joke—Gower's medieval readership would be familiar with the figure of the decrepit poet not only from his descriptions of himself, but from author portraits and miniatures in *Confessio* and elsewhere.[30] A number of manuscript illustrations depicting Amans's confession to Genius appear to represent Amans as Gower: this is clearest in the depictions of Amans as an aged lover, but may also be true of those that depict Amans as youthful.[31] One of the most striking examples is MS Fairfax 3, a manuscript that many see as having some claim to authority, although the illustration may well date to after Gower's death.[32] Here, in a striking reversal of our expectations, and of the other comparable miniatures, a garlanded and youthful Genius appears very much the servant of love, and lacks the priestly garb and *gravitas* characteristic of most of these illustrations. He comforts a shrouded death's-head Amans, who is wearing the collar of S's, awarded to Gower by Henry of Derby, and also visible on the poet's effigy. In this illustration, as in the poem itself, the historical and fictive, real and imaginary, blur and become indistinct as

Amans's double self, his split identity, merges with Gower's actual physical deterioration.

In this context, it is important to take into account two other figures in *Confessio Amantis* with whom Gower's poetic voice has been identified: the harper, Arion, and the confessor, Genius. To start with Gower as Arion, R. F. Yeager contends that Gower likens himself to this mythical harpist who will bring peace to the world through his poetry.[33] Certainly Gower concludes the Prologue with an account of Arion's history and the hope that one like him might appear (Prol.1053–77). But, as Dean observes, at the start of Book I, Gower the poet clearly states that he himself lacks the wisdom to "tempre the mesure" of love (I.23) or to heal the discord in the world.[34] The determination to see Arion as a figure for Gower's voice stems from a need to locate a single authorial voice in all of his major writings. The voice of *Confessio* must be made to conform to the voices of the *Mirour* and *Vox*. Yet, the author here quite deliberately sets this text apart from his previous poetry. He tells us:

> I may noght strecche up to the hevene
> Min hand, ne setten al in evene
> This world, which evere is in balance:
>
> . . .
>
> Forthi the Stile of my writinges
> Fro this day forth I thenke change
> And speke of thing is noght so strange,
>
> . . .
>
> And that is love.... (I.1–15)

Although in the Prologue (with its debt to Old Testament prophecy and estates satire and its development of the microcosm/macrocosm opposition), there are echoes of his earlier writing, in these lines, Gower seeks to distance himself from his former instructive and visionary roles.

The case of Genius is somewhat different. The most important point to note is that, at times, the voice of Genius slides into the narrator's voice of the Prologue and the conclusion to *Confessio*. Some of these occasions are more marked than others, but the merging of the two voices is especially evident in the discussion of the authority of the church in Book II.2803–3071. It is also visible in his comparative account of world religions and identification with Christianity in Book V (esp. 738–1830;

and the attack on Lollardy at 1803–19 that clearly echoes the Prologue). The voices are virtually indistinguishable in the advice to princes section that occupies Book VII. But Genius himself, although a priest and an instructor, is no more a positive model of authority than Amans.[35] He is, as I have already suggested, and as Anne Middleton puts it, "muddled" about his own status: is he a Christian or pagan priest? Does he serve God or Venus? Nor does he seem certain about his own role: is he to encourage or discourage Amans in his love affair? Genius appears at times (as the Fairfax miniature discussed earlier illustrates very vividly) as much the double of Amans as he is that of the poetic persona. And, as his complex literary history reveals, he is very much a divided figure.[36] By allowing his poetic voice to blur with that of Genius, Gower further undermines his own status as *auctor*.

Returning to Strohm's reading of Gower's persona in *Confessio*, I would like to develop and to refine one further point. According to Strohm, the "shifting dedications" of *Confessio* are important because they alert the reader to what he terms "'extrapolitical' considerations": the changing political allegiance of this historical Gower.[37] At the same time, he does not deny that "Gower's passionate concern with politics is one aspect of his poetic stance." But what exactly do Gower's two dedications tell us about Gower's poetic, or for that matter ethical, stance? They reveal that, wherever the truth lies concerning the historical Gower's own political loyalties, Gower the poet, and *auctor* with his divided allegiances, is fully embroiled in the sinful world of his poem: with a foot in two political camps, Gower is not dissimilar to Nebuchadnezzar's fissured and corrupt statue. The two prologues betray a self-interest that seems at odds with the author's self-representation in *Confessio*. In other words it is not simply in respect of his physical appearance ("old, feeble, and vile" though he may be) that the narrator reflects, as Dean suggests, the macrocosm of the corrupt and decaying world, as it is described in the poem's Prologue.[38] My interpretation here is in line with that offered by Dean, in which he contends that at the end of *Confessio*, Gower "humbly acknowledges his complicity in the decay of society."[39]

AMORAL GOWER

Our perception of Gower's self-representation is the key to our understanding of Gower's *Confessio Amantis*, and more specifically its ethical and political content. *Confessio Amantis* is characterized by conflict, and critics have been exercised by what has been referred to as the "unresolved problem of Gower's ethical integrity."[40] David Aers, in a detailed analysis of certain aspects of Gower's ethics and politics, outlines some important internal contradictions in his poetry.[41] Aers notes, for example, that Gower's take on violence is not consistent. The pacifism that critics like R. F. Yeager have identified in both *Vox Clamantis* and *Confessio Amantis* is undermined by his support for the crusades and the wars against France.[42] Likewise, Aers takes issue with Larry Scanlon's reading of *Confessio* that sees the poem as advocating lay power while avoiding an antiecclesiastical position.[43] For Aers, Gower's representation of the church is incoherent, and even his attacks on the Lollard heresy are extremely ambiguous. In the final pages of this book, I will offer my own account of some of the conflicts that cut through Gower's politics, in particular his representation of kingship. Suffice to say here that Aers offers a thoroughly convincing counterargument to the widely held view as put forward by critics such as Minnis, Yeager, Kurt Olsson, and more recently James Simpson that Gower is "a brilliant dialogic and utterly coherent moral and political poet" in the Christian-Aristotelian tradition.[44] The question is, does Gower intend, or even acknowledge, the warring forces within his poetry? Aers thinks not. He dismisses the possibility that Gower's writing might be tinged with irony aimed at sophisticated readers like his friend Chaucer.[45] And he asserts that Gower does not assume an antifoundationalist position, and that he avoids facing up to the "profoundly disturbing consequences" of what he has written.[46] Aers's dismissal is scathing: "'John Gower, *sapiens* in ethics and politics,' for sure."

It is surely indisputable that poetic incoherence and political and moral instruction are fundamentally incompatible, and that ethical confusion undermines the poet's role as adviser and teacher. But what if Gower's poetic persona is not that of "Moral Gower," but that of "Amoral Gower"? What if Gower deliberately steps out of the role assigned to him by Chaucer, and by generation upon generation of poets, scholars, and critics? Perhaps it is not so implausible that Gower is, albeit within a broader Christian framework, assuming an antifoundationalist position. Gower may in fact intend his poem to be dialogic, contradictory, divided. Of course, the danger in following this line of thought is that, against all the evidence, we doggedly look for and therefore find coherence in incoherence, unity in disunity, simply countering claims of authorial dishonesty or incompetence with claims of sophistication and intentionality. For all its risks, this is the line of thought I have followed in this book. Here it has been argued that Gower, in *Confessio*, pursues a negative critique of ethics. Gower may offer an ethical ideal but no one (not the author, not his protagonists, not the models of kingship and authority that he presents to his readers) really succeeds in living up to it. In a divided world, morality is not unified, simple, and transcendent, but multiple, complex, contingent, even contradictory. The evidence to support this approach lies in the formal aspects of Gower's poetry.

Strohm has argued for a connection between the political situations in the reigns of Edward III and Richard II—and in particular the factionalism manifest during the Good Parliament (1376), the Merciless Parliament (1388), and the beginning of Richard II's absolutist rule (1397)—and aesthetic choices, in relation to the writing of Gower, and also Usk and Chaucer.[47] Whereas Usk's writing reflects his desire for personal advancement, Chaucer's is more disinterested, acknowledging and accepting conflict and faction. Strohm notes that Gower's engagement with contemporary issues is far more direct and manifest than Chaucer's. This, he suggests, is a reflection of Gower's social and economic position: because he was not a courtier or public servant, he enjoyed an independence Chaucer lacked.[48] Gower therefore felt able to speak out against division and factionalism. However, Strohm's reading of *Confessio* is oversimplistic. Strohm sees in Gower's *Confessio* a direct correlation between a political and ideological investment in the "proper" hierarchy of society (overtly stated, for example, at Prol.107–08) and the hierarchical form of the poem.[49] Strohm argues that Gower—through the person of Genius—relates the order of society to the order of love, creating "moral hierarchies based on the identification of virtue with acceptance of estate, degree, and natural limits."[50] Yet, he is forced to acknowledge that although in the Prologue to *Confessio*, Gower makes explicit the link between the ethical-political and the erotic aspects of the poem, especially in his discourse on the relationship between macrocosm and microcosm (Prol.954–58), this is not sustained throughout the poem. "The only problem with respect to the unity of the poem," he remarks, "is that these connections between properly-ordered love in the individual and harmony in the state point the *way* to a unified reading of the poem, but are not held very clearly in view as one moves from section to section and tale to tale."[51] His argument that Gower's poem foregrounds "threatening or deviant behaviour," but ultimately transcends "division and disorder" is one that can be contested.[52] Aers's analysis of Gower's style in *Vox Clamantis* and *Confessio Amantis* is apposite here. Aers argues that the dominant mode in these poems is parataxis: the various narratives take the form of self-contained episodes or units that are not brought into dialogue with one another.[53] This mode, so Aers argues, "protects the poet from having to confront sharp contradictions in his ethics ... [and] enabled him to repress ... 'division' from critical exploration."[54] Yet, it is possible that Gower intended the paratactic mode to be a stimulant rather than (again quoting Aers) an "impediment to moral enquiry."[55] A number of critics have argued that Gower's poem is concerned with good and bad reading.[56] Olsson, Theresa Tinkle, Elizabeth Allen, and Siân Echard have all variously argued that Gower's *Confessio Amantis* offers its readers a series of interpretative challenges.[57] Gower places the onus on his readers to spot interconnections between the different episodes in his poem, to identify the parallels, echoes, and contradictions, to transform the paratactic into the dialogic. After all, as a number of critics have noted, there are problems of coherence within many of the episodes themselves, when the tales and their morals do not appear to fit together.[58] Presumably the reader is expected to notice these as well, and to make something of them.

Furthermore, Gower's moral structure and self-glossing on a superficial analysis would seem to stabilize the text, but throughout *Confessio* the exemplary method is undermined, as the status of the Latin commentary and, to use Minnis's phrase (borrowed from Roland Barthes), the final signified are undercut.[59] Let me finish with one last and powerful example: the last gloss, which reads, "Hic in fine recapitulat super hoc quod in principio libri primi promisit se in amoris causa specialius tractaturum. Concludit enim quod omnis amoris delectacio extra caritatem nichil est. Qui autem manet in caritate, in deo manet" (Here at the end he states again that he promised at the beginning of the first book to deal particularly with matters of love. But now he concludes that every delight of love, outside of charity, is nothing. But he who dwells in charity abides in God) (at VIII.3008).[60] The English verses, in contrast, are not so dogmatic: the author may take his leave from earthly love, and turn to that which is heavenly, but he does not reject it completely:

> And thus forthy my final leve
> I take now for evere more,
> Withoute makynge any more
> Of love and of his dedly hele,
> Which no phisicien can hele.
> For his nature is so divers,
> That it hath evere some travers
> Or of to moche or of to lite,
> That pleinly mai no man delite,
> Bot if him faile or that or this. (VIII.3152–61)

Readers may certainly feel that they cannot so easily dismiss the often poignant (sometimes tragic) stories they have encountered earlier, not least those concerning Amans himself. As Minnis finds himself admitting, even at the conclusion of *Confessio,* "the Latin and English do not speak with one and the same voice."[61] Echard goes even further, comparing the Latin ending, in its brevity and its absolute dismissal of all that has gone before, to the palinode at the end of *Troilus and Criseyde.* She asks rhetorically, "Is the reader truly comforted to feel that she's finally come to the real point, or would she perhaps share Amans's frequently expressed frustration over the apparent inability of Genius, and the poem, to get to the point?"[62] Even at its closure, *Confessio Amantis* is characterized not by success but by failure, not by reconciliation but by division.

Notes

Preface

1. Allen, *The Ethical Poetic of the Later Middle Ages*, 3–66.

2. Allen "Chaucer Answers Gower." Allen gives a summary of the debate (649 n. 7).

3. Simpson, *Sciences and the Self*, 203. See also Olsson, "Reading, Transgression, and Judgement"; and Robins, "Romance, Exemplum, and the Subject."

4. Olsson, "Reading, Transgression, and Judgement," 90.

5. Patterson, *Negotiating the Past*, 115–53, at 141.

6. Patterson, *Negotiating the Past*, 137–38 and 140. Joyce Coleman suggests, on the basis of his fictional representations of the process, that Gower finds "secret reading . . . of propriety texts dangerous": *Public Reading and the Reading Public,* 182. In this context, see also Saenger, "Silent Reading"; and Stock, "The Self and Literary Experience."

7. E. Allen, "Chaucer Answers Gower," 653 n. 34.

8. For a useful introduction, see Eaglestone, *Ethical Criticism*. Eaglestone focuses on the writing of Martha Nussbaum, J. Hillis Miller, and Emmanuel Levinas. See also Norris, *Truth and the Ethics of Criticism*.

9. In this context, see McCann, "Distant Voices, Real Lives."

10. Stierle, "Interpretations of Responsibility," 863.

11. Stierle, "Interpretations of Responsibility," 863.

12. Stierle, "Interpretations of Responsibility," 864.

13. See Fish, *Is There a Text in This Class?* esp. 13–15 and 303–71; and the critique of Fish's argument and of reader-reception theory more generally by Pearce, *Feminism and the Politics of Reading,* esp. 4–8, and 211–13.

14. For a provocative example of a study of a range of medieval texts that does just this, see Dinshaw, *Getting Medieval*. See further, my short review article, "Truth or Dare?"

15. Lee Patterson believes that historically sensitive readings can justify the argument that "medieval interests prefigure modern preoccupations" and counter the charge

of what Caroline Walker Bynum has termed "presentism": *Literary Practice and Social Change*, ed. Patterson, 4.

16. See, for example, Norris, *Deconstruction and the Interests of Theory*, 182–83; Morton, "Birth of the Cyberqueer," esp. 378; and Frantzen, *Before the Closet*, 1–29.

17. Stierle, "Interpretations of Responsibility," 864–65. For a defense of queer theory, see Lamos, "The Ethics of Queer Theory."

18. Stierle, "Interpretations of Responsibility," 865.

19. Stierle, "Interpretations of Responsibility," 865.

20. Pearce, *Feminism and the Politics of Reading*, 4–8; see also McCann, "Distant Voices, Real Lives," 73.

21. Simpson, *Sciences and the Self*, 252–71. Of related interest is his "Ethics and Interpretation."

Introduction

1. For Gower's biography see Fisher, *John Gower*. This summary is indebted to the entry on "John Gower" by Fisher, Hamm, Beidler, and Yeager in *A Manual of the Writings in Middle English*.

2. See also Strohm, "Chaucer's Fifteenth-Century Audience," 14. Also relevant is Strohm, "Form and Social Statement," 37–38.

3. For the details, see Fisher, *John Gower*, 51–53 and appendix c, 313–18.

4. Fisher, *John Gower*, 59–60, 116–27, and appendix a, 303–09; Doyle and Parkes, "The Production of Copies," 200 and n. 98. See also Parkes, "Scribal Activity."

5. See Part III, below. See also Manzalaoui, "'Noght in the Registre of Venus,'" esp. 163; and Stow, "Richard II in John Gower's *Confessio Amantis*."

6. On the membership of this circle, see Fisher, *John Gower*, 61–63. On Chaucer's circle, see Pearsall, *Life*, 133–34 and 181–85; Strohm, "Chaucer's Audience"; Strohm, "Chaucer's Fifteenth-Century Audience," 6–18; and Strohm, *Social Chaucer*, 47–83. On Chaucer's social position, see also Patterson, *Chaucer and the Subject of History*, 32–39. On the changing constituency of Chaucer's circle and its political context, see Strohm, *Social Chaucer*, esp. 50. On the absence of women, see Greene, "Women in Chaucer's Audience."

7. For Usk's debt to *Vox Clamantis* in his *Testament of Love*, and his attempt to align himself politically with Chaucer and Gower, see Summers, "Gower's *Vox Clamantis* and Usk's *Testament of Love*." Hoccleve acknowledged the late Gower as his "maister" in *The Regement of Princes*, 1975 (the same term he applied to Chaucer, 2077–78). Reference is to *Hoccleve's Works*, ed. Furnivall.

8. Fisher, *John Gower*, 63. Fisher is of the view that Gower and Chaucer were not in contact for much of the period in which the former was writing *Confessio* (285–86). Strohm discusses the dispersal of Chaucer's circle in "Chaucer's Fifteenth-Century Audience," esp. 14–15. He dates this to around the time of Chaucer's death in 1400 (8); Pearsall, in *Life*, places it a decade earlier (185). For a revision of the traditional view that Gower was Chaucer's mentor, see Axton, "Gower—Chaucer's Heir?"

9. There is some debate over whether or not Chaucer and Gower resumed contact after the former returned to London. Fisher believes they did: *John Gower*, 32–33 and 283–

92. Peter Nicholson is of the view that the two writers were sharing books and ideas in this period: "Chaucer Borrows from Gower," esp. 94–95.

10. Parkes, "Scribal Activity," 97 and 104 n. 85. For Gower's will, see Nicolas, "Gower, the Poet," 103–05 n. 1.

11. Fisher has suggested that his early work, *Cinkante Balades,* was written for a London *puy,* a merchant banquet, or what Derek Pearsall has termed "a kind of bourgeois eisteddfod": Fisher, *John Gower,* 75–83; Pearsall, *Life,* 22. However, according to Ardis Butterfield, "the attempts to link Gower, and even Chaucer, Froissart, and Oton de Graunson with the *puy*... are far-fetched": "French Culture," 88.

12. For a useful discussion of the distinction between different types of audiences, see Strohm, "Chaucer's Audience(s)."

13. On Gower's distancing of his authorial voice in *Vox* from the peasants, see for example, Justice, *Writing and Rebellion,* 210–13; and Aers, "*Vox Populi,*" 439–44; but see the discussion in Chapter 1 below.

14. Bennett, "The Court of Richard II and the Promotion of Literature," 7.

15. Middleton, "The Idea of Public Poetry," 107. She also discusses the meaning of the word *common* (100). Strohm notes in "Chaucer's Audience(s)" that the original dedications of *Confessio* reveal that Richard II was certainly one intended reader of the poem, and that he may have been an actual reader as well. However, he also explains that the king was "not necessarily the sole member of its implied audience, or even very close to the center of that audience" (141).

16. Lynn Staley has argued for the central role of John of Gaunt in framing literary culture in what we often refer to as the Ricardian period. Staley posits that "Gower's changes to the *Confessio* [are] a sign, possibly of dissatisfaction with Richard, but also of Gaunt's subtle coopting of a poet's allegiance": "Gower, Richard II, Henry of Derby," 96.

17. Harris, "Ownership and Readership," esp. 96–208.

18. Strohm, *Social Chaucer,* 60.

19. Staley, "Gower, Richard II, Henry of Derby," 71.

20. Fisher, *John Gower,* 250 and 289.

21. See the notes to *The Legend of Good Women* in *The Riverside Chaucer,* 1059. Critics have variously argued that *The Legend* inspired *The Canterbury Tales,* that part has simply been lost in transmission, and that it is actually complete in its current form. See, for example, Frank, "The Legend of Good Women"; Blake, "Geoffrey Chaucer," 77; and Rowe, *Through Nature to Eternity.*

22. Allen, "Chaucer Answers Gower," 650 n. 9.

23. Fisher, *John Gower,* 26–33, 285–86, 289. See also the notes to the Man of Law's Tale, in *The Riverside Chaucer,* 854 and 856. For a reading of the feud that argues that it is a critical construct built on underlying misogyny, see Dinshaw, "Rivalry, Rape, and Manhood." I do not entirely concur with Dinshaw's reading, as I believe there is evidence in their works of amicable rivalry, although not of an actual feud, between the two poets.

24. For a more pragmatic interpretation that explains the deletion of these lines in terms of manuscript variation, see Macaulay's introduction to Gower, *English Works,* 1:xxvi–xxviii.

25. For a summary of this argument, originally put forward by Thomas Tyrwhitt in his 1775–78 edition of Chaucer's *Canterbury Tales*, see Fisher, *John Gower*, 26–28.

26. Fisher, *John Gower*, 287.

27. Bishop, "*The Nun's Priest's Tale* and the Liberal Arts," 263–64; but cf. Pearsall, *Life*, 147.

28. Justice, *Writing and Rebellion*, 213–18.

29. Pearsall, *Life*, 113.

30. Middleton, "The Idea of Public Poetry," 107; cf. E. Allen, "Chaucer Answers Gower," 650 n. 9.

31. Cf. Middleton, "The Idea of Public Poetry," 98. Unlike Middleton, however, I perceive anxiety in this awareness.

32. See Strohm, *Social Chaucer*, 57–59. Cf. Kerby-Fulton and Justice, "Langlandian Reading Circles," 61; and Lerer, *Chaucer and His Readers*, 10.

33. MED s.v. "zele" (d): "a strong emotion, esp. one of wrath or jealousy..." and OED s.v. "zeal" 1: "ardent feeling or fervour...with contextual tendency to unfavourable implications...." Cf. Yeager, "'O Moral Gower'"; E. Allen, "Chaucer Answers Gower," esp. 627–29. On the medieval imperative to read morally, see J. Allen, *The Ethical Poetic of the Later Middle Ages*.

34. For a discussion of the theoretical concept of interpretative disagreement, in a very different context, see Pearce, *Feminism and the Politics of Reading*, 193–219.

35. MED s.v. "moral" 2(b).

36. E. Allen, "Chaucer Answers Gower," 641.

37. Cf. Pearsall, "Gower Tradition," 180.

38. See the notes to the Man of Law's Tale in *The Riverside Chaucer*, 855.

39. See E. Allen, "Chaucer Answers Gower," and the earlier analysis by Sullivan, "Chaucer's Man of Law as a Literary Critic." For a rather different reading of the Man of Law as arbitrator of literary taste, see Middleton, "Chaucer's 'New Men' and the Good of Literature."

40. See, for example, Kelly, *Love and Marriage in the Age of Chaucer*, 139–40 and 144–45; Woolf, "Moral Chaucer and Kindly Gower," 226–27; Benson, "Incest and Moral Poetry"; Hatton, "John Gower's Use of Ovid," 260–64; Wetherbee, "Constance and the World," 66–68 and 86–87; Donavin, *Incest Narratives*, 33–37; Spearing, "Canace and Machaire," 211–21; Simpson, *Sciences and the Self*, 172–77; E. Allen, "Chaucer Answers Gower," 632–35; Lochrie, *Covert Operations*, 207–09; Bullón-Fernández, *Fathers and Daughters*, 158–72; and White, *Nature, Sex, and Goodness*, 174–219, esp. 194–99.

41. Strohm, "Chaucer's Fifteenth-Century Audience," esp. 18–32. Cf. Lerer, *Chaucer and His Readers*, 7–8, 17–18, and passim. For the application of this argument to Langland, see Middleton, "William Langland's 'Kynde Name,'" 20 n. 7.

42. Lawton, "Dullness," 780.

43. Pearsall, "Gower Tradition," 184; cf. Doyle, "English Books," 169–71; and Harris, "Patrons, Buyers, and Owners," 170. For a fuller discussion, see Harris, "Ownership and Readership," esp. 165–208.

44. Emmerson, "Reading Gower," 176.

45. For a comparison of the two tales, see E. Allen, "Chaucer Answers Gower." Allen argues that Chaucer and Gower share similar concerns about moral choice and reader reception.

46. Fisher, *John Gower*, 1.

47. Fisher, *John Gower*, 3–8.

48. On the Gower tradition of ethical and political poetry in the fifteenth century, see for example Lawton, "Dullness." Cf. Gilroy-Scott, "John Gower's Reputation." Pearsall in "Gower Tradition" covers some of the same ground, but argues that Gower's real influence on later authors was limited (see esp. 184).

49. Caxton, *Book of Curteyse*, 327. Reference is to *Caxton's Book of Curtesye*, ed. Furnivall.

50. *Boethius: De Consolatione Philosophiae*, trans. Walton, ed. Science, 3.

51. Barclay, *The Mirrour of Good Maners*, sig. A2r.

52. Puttenham, *The Arte of English Poesie*, 62.

53. See Dinshaw, "Rivalry, Rape, and Manhood," 130–34, esp. 133.

54. Harris, "John Gower's *Confessio Amantis*," 33–34.

55. Harris, "Ownership and Readership," 226–28.

56. This point was made by Nicola McDonald in her paper "Violence and the Gender of Space." For the fullest account of these illustrations, see Eberle, "Miniatures as Evidence."

57. Macaulay knew of only forty-one of these manuscripts. See Gower, *English Works*, 1:cxxxviii–clxv; Fisher, *John Gower*, appendix a, 303–09; Fisher et al., "John Gower," 2408. See also the forthcoming *Descriptive Catalogue*, ed. Griffiths, Harris, Pearsall, and Smith.

58. Fisher, *John Gower*, 127. Macaulay used MS Fairfax 3 as the base text in his EETS edition (Gower, *English Works*, 1:cxxx and clxx–clxxiii). For the argument that Gower supervised the revisions to this manuscript himself, see also Pearsall, "Gower Tradition," 182. For an opposing view, see Nicholson, "Gower's Revisions," 136–37. However, Nicholson argues here and elsewhere that neither the Fairfax (Oxford, Bodleian Library MS Fairfax 3) nor the Stafford (San Marino, CA, Huntington Library MS Ellesmere 26.A.17) Manuscripts were prepared by Gower as exemplars.

59. See, for example, Gower, *English Works*, 1:xxiii–xxvi. Fisher calls Gower a "sycophant" (*John Gower*, 133). For a recent defense of this view about Gower's politics, see Simpson, *Sciences and the Self*, 293–94 and esp. n. 21.

60. Nicholson, "Dedications," 160–61. Dhira B. Mahoney endorses Nicholson's argument, in "Gower's Two Prologues," 22–23.

61. Nicholson, "Dedications," 175.

62. Simpson, *Sciences and the Self*, 294 n. 21.

63. Fisher, *John Gower*, 116–17. For a concise discussion, see Fredell, "Reading the Dream Miniature," 61.

64. Gower, *English Works*, 1:clii–cliii; Fisher, *John Gower*, 124. See also Nicholson, "Gower's Revisions," 136; Nicholson, "Poet and Scribe," 141; and Doyle, "English Books,"169–70. Emmerson is of the opinion that Stafford "provides the best evidence for

the original *mise en page* of the poem": "Reading Gower," 162. For a newly rediscovered portion of leaves missing from the Stafford Gower, see Edwards and Takamiya, "A New Fragment of Gower's *Confessio Amantis*." Edwards and Takamiya suggest that the excisions to the manuscript "may offer some insight into early responses to the poem" (932).

65. Fredell, "Reading the Dream Miniature," 61 and n. 3.

66. See Gower, *English Works*, 1:xxi–xxviii and cxvii–clxv, esp. the summary on cxxvii–cxxix; Fisher, *John Gower*, 116–27. For an argument that dates the first recension to 1392–93 rather than 1390, and the third recension to the late 1390s, see Astell, *Political Allegory*, 73–93.

67. Some first-recension manuscripts contain a short Latin envoy that includes a second dedication, this time to Henry of Derby: Gower, *English Works*, 1:xxi.

68. Gower, *English Works*, 1:cxxx–cxxxiii and clvii–clix.

69. Nicholson, "Dedications"; "Gower's Revisions"; and "Poet and Scribe."

70. Nicholson, "Poet and Scribe," 138.

71. For a critique of Nicholson's arguments, see Simpson, *Sciences and the Self*, 293–94 n. 21.

72. Fredell "Reading the Dream Miniature," 62.

73. Pearsall, "Gower's Latin"; summarized and revised by Emmerson "Reading Gower," 147–55.

74. See also Gower, *Latin Verses*.

75. See Pearsall, "Gower's Latin"; Copeland, *Rhetoric*, 202–20; Echard, "With Carmen's Help"; and "Glossing Gower"; Wetherbee, "Latin Structure and Vernacular Space"; and Yeager, "English, Latin, and the Text as 'Other'," and "'Oure englisshe' and Everyone's Latin."

76. For the suggestion that Gower did not write the commentary, see J. Griffiths, "*Confessio Amantis*," 174–75.

77. See also Siân Echard's articles, "Designs for Reading" and "Dialogues and Monologues."

78. Gower, *English Works*, 2:479–80; Fisher, *John Gower*, 88–91, and appendix b, 311–12; Gower, *Latin Works*, 343–68. On the status of this Latin see Gower, *English Works*, 2:549–50 n: Macaulay attributes two poems to Strode. See also Pearsall, "Gower's Latin," 24. Some manuscripts of *Confessio* also include Gower's *Traitié pour Essampler les Amantz Marietz* (Pearsall, "Gower Tradition," 183). Reading the two texts together clearly influences our interpretation of them.

79. Echard, "With Carmen's Help," 11; Emmerson, "Reading Gower," 152–53.

80. Emmerson, "Reading Gower," 155.

81. Ibid., 155–66.

82. Ibid., 164.

83. Ibid., 161.

84. Ibid., 171–78.

85. Ibid., 176. Cf. Echard, "Designs for Reading."

86. Ibid., 144.

87. J. Griffiths, "*Confessio Amantis*," esp. 176–77; Fredell, "Reading the Dream Miniature"; Emmerson, "Reading Gower," 167–70 and 184–86.

88. Fisher, *John Gower*, 136 and 354 n. 2; Peck, *Kingship and Common Profit*, 193; Pearsall, "Gower Tradition," 183.

89. See Burrow, "Portrayal of Amans"; Emmerson, "Reading Gower," 169–70; Garbárty, "Description"; J. Griffiths, "*Confessio Amantis*."

90. Emmerson, "Reading Gower," 169–70.

91. Burrow, "Portrayal of Amans"; J. Griffiths, "*Confessio Amantis*," esp. 174–75 and n. 35. Garbárty argues for three overlapping categories of lover in the illustration: old, young, and biographical: "Description," 334.

92. J. Griffiths, "*Confessio Amantis*," 174 n. 33; cf. Burrow, "Portrayal of Amans," 12.

93. Emmerson "Reading Gower," 167–69; Fredell, "Reading the Dream Miniature."

94. Emmerson "Reading Gower," 167.

95. Fredell, "Reading the Dream Miniature."

96. Emmerson, "Reading Gower," 169 and 175.

97. Ibid., 170.

98. See J. Griffiths, "*Confessio Amantis*," 163–66.

99. Emmerson, "Reading Gower," 178–83; Eberle, "Miniatures as Evidence"; and Braeger, "Illustrations."

100. Emmerson, "Reading Gower," 178–83, at 179. See also Eberle, "Miniatures as Evidence," 322–25.

101. Fisher's views have been outlined above. For Minnis's, see for example his essays, "'Moral Gower'"; "John Gower, *Sapiens*"; and his *Medieval Theory of Authorship*, 188–89.

102. Echard, "With Carmen's Help," 26.

103. Ibid., 5.

104. Ibid., 3.

105. For brief discussions of such texts, see Machan, "Thomas Berthelette," 165 and n. 59; and Mahoney, "Gower's Two Prologues," 34.

106. Gower, *English Works*, 1:clxv–clxvii and clxviii–clxx; Fisher et al., "John Gower," 2409. For the Spanish prose translation of *Confessio*, see Gower, *English Works*, 1:clxvii–clxviii. Echard notes, for example, that Caxton's table of contents for his edition of Gower omits the historical and political frame (Echard, "Pre-texts," 278 and 283), while Berthelette's edition privileges the vernacular text over the Latin (Echard, "With Carmen's Help," 40). See also Harris, "John Gower's *Confessio Amantis*" and "Ownership and Readership," 27–75 and "Longleat House"; Blake, "Early Printed Editions"; Machan, "Thomas Berthelette"; Edwards, "Selection and Subversion"; and Driver, "Printing the *Confessio Amantis*."

1. GOWER'S BABEL TOWER

1. For the independence of the literary text from the historical figure of the author and from the constraints of author intentionality, see Barthes, "The Death of the Author." Barthes calls for a criticism that will "consist in *returning* the documentary figure of the author into a novelistic, irretrievable, irresponsible figure, caught up in the plural of its own text" in his *S/Z*, 211–12. Here I do not argue for the complete separation of author and text, but suggest that the author, text, and reader collaborate in the plurality of meaning.

2. See Pearsall, "Gower's Latin," 16–17. On the humility topos generally, see Curtius, *European Literature*, 407–13. For another discussion of Gower's use of it, see Chapter 2, below.

3. Gower, *Latin Verses*, 2 n. 1.

4. Pearsall, however, translates the opening two lines as "Torpor, dullness of perception, little opportunity for learning, and the scantest application are the reason that I, least [of poets], sing of lesser things": "Gower's Latin," 16. He suggests that the comparison implied in *minora* "means that [Gower] also claims to have spoken in the past of greater ones (in the *Vox Clamantis*)."

5. Gower, *Latin Verses*, xxxvii; cf. 2–3 n. 2. Pearsall says that he "was tempted to believe that Gower's Latin was not merely difficult to understand but not meant to be understood": "Gower's Latin," 17. For other, comparable, riddling references to the tongue in Gower's works, see *Confessio Amantis*, III.462–65 and *Vox Clamantis*, V.921–22. See also Echard, "With Carmen's Help," 4.

6. Antiochus's riddle, which reveals his incestuous relationship with his daughter, is (apparently) solved, but never explained, by Apollonius. For a discussion of the riddle, and the tale as a whole, see Chapter 6, below, and Scanlon, "The Riddle of Incest."

7. *The Idea of the Vernacular*, ed. Wogan-Browne, Watson, Taylor, and Evans, 179 n.

8. Cf. Ferdinand's exchange with his sister in *The Duchess of Malfi*, I.ii.255–57: "And women like that part, which, like the lamprey / Hath nev'r a bone in't . . . Nay, / I mean the tongue . . ." (Webster, *The Duchess of Malfi*). There is a long-established English tradition of penis riddles that can be dated back to the Anglo-Saxon period. See, for example, *The Old English Riddles of the Exeter Book*, ed. Williamson, nos. 23 and 42. Echard, Fanger, and Pearsall agree that "[Gower's Latin [is] intrinsically difficult, full of allusions and word-play *(some of it quite obscene)*": Pearsall, "Gower's Latin," 17 n. 8 (my emphasis).

9. See Salisbury, "Remembering Origins," 164; and especially Schibanoff, "Sodomy's Mark," 47–51.

10. I am assuming here that Gower's implied audience is male rather than female or mixed (a point I will return to later), but not of course that the actual reader, perverse or otherwise, has to be a man.

11. See Bakhtin's *Rabelais and His World;* and especially his *Dialogic Imagination*. See also A. White, *Carnival, Hysteria, and Writing*, 135–59.

12. Bakhtin, *Dialogic Imagination*, 431. On the language situation in late medieval England, see Watson, "Politics."

13. Bakhtin, *Dialogic Imagination*, 68.

14. This paraphrase is taken, almost verbatim, from the translation by Götz Schmitz, "Rhetoric and Fiction," 135.

15. Cooper, "Gender and Personification." See also L. Griffiths, *Personification in Piers Plowman;* C. Murphy, "Lady Holy Church and Meed the Maid"; and Lees, "Gender and Exchange." For female personifications more generally, see Warner, *Monuments and Maidens*, esp. 63–87.

16. Cooper, "Gender and Personification," 35.

17. Gower, *Major Latin Works*, 258.

18. Stallybrass and White, *The Politics and Poetics of Transgression*, 10–11.

19. Minnis, *Medieval Theory of Authorship*, 177. Minnis is, however, referring specifically to the Latin glosses and summaries rather than the Latin verses.

20. Fleming, *The Roman de la Rose*, 45.

21. On Sin (whom Gower describes in *Confessio*, Prol.1029–30, as the masculine mother of division) as a monstrous portent, see Chambers, "'Sin' and 'Sign.'" On the representation of Death and the connection between Gower and Milton, see Chapter 4, below.

22. I am grateful to Ros Allen for drawing the following passage to my attention, and to Catherine Batt and David Trotter for discussing it with me.

23. Gower, *French Works*, xvii.

24. The standard study is Ziolkowski, *Alan of Lille's Grammar of Sex*. I have been particularly influenced by the readings offered in Bloch's *Etymologies and Genealogies*, 133–36; Pittenger, "Explicit Ink"; Keiser, *Courtly Desire*, 71–92; Jordan, *Invention of Sodomy*, 67–91; and Schibanoff, "Sodomy's Mark," 28–35. Two important flaws in Alan's logic are that heterosexual reproduction would seem to *contradict* rules of grammatical copulation (in which agreement in gender is the norm) and that Nature appears to be responsible for homosexuality. Jordan suggests that in the *Plaint*, "everywhere we turn, Nature's rules seem to spawn their own violations in same-sex fertilities" (*Invention of Sodomy*, 86). See also the discussion in Chapter 2.

25. "Heteroglossia implies dialogic interaction in which the prestige languages try to extend their control and subordinated languages try to avoid, negotiate, or subvert that control": A. White, *Carnival, Hysteria, and Writing*, 137.

26. For a discussion of the debate, see Watson, "Censorship and Cultural Change," especially his discussion of the views of Richard Ullerston (844–45). For the Lollard version of Ullerston's text (mistakenly ascribed to John Purvey), see Deanesly, *Lollard Bible*, 437–45. See also Watson, "Politics."

27. Watson, "Censorship and Cultural Change," 836–40.

28. Minnis and Scott, eds., with Wallace, *Medieval Literary Theory and Criticism*, 374; Copeland, *Rhetoric, Hermeneutics, and Translation*, 202–20, esp. 202–03.

29. This identification with lay rather than clerical learning is made even more explicit in *Mirour de l'Omme*, 21769–80, and *Vox Clamantis*, III.2141–42. See also Scanlon, *Narrative, Authority, and Power*, 245–97, esp. 248–67.

30. On Genius as lay clerk, see Scanlon, *Narrative, Authority, and Power*, 255–56. Genius is himself aware of his double role as priest and servant to a pagan goddess (I.233–88). At the same time as he castigates "lewed" priests (274), Genius admits his own ignorance about "thinges that ben wise" (265).

31. Crane, "Writing Lesson"; and Galloway, "Gower in His Most Learned Role."

32. See, for example, Palmer, "De translatione sacræ scripturæ in linguam Anglicanam," 428.

33. Aers, "*Vox Populi*," 439–44; Justice, *Writing and Rebellion*, 211–13.

34. Aers, "*Vox Populi*," 439. See also Aers, *Chaucer, Langland, and the Creative Imagination*, 1–79.

35. Aers, "*Vox Populi*," 438–39. Aers's definition of the "radical reader" is distinct from but comparable with my own notion of the "perverse reader."

36. Salisbury, "Remembering Origins," 159–84.

37. Ibid., 161.

38. Ibid., 161; cf. Yeager, "Did Gower Write *Cento*?"; and also his *John Gower's Poetic*, 52–60. Yeager argues that the *cento* technique is also demonstrated in *Confessio Amantis*.

39. Bakhtin, *Dialogic Imagination*, 69.

40. Salisbury, "Remembering Origins," 162–63.

41. Ibid., 168–69.

42. Judith Ferster thinks that the narrator's voice has certainly merged with that of the masses by the end of *Vox Clamantis*. She reminds us that the first book, with its attack on "the people and their inhuman voices," was added later, but suggests that the final version of the text is intended to be read in linear order: *Fictions of Advice*, 108–34, at 130.

43. Copeland, *Rhetoric, Hemeneutics, and Translation*, 217.

44. Ibid., 215.

45. Cf. John Trevisa's claim that translation into the vernacular can resolve the problems brought about by Babel: "Dialogue between the Lord and the Servant," 131–32.

46. Keiser, *Courtly Desire*, 42, 45–48, 70, and 100.

47. Gaunt, "Bel Acueil and the Improper Allegory." Gaunt reads into the *Roman de la Rose* a tension between the super-text (the literal narrative of the homosexual relationship between Bel Acueil and Amant) and the allegorical plot of heterosexual seduction, and he concludes that allegory and sexuality are "profoundly imbricated."

48. Jordan, *Invention of Sodomy*, 34.

49. See, for example, Prol.111–14, in which the author-narrator laments the passing of a Golden Age when "Of mannes herte the corage / Was schewed thanne in the visage; / The word was lich to the conceite / Withoute semblant of deceite."

50. The pun on "semblant" is interesting here, because in addition to meaning "kind" or "like" (the dominant sense here), it can also mean "outward" or "deceptive appearance." The wordplay thus encapsulates the meaning of Hypocrisy, whose "real" nature is only betrayed by those with whom she associates because she is never quite what she seems.

51. Wetherbee, "Latin Structure and Vernacular Space," 20–22.

52. Watson, "Censorship and Cultural Change," 842–43. For a defense of the "grammatical" nature of the English language, see extract 2.4, "On Translating the Bible Into English" in *The Idea of the Vernacular*, ed. Wogan-Browne et al., 146–47.

53. Bakhtin, *Dialogic Imagination*, 282.

54. According to Wetherbee, "the occasion and intended audience of the *Mirour* remains obscure": "John Gower," 594. For the continuing importance of Anglo-Norman in the court after 1350, see Machan, "Language Contact," 383.

55. Watson, "Censorship and Cultural Change," 857; and "Politics," 345.

56. See Hudson, "Lollardy: The English Heresy?" 142 and n. 5.

2. WRITING LIKE A MAN

1. *Inferno*, XV.25–30. All quotations are from Dante Alighieri, *The Divine Comedy*, ed. and trans. Bickersteth.

2. For an overview of critical responses, see Pequigney, "Sodomy," 26–27. In addition, see also Holsinger, "Sodomy and Resurrection"; and Camille, "The Pose of the Queer."

3. See Michel Foucault's widely accepted description of sodomy as an "utterly confused category" in *The History of Sexuality*, 101. An important recent study of the meaning or grammar of sodomy in the Middle Ages is Jordan's *Invention of Sodomy*, esp. 1–9.

4. It is remarkable that the words *sodomita* (sodomite) and *sodomia* (sodomy) are never actually applied to Brunetto Latini or his sins. Nor, for that matter, as Joseph Pequigney observes, do they occur anywhere in the *Commedia*: Pequigney, "Sodomy," 22. Pequigney explains that the sin is designated by the proper noun *Soddoma* (Sodom) that occurs on only three occasions: *Inferno*, XXI.50, *Purgatorio*, XXVI.40, and *Purgatorio*, XXVI.79. He sees Dante's conception of and attitude toward sodomy as influenced by but distinct from that of St. Thomas Aquinas, and convincingly argues that Dante's attitude to sodomy undergoes "a sea-change" as the *Commedia* progresses. Certainly, whereas in *Inferno* it is viewed as more serious than sinful heterosexual desire, in *Purgatorio* sodomy is represented as a species of lust, the most excusable of the seven capital sins.

5. For examples of connections being made between idolatry and sodomy in the writings of St. Jerome and Gregory the Great, see Jordan, *Invention of Sodomy*, 36.

6. Vance, "The Differing Seed," 253.

7. See Bloch, *Etymologies and Genealogies*, esp. 135.

8. On the "outdoing topos," see Curtius, *European Literature*, 162–65.

9. Bloom, *The Anxiety of Influence*.

10. Latini, *Li Livres dou Trésor*.

11. For Gower's possible familiarity with Dante's *Commedia*, see Lynch, *The High Medieval Dream Vision*, 163–98, esp. 190–98; Simpson, *Sciences and the Self*, 173–4 n. 6.

12. Murphy, "John Gower's *Confessio Amantis*." On Gower's other sources, see Chapter 5 below.

13. Minnis, *Medieval Theory of Authorship*, 184.

14. Wetherbee, "John Gower," 604.

15. Gower does however cut down considerably the discussion of rhetoric. On Gower's debt to Latini, see especially Copeland, *Rhetoric*, 207–11, and Schmitz, "Rhetoric and Fiction," 121–29.

16. J. Murphy ("John Gower's *Confessio Amantis*") argues that Gower had no real technical understanding of rhetoric, but more nuanced recent studies reveal that *Confessio Amantis* has a developed and sophisticated rhetorical structure. See, for example, Schmitz, "Rhetoric and Fiction"; Yeager, *John Gower's Poetic*; Copeland, *Rhetoric, Hermeneutics, and Translation*, 202–20; Olsson, *John Gower*; and Craun, *Lies, Slander, and Obscenity*, 113–56. For a reading of Gower's discussion of rhetoric that finds in it contemporary political allusions, see Astell, *Political Allegory*, 83–91.

17. Copeland, *Rhetoric, Hermeneutics, and Translation*, 210.

18. Craun, *Lies, Slander, and Obscenity*, 119 (my emphasis).

19. Craun, *Lies, Slander, and Obscenity*, 121.

20. See Schmitz, "Rhetoric and Fiction," 126–27.

21. For an analysis of Medea's "jargoun," see Nicola F. McDonald's forthcoming article, "John Gower's *Medea Genetrix*." Having had her tongue torn out, Philomele is also described as chattering "as a brid jargoune" (V.5700).

22. For the connection between women and excessive desire and the association of feminine language with the disruption of rhetoric (both of which date back to the teach-

ings of the ancient Greek philosophers, especially Aristotle), see Cixous, "Sorties: Out and Out." See also Cixous, "The Laugh of the Medusa." For an overview on *écriture féminine*, see Moi, *Sexual/Textual Politics*.

23. Schmitz, "Rhetoric and Fiction," 127.

24. Cf. the depiction of Malebouch, who is unable to pronounce "A plein good word withoute frounce" (II.392). For the meanings of "frounce" as "frown or sneer" and "complication, ambiguity," see MED s.v. "frounce"1(b) and 1(c).

25. Echard and Fanger, in Gower, *Latin Verses*, note that the second line echoes the description of False-seeming in II.1878g–h, "politi / Principium pacti finis habere negat," which they translate as "the end / Of his smooth pledge denies what's first implied."

26. Craun, *Lies, Slander, and Obscenity*, 125.

27. For Gower's distrust of the royal advisers see Mathew, *The Court of Richard II*, 81. Other important studies of the reign of Richard II (in chronological order) include Steele, *Richard II*, which should be read alongside the review by Galbraith, "A New Life of Richard II"; Jones, *The Royal Policy of Richard II;* Tuck, *Richard II and the English Nobility;* and Saul, *Richard II*. Criticism of flattery in the court is of course found in earlier texts, such as John of Salisbury's *Policraticus*, III.4: quoted by Echard, *Arthurian Narrative*, 13.

28. See Saul, *Richard II*, 456–57. I am grateful to Alfred Thomas for suggesting to me the significance of Richard II's lack of an heir.

29. *Vox Clamantis*, VI.643.

30. *Vox Clamantis*, VI.853–916.

31. Curtius, *European Literature*, 62–78, esp. 75–77.

32. Schmitz, "Rhetoric and Fiction," 124.

33. Schmitz, "Rhetoric and Fiction," 122–26, at 125. The *Historia Meriadoci* provides us with a comparable example of rhetorical speech being used to deceive in a legal (as well as courtly) context: see Echard, *Arthurian Narrative*, 159–92, esp. 168–70.

34. MED s.v. "colouren" 2(a); OED s.v. "colour" 3(b).

35. These contrasting definitions can be explained by the two different meanings of the word. According to Schmitz, *colour* could both be "a synonym of *ornatus*" and mean "the glossing necessary to give a fair appearance to a dubious case" ("Rhetoric and Fiction," 124–25 n. 13 and n. 14). Murphy oversimplifies when he contends that Gower "uses the term 'colour' only in the classical Latin sense of 'semblance or appearance'" ("John Gower's *Confessio Amantis*," 408).

36. Schmitz, "Rhetoric and Fiction," 133.

37. Colish, "Cosmetic Theology," 10.

38. Alain de Lille, *De Planctu Naturae*, prosa 7.34; contrast the depiction of manly Hymenaeus in prosa 8.1–21.

39. Guillaume de Lorris and Jean de Meun, *Le Roman de la Rose*, 2170–74; cf. Alain de Lille, *De Planctu Naturae*, prosa 8.48–50.

40. Quintilian, *Institutio oratoria*, II.v.11–12. All references are to *Institutio Oratoria*, ed. and trans. Butler.

41. Lichtenstein, "Making Up Representation," 78.

42. Cf. the Latin verses describing Ypocrisis (I.574e–h).

43. MED s.v. "coveture" 5 and 6(a). See Pickles and Dawson, eds., *A Concordance to John Gower's Confessio Amantis*.

44. Lichtenstein, "Making Up Representation," 79. See also Parker, "Virile Style." Parker argues that, although indebted to the Roman authors, "anti-Ciceronianism . . . [with] its anxieties of virility haunted by both the female and the effeminate" was a new development in sixteenth-century discussions of rhetoric ("Virile Style," 206). Gower's text suggests that these ideas were also in circulation in the late medieval period. Of related interest is Enders, "Delivering Delivery."

45. Quintilian, *Institutio oratoria*, II.v.10.

46. Ziolkowski, *Alan of Lille's Grammar of Sex*, 29.

47. See Alain de Lille, *De Planctu Naturae*, prosa 4.170–72 and prosa 3.121–24.

48. "Sed si muneris anthonomasia uideatur laudum tympana postulare, adulationis poeta stilo conmendationis turget altiloquo. Si uero muneris pauperies fame mendicat suffragia, humiliori stilo fame depauperat dignitatem" (However, if an expression to describe the gift seems to call for the drums of praise, the poet of flattery grows swollen in a bombastic style of eulogy. If, however, a poor gift begs aid for fame, he robs the account of it by a more lowly style): Alain de Lille, *De Planctu Naturae*, prosa 7.108–11.

49. Alain de Lille, *De Planctu Naturae*, prosa 5.35–42; cf. *De Planctu Naturae*, prosa 5.108–14. The source of Nature's teaching here can once again be traced back to Quintilian, who drew a distinction between "proper" and "improper" or "figurative" language. He argued, "propria sunt verba, cum id significant, in quod primo denominata sunt; translata, cum alium natura intellectum alium loco praebent" (words are *proper* when they bear their original meaning; *metaphorical*, when they are used in a sense different from their natural meaning): Quintilian, *Institutio oratoria*, I.v.71.

50. For the distinction between "tropus" and "vitium" see Ziolkowski, *Alan of Lille's Grammar of Sex*, 17.

51. Alain de Lille, *De Planctu Naturae*, metrum 1.21–24.

52. Alain de Lille, *De Planctu Naturae*, prosa 5.142–44; cf. the discussion of the sophistic pseudographer in prosa 4. In this context, see also *Le Roman de la Rose* and Simon Gaunt's analysis in "Bel Acueil and the Improper Allegory," 86–93; and Schibanoff, "Sodomy's Mark."

53. Commenting on the dire warnings that Nature has to give Venus against unnatural unions, Elizabeth Keiser remarks that "Apparently, same-sex union is thought to be so desirable that only the severest threats and combinations can deter the human male from finding it preferable to heterosexual intercourse": *Courtly Desire*, 75.

54. Ziolkowski, *Alan of Lille's Grammar of Sex*, 29; see also Bloch, *Etymologies and Genealogies*, 133–35.

55. See, for example, Orderic Vitalis, *The Ecclesiastical History*, 4:188–89. On courtly literature and the meaning of effeminacy in the Middle Ages, see Jaeger, *The Origins of Courtliness*, 176–94; Keiser, *Courtly Desire*; Putter, "Arthurian Literature."

56. Walsingham, *Historia Anglicana*, 2:156 (my emphasis). Translated by Patricia J. Eberle in "Politics of Courtly Style," 169.

57. Walsingham, *Historia Anglicana*, 2:148. See Stow, "Richard II in Thomas Walsingham's Chronicles." John Boswell points out that accusations of sodomy were often made against unpopular monarchs: *Christianity, Social Tolerance, and Homosexuality*, 229. Writing after the deposition, Adam of Usk explicitly accused Richard II of sodomy: Hanrahan, "Speaking of Sodomy," 433.

58. See the discussions about the occurrence of the words "disgysing"/ "disfigura-cione" (disguising, disfiguring) and "mollicia" (effeminacy, softness) in the Lollards' *Twelve Conclusions* and Roger Dymmok's response in Eberle, "Politics of Courtly Style," 174; and Somerset, "Answering the *Twelve Conclusions*," 62–63. For a full discussion of the "innuendos" about Richard II's sexuality, see Hanrahan, "Speaking of Sodomy."

59. Quoted and translated by Putter in "Arthurian Literature," 38. I am grateful to Ad Putter for this reference.

60. See his intervention in the story of Achilles and Deidamia at V.3126–34, dis-cussed in Chapter 3.

61. *Suetonius,* I.52, ed. and trans. Rolfe.

62. *Catullus,* ed. and trans. Cornish, rev. Goold, no. 57.

63. On the topos see Curtius, *European Literature,* 407–13.

64. Barclay, *The Mirrour of Good Maners,* sig. A2r; see also the Latin marginal glosses to the text.

65. For the argument that this commissioning passage is fictional, see Barclay, *The Life of St. George,* xiv–xv.

66. Translation by Echard, "With Carmen's Help," 32.

67. Minnis, *Medieval Theory of Authorship,* 189.

68. It is pertinent to this discussion to note that Amans borrows rhetorical terms to describe his activities, e.g., at I.2726–31 or II.1962–65.

69. "quodsi nulla contingit excusatio, sola colorem habet paenitentia" (when there is no other excuse, penitence can lend color to a confession): Quintilian, *Institutio oratoria* XI.i.81 (trans. Schmitz, "Rhetoric and Fiction," 125 n. 14).

70. See Mahoney, "Gower's Two Prologues," esp. 18–19. For recent readings of this passage, which argue that Gower's claim that he received royal patronage is heavily fic-tionalized, see Astell, *Political Allegory,* 77–83, and Grady, "Gower's Boat, Richard's Barge."

71. On the overlap between the erotic and the political in relations between powerful men (kings and other kings, kings and their courtiers, etc.) and on the exclusion of sodomy from such elite homosocial structures, see Jaeger, *Ennobling Love,* esp. 11–26 and 36–53. Also cf. Hanrahan, "Speaking of Sodomy," 443.

72. Barclay, *The Mirrour of Good Maners,* sig. A2r.

3. Transgressive Genders and Subversive Sexualities

1. See Foucault, *The History of Sexuality;* and also Tambling, *Confession,* esp. 35–65.

2. Murray, "Gendered Souls in Sexed Bodies," 80–81.

3. Foucault, *History of Sexuality,* 59.

4. Frantzen, "Disclosure of Sodomy," 455.

5. *The Book of Vices and Virtues,* ed. Francis, 46.

6. St. Thomas Aquinas defined sodomy as intercourse "with a person of the same sex, male with male and female with female": *Temperance* (2a2ae), q.154, a.11.

7. On the poem's penitential framework, see McNally, "The Penitential and Courtly

Tradition"; Braswell, *Medieval Sinner*, 81–87; Kinneavy, "Gower's *Confessio Amantis*"; and Craun, *Lies, Slander, and Obscenity*, 113–56, esp. 115–18.

   8. There have been a number of fascinating recent readings of *Confessio* that focus on the treatment of women and incest, but the studies most relevant to my own approach are Woolf, "Moral Chaucer and Kindly Gower," and chapter five of Karma Lochrie's *Covert Operations*, 177–227.

   9. Lochrie, *Covert Operations*, 226.

   10. Ibid., 221.

   11. Ibid., 225.

   12. Ibid., 226.

   13. Halberstam, *Female Masculinity*, esp. 1–43.

   14. Lochrie acknowledges the absence of sodomy in Gower's text, but only in passing. She does not explore the significance of this silence. See also Hanrahan, "Speaking of Sodomy," 436.

   15. On the cultural significance of cross-dressing, see Garber, *Vested Interests*.

   16. See, for example, Keiser, *Courtly Desire*, 85. For a fuller analysis, see Lochrie, *Covert Operations*, 177–227, and Hanrahan, "Speaking of Sodomy."

   17. See Sedgwick, *Between Men*; and Irigaray, "Women on the Market" and "Commodities Among Themselves," in *The Sex Which Is Not One*, 170–91 and 192–97.

   18. Kinneavy, "Gower's *Confessio Amantis*," 152.

   19. Cf. *Troilus and Criseyde* I.206–10, in which Cupid's dart is immediately responsible for Troilus's sudden passion.

   20. Eberle, "Miniatures as Evidence," 326.

   21. Kathleen L. Scott identifies the female figure as Amans's beloved: *Later Gothic Manuscripts*, 322–325, esp. 322. This seems unlikely given the absence of the woman from the narrative. Eberle assumes the woman is Venus ("Miniatures as Evidence," 326).

   22. See Merivale, *Pan the Goat-God*.

   23. Cf. VIII.2287–90.

   24. "Gropen" can mean "to feel with the hand or fingers, touch, stroke" and "to touch amorously, play with, fondle": MED s.v. "gropen" 1(a) and 1(d). For the possible figurative use of the word "launce" to mean "penis" see MED s.v. "launce" 3(e). For a detailed discussion of "gropen," see Cox, "'Grope wel bihynde,'" esp. 154–55.

   25. Norton, "Lovely Lad and Shame-Faced Catamite."

   26. Cf. I.267–69.

   27. Braswell draws this comparison in *Medieval Sinner*, 82. In his *History of Sexuality*, Foucault argued that confession and psychoanalysis were part of the same tradition. See also his "Confession of the Flesh," 209–22.

   28. This episode of the tale does not occur in Ovid's *Metamorphoses*, IX.101–210, Gower's main source for the tale. Analogies can be found in Ovid's *Herodites* and Pierre Bersuire's *Ovidius Moralizatus*. See Brown, "The Tale of Deianira and Nessus," 18; and C. Mainzer, "John Gower's Use of the 'Mediaeval Ovid,'" 217.

   29. "Wommanysshe" is glossed by Macaulay as "womanly" or "effeminate."

   30. Other examples of such folly include the Lydians (VII.4361–4405) and the Hebrews (VII.4406–45). The folly of the Hebrews is also described in *Vox Clamantis*, VI.871–

902, in the context of an admonition to the king to marry and to avoid the allurement of sins of the flesh.

31. Gower's portrayal of Hercules' divided nature is traditional. From the classical period onward, Hercules was renowned not only for his great strength but also for his intemperance and lascivious nature: see Galinsky, *Herakles Theme*. As Robert Yeager puts it, Hercules' reputation is "piebald": *John Gower's Poetic*, 89.

32. By the seventeenth century to "procure" could mean "to obtain (women) for the gratification of lust" (OED s.v. "procure" 5[b]), and a "procurer" could have the sense of "one who procures women for the gratification of lust; a pander" (OED s.v. "procurer" 4). The MED does not offer comparable definitions, but Gower's use of the word "procurours" suggests that in the late Middle Ages it had similar connotations.

33. Woolf, "Moral Chaucer and Kindly Gower," 224. See also Lochrie, *Covert Operations*, 216–17. This "moment" is not conveyed in the illustration to this story in Pierpont Morgan Library M.126 (fol. 106v), which depicts a clearly male Achilles in bed alongside Deidamia.

34. Alain de Lille, *Anticlaudianus*, ed. Bossuat, 9.265–69; trans. Sheridan, 211.

35. For another, briefer, analysis of Achilles' effeminacy, see Putter, "Arthurian Literature," 42.

36. See King, *Achilles*, esp. 180–84.

37. See, for example, Chrétien de Troyes, "Perceval," 375–78. For a reading of the Middle English *Sir Perceval of Galles* that argues that Perceval moves from the maternal sphere into the paternal and then back into the maternal, see Baron, "Mother and Son in *Sir Perceval of Galles*."

38. Ricks, "Metamorphosis in Other Words," 43.

39. Woolf, "Moral Chaucer, Kindly Gower," 225; Gallacher, *Love, the Word, and Mercury*, 67. See also Lochrie, *Covert Operations*, 213–16, and Dinshaw, *Getting Medieval*, 10–11.

40. Woolf, "Moral Chaucer, Kindly Gower," 225.

41. In Ovid, it is Isis, the goddess of good hope, who intervenes: *Metamorphoses*, IX.782–84. Cupid's intervention here points outward to the frame narrative in which Cupid's interventions both cause Amans's obsession and release him from it.

42. For an attempt to resolve the confusion surrounding Nature and "kinde" in the Tale of Iphis and Ianthe, see Yeager, "Learning to Read in Tongues," 120–26. For more recent responses, see Lochrie, *Covert Operations*, 214–15; Dinshaw, *Getting Medieval*, 10–11; and H. White, *Nature, Sex, and Goodness*, 174–299, esp. 192–94. White's analysis of the Tale of Iphis and Ianthe demonstrates how Gower's anarchic Nature manages to be "moral" and "immoral" simultaneously.

43. MED s.v. "wonder" 1, 2(a), 2(b), 3(a), 4, 7(a), and 7(b).

44. For an overview of surviving evidence in Europe, see Murray, "Twice Marginal and Twice Invisible"; most of the examples cited are from continental Europe.

45. Twelve seems to have been the crucial age for girls (fourteen for boys): see Shahar, *Childhood*, 24–26. If found guilty of a sexual sin, a child under the age of legal responsibility would usually be treated more leniently than an adult would.

46. See Shahar, *Childhood*, 23–26, 77–120, and 162–82. Gower does not specify Achilles' age when he is cross-dressing, but despite his childish appearance he is evidently not in his infancy because (all other factors, including sexual maturity, apart) in the Middle Ages girls and boys would generally have been dressed the same in the first age of childhood. For a further important example of childhood as a space for legitimate transgression (in this case, incest), see the Tale of Canace and Machaire (III.143–336).

47. See Laqueur, *Making Sex,* esp. 134–42; but also Cadden, *The Meanings of Sex Difference,* esp. 3.

48. See Tyrrell, *Amazons,* 49–52.

49. Lochrie views Gower's Iphis more negatively, arguing that by cross-dressing she becomes a caricature of a prince and "of the masculinity it implies": *Covert Operations,* 216. Halberstam's analysis of female masculinity suggests that it should not be so readily dismissed as simple parody.

50. I use the list of *Metamorphoses* provided by Jordan, *Invention of Sodomy,* 81 n. 70: Narcissus, Athis and Lycabas, Cycnus and Phyllius, Iphis and Ianthe, Orpheus, Cyparissus and Apollo, Ganymede and Jupiter, and Hyacinth and Apollo.

51. Jordan, *Invention of Sodomy,* 83.

52. Translated by Echard, "With Carmen's Help," 36.

53. Echard, "With Carmen's Help," 37. Echard's main point is, however, that at the same time Gower is "drawing attention to the unreliability of both the English *and* the Latin parts of the text" (Echard's emphasis). Again my reading of this episode can be compared to that by Lochrie, *Covert Operations,* 219–21.

54. Pierpont Morgan MS M.126 fol. 21v. Eberle believes that the illustrator here was following instructions based in part on the Latin gloss: "Miniatures as Evidence," 338–39.

55. See Galinsky, *Herakles Theme,* 109–22.

56. Jordan claims that the "literate reader" would automatically think of Achilles in terms of his relationship with Patroclus: *Invention of Sodomy,* 73–74; but see also King, *Achilles,* 171–72. For the passage in Alain de Lille that seems to refer to Achilles' homosexuality, see *De Planctu Naturae,* metrum 1 lines 55–56.

57. Lochrie does not see any homoeroticism in this passage, but observes that the narrative functions to trivialize rape and thus overlooks the violation of women inherent in the medieval ideology of romantic love: *Covert Operations,* 218–19.

58. Merivale, *Pan the Goat-God,* 8–9.

59. I see many more of Genius's failings as a confessor than Kinneavy does in "Gower's *Confessio Amantis.*"

60. Payer, "Sex and Confession," 127.

61. John Mirk, *Instructions for Parish Priests,* lines 223 and 230–31.

62. MED "gropen" 5(b) and 5(c).

63. One of the most recent critics to argue this case is Wallace, *Chaucerian Polity,* 337–78. As an illustration of Richard II's hot temper, Wallace cites an incident, recorded in the *Westminster Chronicle,* that took place in 1385 on board the royal barge: the king drew his sword on the archbishop of Canterbury, who was then forced to kneel and to beg forgiveness (347). See also Astell, *Political Allegory,* 95–100.

64. In this context, see the discussion of "Cupid's Bohemian Court" in Book VIII of *Confessio* in Hanrahan, "Speaking of Sodomy," 444–45.

65. Jaeger, *Ennobling Love,* 20.

4. SEXUAL CHAOS AND SEXUAL SIN

1. Lochrie, *Covert Operations*, 177–27, esp. 225.

2. Ibid., 223–24.

3. See the Introduction, n. 40.

4. Macaulay, for example, describes this digression as "ill-advised," arguing that, if it had to occur at all, it should have occurred much earlier, and concluding that "the awkwardness of putting it all into the mouth of the priest of Venus is inexcusable" (Gower, *English Works*, 1:515 n. 729).

5. For an examination of Amans's religion of love that argues for the lover's "conversion" in Book VIII, see, Gallacher, *Love, the Word, and Mercury*.

6. Tinkle, *Medieval Venuses and Cupids*, 184.

7. For the link between femininity and sodomy, see Alain de Lille, *De Planctu Naturae*, metrum I and passim. See also Keiser, *Courtly Desire*, esp. 85; and Lochrie, *Covert Operations*, 189. On the link between perversion and femininity in the *Roman de la Rose*, see 20058–66; and Kay, "Birth of Venus," 25.

8. *Cleanness*, 695–96; quoted from *Sir Gawain and the Green Knight, Pearl, Cleanness, Patience*, ed. Anderson.

9. In this context, see the discussion of Venus in Lochrie, *Covert Operations*, 177–27, esp. 209–11.

10. Lochrie, *Covert Operations*, 211 and 225.

11. Donavin, *Incest Narratives*, 25.

12. Reference is to John Milton, *Paradise Lost*, ed. Fowler. On Gower's sources and the parallels with Milton, see Steadman, "Grosseteste on the Genealogy of Sin and Death"; and Steadman, "Milton and St Basil."

13. Kay, "Birth of Venus," 9. Kay cites representative examples of this birth narrative in an appendix to her article, 29–37.

14. Tinkle discusses Venus's birth in the context of other works; e.g., *Medieval Venuses and Cupids*, 83–84.

15. Kay, "Birth of Venus," 11–15. On Venus generally, see Economou, "The Two Venuses and Courtly Love"; and Tinkle, *Medieval Venuses and Cupids*.

16. Kay, "Birth of Venus," 13–21.

17. Tinkle, *Medieval Venuses and Cupids*, 192.

18. Donavin, *Incest Narratives*, 23.

19. Kay, "Birth of Venus," 21.

20. Ibid., 21.

21. Ibid., 28.

22. On the ambiguity of Nature, see H. White, *Nature, Sex, and Goodness*, 174–219.

23. This, of course, echoes Alain de Lille, *De Planctu Naturae*, metrum I.

24. Tinkle, *Medieval Venuses and Cupids*, 191.

25. MED s.v. "ravin(e)" 1(a): "robbery, rapine"; and 1(d): "forcible seizing of a woman, rape."

26. Rubin, "Traffic in Women."

27. Dinshaw, "Rivalry, Rape, and Manhood," 134. See also Sedgwick, *Between Men*;

and Irigaray, "Women on the Market" and "Commodities Among Themselves," in *The Sex Which Is Not One*, 170–91 and 192–97.

28. Dinshaw, "Rivalry, Rape, and Manhood," 138.

29. Ibid., 136–40.

30. Fanger, "Magic and the Metaphysics of Gender," 218.

31. Jocelyn Wogan-Browne opens her essay on the chaste female body with reference to male models of chastity, such as Christ, St. John, Galahad, and Perceval: "Chaste Bodies," 24.

32. Dinshaw, "Rivalry, Rape, and Manhood," 138–39.

33. *Troilus and Criseyde*, II.925–30, analyzed in Dinshaw, "Rivalry, Rape, and Manhood," 139–41; *The Parliament of Fowls*, 392–665, analyzed by Chatten, "'With Diverse Spieces.'"

34. Dinshaw, "Rivalry, Rape, and Manhood," 135.

35. Even before her transformation, Philomela is compared to a bird (e.g., at V.5700).

36. In this context, see the famous essay by Patricia Klindienst, "The Voice of the Shuttle," and also Jane Marcus's discussion of Virginia Woolf's adaptation of the Procne and Philomela myth, in "Liberty, Sorority, Misogyny," 88–89.

37. Dinshaw, "Rivalry, Rape, and Manhood," 139.

38. Ibid., 140.

39. Ibid., 138.

40. Gower also omits Ovid's description of Philomela throwing the child's head into Tereus's face: *Metamorphoses*, VI.656–59.

41. On the role of the five senses as servants to reason and guardians of the soul, see, for example, *Sawles Warde*, 1–25. Reference is to *Medieval English Prose for Women*, ed. Millett and Wogan-Browne.

42. Woolf, "Moral Chaucer and Kindly Gower," 228–29; H. White, "Sympathetic Villain," 223–28.

43. MED s.v. "lust." This line is cited under 3(c): "a woman's attractions, charms"; but for the sexual connotations of the word, see also 2(c): "sexual gratification."

44. See, for example, Gallacher, *Love, the Word, and Mercury*, 36.

45. In the Latin commentary to this tale (at I.763), no moral distinction seems to be drawn between the priests and Mundus. For the gap between commentary and text in this instance, see H. White, "Sympathetic Villain," 224–25 and n. 6.

46. Gallacher suggests that Mundus also represents *Verbum*, or the Word: *Love, the Word, and Mercury*, 35.

47. Simpson, *Sciences and the Self*, 134–229, esp. 216.

48. For a full list, see Gallacher, *Love, the Word, and Mercury*, 26–43. Gallacher analyzes examples of the annunciation pattern in this chapter.

49. For Gower's sources of the story of the birth of Alexander, see Beidler, ed., *John Gower's Literary Transformations*, part 2, 79–141.

50. Fanger, "Signs of Power," 302–03.

51. On Gower's ambivalent attitude to the power of magic, which is not viewed as inherently sinful and seemingly can be used for good as well as evil, see Fanger, "Signs of Power," 278–318.

52. Fanger, "Magic and Metaphysics," 210–11.

53. An alternative name for the god is Ammon, an African name for Jove: see Fanger, "Signs of Power," 278–318, esp. 303 n. 24.

54. Gallacher, *Love, the Word, and Mercury,* 41 and 42; cf. Fanger, "Signs of Power," 309.

55. Dinshaw, "Rivalry, Rape, and Manhood," 138.

56. Kay, "Birth of Venus," 26.

57. Tinkle, *Medieval Venuses and Cupids,* 195.

58. Tinkle does however note that Venus and Cupid play a role in the lover's cure: *Medieval Venuses and Cupids,* 192–95. See also H. White, *Nature, Sex, and Goodness,* 205–06, and 219.

5. TYRANNY, REFORM, AND SELF-GOVERNMENT

1. Dean, *World Grown Old,* 257.

2. Ibid., 255.

3. See *Jerome's Commentary on Daniel,* trans. Archer, 30–33.

4. Dean, *World Grown Old,* 257–58; Fredell, "Reading the Dream Miniature," 64.

5. Peck, "John Gower and the Book of Daniel," 174.

6. See J. Griffiths, *"Confessio Amantis"*; Fredell, "Reading the Dream Miniature"; and Emmerson, "Reading Gower."

7. Emmerson, "Reading Gower," 170,

8. Ibid., 167–70.

9. Fredell, "Reading the Dream Miniature," 64; see Doob, *Nebuchadnezzar's Children,* 63.

10. Gower himself sees Richard in terms of this tradition in the final version of the *Confessio Amantis* Col. 16–18: Fredell, "Reading the Dream Miniature," 69. Fredell also notes that revised glosses and passages in *Confessio* (specifically the glosses at Prol.94 and 194, and revisions to Prol.495–98 and 579–84) "identify specific events in Richard's reign with the historical low point in morality and good governance epitomized by Gower's application of Daniel's prophecy" (69 and 89 n. 35).

11. Fredell, "Reading the Dream Miniature," 83. As noted in the Introduction, Emmerson is not convinced and argues instead that the placement and form of miniatures reflects changing reading practices: "Reading Gower," 169.

12. See Kantorowicz, *The King's Two Bodies,* esp. 24–41 (on Shakespeare's portrayal of Richard II). Nigel Saul, however, suggests that by the fourteenth century, and Richard's reign in particular, emphasis was placed on the "personal and outward marks of autocracy" rather than on the sanctity of kingship, and that consequently "it became more difficult than before to distinguish the man from his kingly persona": *Richard II,* 446. For a recent reassessment of *The King's Two Bodies,* see Norbrook, "The Emperor's New Body?"

13. Salisbury, "Remembering Origins," 174.

14. Gower, *Major Latin Works,* 459 n. 1.

15. Salisbury, "Remembering Origins," 174.

16. For the argument that the apocalypticism is developed in the Lancastrian Prologue, see Mahoney, "Gower's Two Prologues," 33.

17. Peck, "John Gower and the Book of Daniel," 180.

18. Whiting and Whiting, *Proverbs, Sentences, and Proverbial Phrases*, P393.

19. Doob, *Nebuchadnezzar's Children*, 89.

20. For an overview of Gower's sources for the Alexander narratives, see Hamilton, "Studies in the Sources of Gower," esp. 504–16; and Mainzer, "A Study of the Sources of the *Confessio Amantis* of John Gower," 52–56, 57–59, 123–30, 157–62, and 166–68.

21. See Porter, "Gower's Ethical Microcosm." The Pseudo-Aristotle and Giles of Rome were translated into English in the later Middle Ages. See *Three Prose Versions of the Secreta Secretorum*, ed. Steele; *Secretum Secretorum*, ed. Manzalaoui; and Giles of Rome, *The Governance of Kings and Princes*. For Brunetto Latini's text, see *Li Livres dou Trésor*.

22. For an analysis of the relationship between this tale and its Latin gloss, see Batchelor, "Feigned Truth and Exemplary Method," 10–15.

23. Oxford, New College MS c.266, fol. 68r; and New York, Pierpont Morgan Library MS M.126, fol. 65r. Cf. Braeger, "Illustrations," 290 and fig. 7; and Eberle, "Miniatures as Evidence," 337 and fig. 6.

24. Porter, "Gower's Ethical Microcosm," 158.

25. Grady, "Lancastrian Gower," 561 n. 33.

26. Simpson, *Sciences and the Self*, 211.

27. Porter, "Gower's Ethical Microcosm," 140 and 146. In *Vox Clamantis* there is a key reference to Alexander as one who could not overcome the immoral teaching of his youth (VI.631–36). It is unclear whether this refers to the instruction by Nectanabus or Aristotle.

28. Contemporary readers evidently considered this section significant. As Eberle notes, Book VII as a whole, and the section on astronomy and astrology in particular, is more fully illustrated than the rest of Pierpont Morgan Library MS M.126: "Miniatures as Evidence," 320–24. She believes that "in concentrating by far the largest proportion of miniatures in Book VII, the program of Morgan M.126 is faithful to Gower's own estimation of its special importance" (322).

29. Simpson, *Sciences and the Self*, 297. Nectanabus must also have failed, as he too instructed Alexander about astronomy and astrology (VI.2289–94 and VII.1290–1438). Theresa Tinkle states that the Tale of Nectanabus "acknowledges and denounces the power of astrology" prior to Book VII (*Medieval Venuses and Cupids*, 185).

30. Cary, *The Medieval Alexander*, 99–100, 218–20, and 231–33; Cary also discusses Gower (253–55). See Quintus Curtius Rufus, *History of Alexander*, VI.2.1–5, VI.5.23, and VI.5.29–32. Reference is to the edition by Bardon and the translation by Yardley. For Petrarch, see Cary, "Petrarch and Alexander the Great," 48–49. I am grateful to Telfryn Pritchard for discussing with me the medieval legends of Alexander.

31. Cf. *In Praise of Peace*, 281–87 (Gower, *English Works*, 2:489).

32. Simpson, *Sciences and the Self*, 294 n. 21.

33. Grady, "Lancastrian Gower," 562 n. 34. See also Hanrahan, "Speaking of Sodomy," 438–41.

34. Gower's major sources for the Tales of Tarquin and Arrons and Lucrece are Ovid, *Fasti*, II.685–852, and *Livy*, I.liii.4–lx.4. All references to Ovid's *Fasti* are to the edition and translation by Frazer. All references to Livy are to the edition and translation by Foster. For an edition and sixteenth-century translation of Boccaccio's *De Claris Mulieribus*, see *Forty-Six Lives*, trans. Parker, ed. Wright. See also Augustine's influential analysis of the dilemma of Lucretia in *The City of God Against the Pagans*, I.xix. For analyses of this and other versions, see Weiher, "Chaucer's and Gower's Stories"; Donaldson, *Rapes of Lucretia*; and Bertolet, "From Revenge to Reform," 407–11. See also C. Mainzer, "John Gower's Use of the 'Mediaeval Ovid,'" 222–23.

35. Cf. Ovid, *Fasti*, II.807–09; *Livy*, I.lviii.4.

36. Bertolet, "From Revenge to Reform," 412.

37. Ibid., 414.

38. Contrast *Livy*, in which Lucretia demands vengeance (I.lviii.10), and Ovid's *Fasti*, in which her spirit ratifies Brutus's vow to take revenge (II.845–46).

39. See Peck, *Kingship and Common Profit*, 156.

40. Donaldson notes that in the classical versions of this narrative, Collatinus, Lucretius, and the Romans are condemned as effeminate (for their failure to act), while Lucretia is praised for her manly self-sacrifice: *Rapes of Lucretia*, 10.

41. Scanlon, *Narrative, Authority, and Power*, 294. *Livy*, I.lx.4.

42. Bertolet, "From Revenge to Reform," 416–17.

43. Ibid., 417.

44. Ibid., 418.

45. *Livy*, III.xliv.1–lviii.11.

46. Bullón-Fernández, *Fathers and Daughters*, 146.

47. Weiher, "Chaucer's and Gower's Stories," 8.

48. In *Livy*, Virginia's ghost is only laid to rest after vengeance has been done: III.lviii.11.

49. *Livy*, III.xlviii.5.

50. Bullón-Fernández, *Fathers and Daughters*, 151–57.

51. Ibid., 153.

52. MED s.v. "riote" 1(c): "a lecherous disposition."

53. Ferster, *Fictions of Advice*, 121. See also Scanlon, *Narrative, Authority, and Power*, 295, and Bullón-Fernández, *Fathers and Daughters*, 154. Ferster also looks at the contemporary political significance of the qualifying phrase "of hem alle" (VII.5294): *Fictions of Advice*, 121–22.

54. Ferster, *Fictions of Advice*, 121.

55. Scanlon, *Narrative, Authority, and Power*, 282–97.

56. Scanlon, *Narrative, Authority, and Power*, 286. Simpson argues that Gower's model of kingship is "consensual" and "constitutionalist": *Sciences and the Self*, 284; but these claims are challenged by David Aers in "Reflections," 104 n. 9. See also Blythe, *Ideal Government and the Mixed Constitution*.

57. In his review of Ferster's book, John Watts argues (475) that, even in the late fourteenth and early fifteenth centuries, "counsel was an uncontroversial matter: everyone knew the basic rules and stating them—particularly in a literary format—was unlikely to be a subversive act."

58. Ferster, *Fictions of Advice*, 112.

59. Scanlon, *Narrative, Authority, and Power*, 293.

6. Oedipus, Apollonius, and Richard II

1. See the preface to Derrida, *Of Grammatology*, lxxxiv.

2. Middleton, "William Langland's 'Kynde Name,'" 27.

3. Middleton, "William Langland's 'Kynde Name,'" 24; Huizinga, *The Waning of the Middle Ages*, 233.

4. Tinkle, *Medieval Venuses and Cupids*, 178–97, esp. 179.

5. See Constans, *La Légende d'Oedipe*; Rank, *The Incest Theme in Literature and Legend*, 271–99, and 300–37; Edmunds, "Oedipus in the Middle Ages"; and Archibald, "Sex and Power in Thebes and Babylon." See also Archibald's *Incest and the Medieval Imagination*.

6. All references to the *Historia Apollonii* are to Elizabeth Archibald's parallel Latin text and modern English translation: *Apollonius of Tyre*, 112–79.

7. Scanlon, "The Riddle of Incest."

8. Archibald, *Apollonius of Tyre*, 29.

9. For a concise overview of the ambiguities of the riddle, see Scanlon, "The Riddle of Incest," 124–25.

10. MED s.v. "privete" 1(d) and 1(g). Significantly "privete" can also mean "a relative": MED s.v. "privete" 4. See also MED s.v. "touchen" 6.

11. MED s.v. "fare" 8(a) and 4.

12. Scanlon, "The Riddle of Incest"; and cf. Donavin, *Incest Narratives*, esp. 71–72. See also Watson, "The Monstrosity of the Moral Pig," 20–21.

13. Archibald, *Apollonius of Tyre*, 112–13.

14. Ibid.

15. Gower significantly reduces the role of Thaise's nurse, thus making the parallel more explicit: see Archibald, *Apollonius of Tyre*, 142–45.

16. See *Suetonius*, IV.24, ed. and trans. Rolfe; 2 Samuel 13:5–14; Genesis 19:32–36.

17. See, for example, Bynum, *Holy Feast and Holy Fast*; Purkiss, *The Witch in History*, 277–81.

18. Archibald, *Apollonius of Tyre*, 114–15.

19. See Goolden, "Antiochus's Riddle," 248.

20. Ibid., 249.

21. Freud, "Parapraxes," 96–99.

22. Scanlon, "The Riddle of Incest," 125.

23. Freud argues that father fixations are usually caused by the displacement of feelings for the mother: see Freud, "A Seventeenth-Century Demonological Neurosis," 406. For Freud's association of mother fixations with homosexuality, see "The Psychogenesis of a Case of Homosexuality in a Woman," 230.

24. Archibald notes the possibility that in the early sources Apollonius may actually have been Antiochus's son: *Apollonius of Tyre*, 17 and n. 33.

25. Irigaray, "Women on the Market," in *This Sex Which Is Not One*, 170–191, at 171. Cf. also Sedgwick, *Between Men*, esp. 1–2.

26. Bullón-Fernández, *Fathers and Daughters*, 14. Cf. Judith Butler who argues that "The resolution of the oedipal complex affects gender identification through not only the incest taboo, but, prior to that, the taboo against homosexuality. The result is that one identifies with the same-sexed object of love, thereby internalizing both the aim and object of homosexual cathexis": *Gender Trouble*, 63.

27. Bullón-Fernández, *Fathers and Daughters*, 15.

28. Irigaray, "Commodities among Themselves," in *This Sex Which Is Not One*, 192–97, at 192–93.

29. Ibid., 192.

30. Freud sees megalomania as a form of narcissism: "On Narcissism," 67.

31. On the double as "the uncanny harbinger of death," see Freud, "The Uncanny," 356–57.

32. Gower, *English Works*, 2:538 n.

33. Freud, *Totem and Taboo*, 77. Freud views the persecution complex as another form of megalomania: "The Libido Theory and Narcissism," 471.

34. Freud, "A Seventeenth-Century Demonological Neurosis," 405–08; "The Uncanny," 353–54 and note.

35. Propp, "Oedipus," 110.

36. Archibald, *Apollonius of Tyre*, 142–43.

37. Cf. Freud, "The Uncanny," 353 note.

38. The relationship between the two men described here can be understood in terms of the courtly phenomenon that C. Stephen Jaeger terms "charismatic friendship": *Ennobling Love*, 36–41.

39. Archibald, *Apollonius of Tyre*, 124–25; cf. 72–75.

40. Bullón-Fernández remarks that "the game has homoerotic connotations": *Fathers and Daughters*, 50. She also notes that Genius suppresses any hint of homosexuality, *Fathers and Daughters*, 16.

41. Archibald, *Apollonius of Tyre*, 75–76.

42. Jordan, *Invention of Sodomy*, 14, 81.

43. See Freud's famous discussion in *The Interpretation of Dreams*, 362–66.

44. See Fanger, "Magic and Metaphysics of Gender."

45. Scanlon, "The Riddle of Incest," 118–27.

46. There is a similar description in the reconciliation scene between Constance's son and his father in the Tale of Constance: II.1381–82. For a discussion of the treatment of the theme of incest in this tale, see Bullón-Fernández, *Fathers and Daughters*, 75–101, esp. 97. See also Archibald, "The Flight from Incest"; and Wetherbee, "Constance and the World."

47. Archibald, *Apollonius of Tyre*, 150–51.

48. Scanlon, "The Riddle of Incest," 118.

49. Ibid., 120.

50. Teresa de Lauretis, "Desire in Narrative."

51. Ibid., 109.

52. *Le roman d'Apollonius de Tyr*, ed. Zink, 13–58, esp. 25–26.

53. The equivalent miniatures (possibly three in total) seem to have been removed from Oxford, New College MS c.266, fol. 178r.

54. Peter C. Braeger argues that many of the illustrations in the New College manuscript represent a character encountering his or her alter ego: "Illustrations," 290. The same might be said of this remarkably symmetrical illustration, in which Antiochus encounters his double: the two male figures flank the woman and the corpses, and their stances, facial expressions, hand gestures, and even the angles of their heads are mirrored in one another.

55. Eberle, "Miniatures as Evidence," 340–41.

56. Goolden, "Antiochus's Riddle," 245 and 247 n. 3.

57. Freud, "Femininity," 146.

58. de Lauretis, "Desire in Narrative," 110.

59. Propp, "Oedipus," 109.

60. Archibald, *Apollonius of Tyre*, 136–37.

61. Ibid., 162–67.

62. Ibid., 150–51.

63. Cf. ibid., 170–71.

64. de Lauretis, "Desire in Narrative," esp. 136–55.

65. Scanlon, "The Riddle of Incest," 117–18, 120–24.

66. Steele, *Richard II*. Steele believes that by the time of his deposition, Richard had lost his sanity. See also McKisack, *The Fourteenth Century*, 424–98, esp. 497.

67. Steele, *Richard II*, 39.

68. V. H. Galbraith offers an important critique of this analysis: "A New Life of Richard II." See also J. Taylor, "Richard II's Views on Kingship," 200.

69. Saul, *Richard II*, 459–62. However Saul also warns: "In forming a view of Richard's career, it should not be supposed that we are studying the working out of a neurosis," *Richard II*, 464.

70. Walsingham, *Historia Anglicana*, 2:148. See Stow, "Richard II in Thomas Walsingham's Chronicles."

71. Porter, "Gower's Ethical Microcosm," 160.

72. Ibid., 160.

73. Peck, *Kingship and Common Profit*, 171; Bullón-Fernández, *Fathers and Daughters*, 45–64.

74. Porter, "Gower's Ethical Microcosm," 152.

75. Simpson, *Sciences and the Self*, 297–98.

76. Archibald, *Apollonius of Tyre*, 18–22.

77. Bullón-Fernández, *Fathers and Daughters*, 23; for her analysis of Antiochus, see 48–50 and 59–61.

78. Ibid., 21. Cf. Jones, *The Royal Policy of Richard II*, 167; Saul, *Richard II*, 366; Staley, "Gower, Richard II, Henry of Derby," 79.

79. Strohm, "Queens as Intercessors," in his *Hochon's Arrow*, 95–119; Saul, *Richard II*, 11–12, 51, 455–57; A. Taylor, "Anne of Bohemia and the Making of Chaucer"; Wallace, *Chaucerian Polity*, 355–70; and Thomas, *Anne's Bohemia*. Particularly useful is Strohm's

discussion of the way in which fictional figures may have reminded contemporary audiences of historical figures, not because they actually represented or symbolized them, but because of "a recognition of the environment of interpretative structures" common to both ("Queens as Intercessors," 116).

    80. Wallace, *Chaucerian Polity,* 295–98.

    81. Cf. E. Allen, "Chaucer Answers Gower," 633.

    82. Saul, *Richard II,* esp. 108–34, 176–204, and 366–404; Ferster, *Fictions of Advice,* 108–34, esp. 119.

    83. Scanlon, "The Riddle of Incest," 121.

    84. Cf. Simpson, *Sciences and the Self,* 283–84.

    85. Bullón-Fernández, *Fathers and Daughters,* 63.

    86. For the opposite view, see E. Allen, "Chaucer Answers Gower," 637.

    87. Porter, "Gower's Ethical Microcosm," 146.

    88. Hanrahan argues that Gower "has reproduced himself" as a potentially bad adviser to the king ("Speaking of Sodomy," 443).

EPILOGUE

    1. This colophon appears at the end of *Confessio Amantis* as it appears in Macaulay's edition, Gower, *English Works,* 2:479–80. The main variations, but not all variants, are reproduced by Fisher, *John Gower,* appendix a, 311–12, who also translates them (88–91). The earliest form of this colophon also appears in the earliest versions of *Vox Clamantis.*

    2. Pearsall, "Gower's Latin," 24. Cf. Pearsall, "Gower Tradition," 183. Fisher notes, however, that at least one of the changes in an "interim" version of the colophon must be scribal as it appears to have been written after Gower's death: *John Gower,* 90.

    3. The extent to which Richard II is held responsible for the Peasants' Revolt, or exonerated from blame because of his youth, varies considerably in the different versions of this colophon.

    4. For these variations, see the text and textual apparatus: Gower, *English Works,* 2:480; and Pearsall, "Gower's Latin," 24–25. In revising the colophon, Gower also takes out lines explaining that in *Confessio* he has compiled the exemplary narratives from a variety of historical, poetic, and literary sources.

    5. Pearsall, "Gower Tradition," 183.

    6. Ibid., 183. These poems are found in Gower, *Latin Works,* 343–68.

    7. For the parallel between Gower and Langland, see Middleton, "The Idea of Public Poetry."

    8. See, for example, Pearsall, "Gower Tradition," 182–83.

    9. See Pearsall, "Gower Tradition," 183–84; and Doyle and Parkes, "The Production of Copies," 201. For examples of uniformity in the production of Lydgate's poetry, see also, Scott, "Lydgate's *Lives of Saints Edmund and Fremund.*"

    10. Fisher, *John Gower,* esp. 121 and 135–36.

    11. Pearsall, "Gower Tradition," 183.

    12. Pearsall, "Gower's Latin," 24.

13. Ibid., 25.
14. Pearsall, "Gower Tradition," 182–83.
15. Iser, *The Act of Reading*, 180–231.
16. Gower, *English Works*, 2:549–50 n.
17. Gower, *Latin Works*, 361; translated by Fisher, *John Gower*, 4.
18. Pearsall, "Gower's Latin," 24.
19. Tatlock, "The Epilog of Chaucer's *Troilus*."
20. Strohm, "Note," 295.
21. Minnis, "'Moral Gower'"; "John Gower, *Sapiens*"; and "*De Vulgari*." See also Butterfield, "Articulating the Author." Locating *Confessio Amantis* within French traditions, Butterfield argues for the originality of Gower's authorial representations.
22. Manzalaoui, "'Noght in the Registre of Venus.'"
23. Simpson, *Sciences and the Self*, esp. 134–66. Cf. Minnis, "*De Vulgari*," 51–65.
24. See Echard, "With Carmen's Help," 39. Echard argues that no single voice is more authoritative than any other in the poem.
25. Strohm, "Note," 296.
26. Translation by Echard, "With Carmen's Help," 32. This distinction is reiterated in a gloss at IV.1454, which states that the opinion expressed is not true, and therefore (by implication) not that of the author "set opinio Amantum" (but the opinion of lovers).
27. Minnis, "*De Vulgari*," 52–53.
28. Strohm, "Note," 297. Minnis himself acknowledges that Gower's authorial voice and his persona do become confused at the end of the poem: "*De Vulgari*," 56–58.
29. Dean, *World Grown Old*, 233–70, at 267.
30. See Burrow, "Portrayal of Amans," 11; and Garbáty, "Description." Of related interest is the article by Wright, "Author Portraits."
31. For the argument that the youthful Amans depicts Gower in his prime, as he appears in his (extensively restored) tomb in Southwark Cathedral, see Garbáty, "Description," 335–39.
32. Oxford, Bodleian Library MS Fairfax 3, fol. 8v. For an analysis, see Garbáty, "Description," 331–32 and 335; cf. n. 7 and n. 13. Kathleen L. Scott argues that this confessor miniature may correspond to Gower's own conception of the illustration: *Later Gothic Manuscripts*, 110.
33. Yeager, *John Gower's Poetic*, 230–79; Olsson, *John Gower*, 35–36.
34. Dean, *World Grown Old*, 263.
35. Middleton, "The Idea of Public Poetry," 110. On Genius as a divided counselor, see Olsson, *John Gower*, 23–24
36. See Baker, "The Priesthood of Genius"; Economou, "The Character Genius"; Nitzsche, *The Genius Figure*, 115–36; and H. White, *Nature, Sex, and Goodness*, 174–219, esp. 211–15.
37. Strohm, "Note," 296.
38. Dean, *World Grown Old*, 267.
39. Ibid., 270.
40. Coffman, "John Gower, Mentor for Royalty," 953.
41. Aers, "Reflections."

42. Yeager, "*Pax Poetica*"; Aers, "Reflections," 105–11.

43. Scanlon, *Narrative, Authority, and Power*, 245–97; Aers, "Reflections," 111–18.

44. Aers, "Reflections," 103; Minnis, "'Moral Gower'" and "John Gower, *Sapiens*"; Yeager, *John Gower's Poetic*; Olsson, *John Gower*; Simpson, *Sciences and the Self*. In this context, see also Peck, *Kingship and Common Profit*. For an alternative view, see Bullón-Fernández, *Fathers and Daughters*.

45. Aers, "Reflections," 115.

46. Ibid., 118.

47. Strohm, "Form and Social Statement"; "Politics and Poetics"; and *Social Chaucer*.

48. Strohm, "Form and Social Statement," 38.

49. Ibid., 27.

50. Ibid., 30.

51. Ibid., 29.

52. Ibid., 35.

53. Aers, "Reflections," 110–11 and 116.

54. Ibid., 110.

55. Ibid., 110. Aers draws a distinction between Gower's poetic technique and that of Langland. I believe they are closer than he allows. See Middleton, "Narrative and the Invention of Experience."

56. For Amans as a reader, see Simpson, *Sciences and the Self*, 252–71; E. Allen, "Chaucer Answers Gower," 634–35; and Robins, "Romance, Exemplum, and the Subject," esp. 163–65.

57. Tinkle, *Medieval Venuses and Cupids*, 178–97, esp. 187; Echard, "With Carmen's Help," passim; E. Allen, "Chaucer Answers Gower," 647 and n. 44; Olsson, "Reading, Transgression, and Judgement."

58. See, for example, Batchelor, "Feigned Truth and Exemplary Method," 10.

59. Minnis, "*De Vulgari*," 65.

60. Trans. Echard, "With Carmen's Help," 29.

61. Minnis, "*De Vulgari*," 62; cf. Pearsall "Gower's Latin," 21.

62. Echard, "With Carmen's Help," 29.

Bibliography

Abbreviations

MED   *Middle English Dictionary,* ed. Hans Kurath et al. 13 vols. (Ann Arbor, MI: University of Michigan Press, 1956–99).

OED   *The Oxford English Dictionary,* 2nd ed., ed. J. A. Simpson and E. S. C. Weiner, 20 vols. (Oxford: Clarendon Press, 1989).

Manuscripts

London, British Library MS Add. Harley 3869.
New York, Pierpont Morgan Library MS M.126.
Oxford, Bodleian Library MS Fairfax 3.
Oxford, New College MS c.266.
San Marino, California, Huntington Library MS Ellesmere 26.A.17.

Primary Texts

Alain de Lille. *Anticlaudianus.* Ed. R. Bossuat. Paris: Librairie de Philosophique J. Vrin, 1955.
———. *Anticlaudianus.* Trans. James J. Sheridan. Toronto: Pontifical Institute of Mediaeval Studies, 1973.
———. "De Planctu Naturae." Ed. Nikolaus M. Häring. *Studi medievali,* series 3, 19 (1978): 797–879.
———. *The Plaint of Nature.* Trans. James J. Sheridan. Toronto: Pontifical Institute of Mediaeval Studies, 1980.
Aquinas, St. Thomas. *Temperance.* Vol. 43 of *Summa Theologiae,* ed. and trans. Thomas Gilby (London: Blackfriars, 1964–76).

Augustine. *The City of God Against the Pagans*. Vol. 1. Ed. and trans. George E. McCracken. Loeb Classical Library. London: Heinemann, 1957.

Barclay, Alexander. *The Mirrour of Good Maners*. London: John Cawood, 1570. Reprint, Manchester: Spenser Society, 1885.

———. *The Life of St. George*. Ed. William Nelson. EETS o.s. 230. Oxford: Oxford University Press, 1955.

Boccaccio, Giovanni. *Forty-Six Lives [De Claris Mulieribus]*, trans. Henry Parker, Lord Morley, ed. Herbert G. Wright, EETS 214. London: Oxford University Press, 1943.

Boethius: De Consolatione Philosophiae. Trans. John Walton. Ed. Mark Science. EETS 170. London: Oxford University Press, 1927.

The Book of Vices and Virtues. Ed. W. Nelson Francis. EETS o.s. 217. London: Oxford University Press, 1942.

Catullus. Ed. and trans. Francis Warre Cornish. Rev. G. P. Goold. Loeb Classical Library. London: Heinemann, 1988.

Caxton, William. *Caxton's Book of Curtesye*. Ed. Frederick J. Furnivall. EETS e.s. 3. London: Trübner: 1868.

Chaucer, Geoffrey. *The Riverside Chaucer*. Ed. Larry D. Benson. Oxford: Oxford University Press, 1988.

Chrétien de Troyes. "Perceval: The Story of the Grail." In *Arthurian Romances*, trans. D. D. R. Owen, 394–495. London: Everyman, 1993.

Dante Alighieri. *The Divine Comedy*. Ed. and trans. Geoffrey L. Bickersteth. Oxford: Basil Blackwell, 1981.

Giles of Rome. *The Governance of Kings and Princes: John Trevisa's Middle English Translation of the De regimine principum of Aegidius Romanus*. Ed. David C. Fowler, Charles F. Briggs, and Paul G. Remley. New York: Garland, 1997.

Gower, John. *The French Works of John Gower*. Ed. G. C. Macaulay. Oxford: Clarendon Press, 1899.

———. *The English Works of John Gower*. Ed. G. C. Macaulay. EETS e.s. 81, 82. London: Kegan Paul, Trench, Trübner, 1900–01. Reprint Oxford: Oxford University Press, 1979.

———. *The Latin Works of John Gower*. Ed. G. C. Macaulay. Oxford: Clarendon Press, 1902.

———. *The Major Latin Works of John Gower*. Trans. Eric W. Stockton. Seattle: University of Washington Press, 1962.

———. *The Latin Verses in the Confessio Amantis: An Annotated Translation*. Ed. and trans. Siân Echard and Claire Fanger. East Lansing: Colleagues Press, 1991.

———. *Mirour de l'Omme (The Mirror of Mankind)*. Trans. William Burton Wilson. Rev. Nancy Wilson Van Baak. East Lansing: Colleagues Press, 1992.

Guillaume de Lorris and Jean de Meun. *Le Roman de la Rose*. Ed. Ernest Langlois. 5 vols. Société de Anciens Textes Français. Paris: Firmin-Didot, 1914–24.

———. *The Romance of the Rose*. Trans. Frances Horgan. Oxford: Oxford University Press, 1994.

Hoccleve, Thomas. *Hoccleve's Works*. Vol. 3. Ed. Frederick J. Furnivall. EETS e.s. 72. London: Kegan Paul, Trench, Trübner, 1987.

Jerome's Commentary on Daniel. Trans. Gleason L. Archer Jr. Grand Rapids, MI: Baker Book House, 1958.

Latini, Brunetto. *Li Livres dou Trésor de Brunetto Latini.* Ed. F. J. Carmody. Berkeley and Los Angeles: University of California Press, 1948.

Livy. Ed. and trans. B. O. Foster. 14 vols. Loeb Classical Library. London: Heinemann, 1919–59.

Medieval English Prose for Women: From the Katherine Group and Ancrene Wisse. Ed. Bella Millett and Jocelyn Wogan-Browne. Oxford: Oxford University Press, 1992.

Milton, John. *Paradise Lost.* Ed. Alastair Fowler. London: Longman, 1971.

Mirk, John. *John Mirk's Instructions for Parish Priests.* Ed. Gillis Kristensson. Lund Studies in English 49. Lund: Gleerup, 1974.

The Old English Riddles of the Exeter Book. Ed. Craig Williamson. Chapel Hill: University of North Carolina Press, 1977.

Ovid. *Metamorphoses.* Ed. and trans. Frank Justus Miller. 2 vols. Loeb Classical Library. London: Heinemann, 1916.

———. *Fasti.* Ed. and trans. James George Frazer. Loeb Classical Library. London: Heinemann, 1959.

Palmer, Thomas. "De translatione sacræ scripturæ in linguam Anglicanam." Printed in Deanesly, *Lollard Bible,* appendix 2, 418–37.

Puttenham, George. *The Arte of English Poesie.* Ed. Gladys Doidge Willcock and Alice Walker. Cambridge: Cambridge University Press, 1936.

Quintilian. *The Institutio Oratoria of Quintilian.* Ed. and trans. H. E. Butler. 4 vols. Loeb Classical Library. London: Heinemann, 1920.

Quintius Curtius Rufus. *Histoires.* Ed. H. Bardon. 2 vols. Paris: Société D'Édition "Les Belles Lettres," 1961–65.

———. *History of Alexander.* Trans. John Yardley. Intro. Waldemar Heckel. Penguin: Harmondsworth, 1984.

Le roman d'Apollonius de Tyr. Ed. Michel Zink. Paris: Union Générale D'Éditions, 1982.

Secretum Secretorum: Nine English Versions. Ed. M. A. Manzalaoui. EETS 276. Oxford: Oxford University Press, 1977.

Sir Gawain and the Green Knight, Pearl, Cleanness, Patience. Ed. J. J. Anderson. London: Everyman, 1996.

Suetonius. Ed. and trans. J. C. Rolfe. 2 vols. Loeb Classical Library. London: Heinemann, 1914.

Three Prose Versions of the Secreta Secretorum. vol. 1. Ed. Robert Steele, EETS e.s. 74. London: Kegan Paul, Trench, Trübner, 1898.

Trevisa, John. "Dialogue between the Lord and the Servant." Extracted in *The Idea of the Vernacular,* ed. Wogan-Browne et al., 130–38.

Vitalis, Orderic. *The Ecclesiastical History of Orderic Vitalis.* Ed. and trans. Marjorie Chibnall. 6 vols. Oxford Medieval Texts. Oxford, Oxford University Press, 1969–80.

Walsingham, Thomas. *Historia Anglicana.* Ed. H. T. Riley. 2 vols. Rolls Series. London: Longman, 1863–64.

Webster, John. *The Duchess of Malfi.* Ed. Elizabeth M. Brennan. London: A. & C. Black, 1993.

SECONDARY TEXTS

Aers, David. *Chaucer, Langland, and the Creative Imagination.* London: Routledge and Kegan Paul, 1980.

———. "*Vox Populi* and the Literature of 1381." In *The Cambridge History of Medieval English Literature,* ed. Wallace, 432–53.

———. "Reflections on Gower as '*Sapiens* in Ethics and Politics.'" In his *Faith, Ethics, and Church: Writing in England, 1360–1409,* 102–18. Cambridge: D.S. Brewer, 2000.

Allen, Elizabeth. "Chaucer Answers Gower: Constance and the Trouble with Reading." *English Literary History* 63 (1997): 627–55.

Allen, Judson Boyce. *The Ethical Poetic of the Later Middle Ages: A Decorum of Convenient Distinction.* Toronto: Toronto University Press, 1982.

Archibald, Elizabeth. "The Flight from Incest: Two Classical Precursors to the Constance Theme." *The Chaucer Review* 20 (1986): 259–72.

———. *Apollonius of Tyre: Medieval and Renaissance Themes and Variations, Including the Text of the Historia Apollonii Regis Tyri with an English Translation.* Cambridge: D.S. Brewer, 1992.

———. *Incest and the Medieval Imagination.* Oxford: Clarendon Press, 2001.

———. "Sex and Power in Thebes and Babylon: Oedipus and Semiramis in Classical and Medieval Texts." *The Journal of Medieval Latin* 11 (2001): 27–49.

Astell, Ann W. *Political Allegory in Late Medieval England.* Ithaca: Cornell University Press, 1999.

Axton, Richard. "Gower—Chaucer's Heir?" In *Chaucer Traditions: Studies in Honour of Derek Brewer,* ed. Ruth Morse and Barry Windeatt, 21–38. Cambridge: Cambridge University Press, 1990.

Baker, Denise N. "The Priesthood of Genius: A Study of the Medieval Tradition," reprinted in *Gower's Confessio Amantis,* ed. Nicholson, 143–57. (First published *Speculum* 51 [1976]: 277–91.)

Bakhtin, Mikhail. *Rabelais and His World.* Trans. Hélène Iswolsky. Cambridge, MA: M.I.T. Press, 1968.

———. *The Dialogic Imagination.* Ed. Michael Holquist. Trans. Caryl Emerson and Michael Holquist. Austin, TX: University of Texas Press, 1981.

Baron, F. Xavier. "Mother and Son in *Sir Perceval of Galles.*" *Papers in Language and Literature* 8 (1972): 3–14.

Barthes, Roland. *S/Z.* Trans. Richard Miller. London: Jonathan Cape, 1975.

———. "The Death of the Author." In *Image-Music-Text.* trans. Stephen Heath, 142–48. London: Fontana, 1977.

Batchelor, Patricia. "Feigned Truth and Exemplary Method in the *Confessio Amantis.*" In *Re-Visioning Gower,* ed. Yeager, 1–15.

Beidler, Peter G., ed. *John Gower's Literary Transformations in the Confessio Amantis: Original Articles and Translations.* (Washington, DC: University Press of America, 1982).

Bennett, Michael J. "The Court of Richard II and the Promotion of Literature." In *Chaucer's England,* ed. Hanawalt, 3–20.

Benson, C. David. "Incest and Moral Poetry in Gower's *Confessio Amantis.*" *The Chaucer Review* 19 (1984): 100–109.

Bertolet, Craig. "From Revenge to Reform: The Changing Face of 'Lucrece' and Its Meaning in Gower's *Confessio Amantis.*" *Philological Quarterly* 70 (1991): 403–21.

Bishop, Ian. "*The Nun's Priest's Tale* and the Liberal Arts." *Review of English Studies*, n.s. 30 (1979): 257–67.

Blake, N. F. "Geoffrey Chaucer: The Critics and the Canon." *Archiv* 221 (1984): 65–79.

———. "Early Printed Editions of *Confessio Amantis.*" *Mediaevalia* 16 (1993 [for 1990]): 289–306.

Bloch, R. Howard. *Etymologies and Genealogies: A Literary Anthology of the French Middle Ages.* Chicago: University of Chicago Press, 1983.

Bloom, Harold. *The Anxiety of Influence: A Theory of Poetry.* New York: Oxford University Press, 1973.

Blythe, James M. *Ideal Government and the Mixed Constitution in the Middle Ages.* Princeton: Princeton University Press, 1992.

Boswell, John. *Christianity, Social Tolerance, and Homosexuality: Gay People in Western Europe from the Beginning of the Christian Era to the Fourteenth Century.* Chicago: University of Chicago Press, 1980.

Braeger, Peter C. "The Illustrations in New College MS. 266 for Gower's Conversion Tales." In *John Gower,* ed. Yeager, 275–309.

Braswell, Mary Flowers. *The Medieval Sinner: Characterization and Confession in the Literature of the English Middle Ages.* Rutherford: Fairleigh Dickinson University Press, 1983.

Brown, Carole Koepke. "The Tale of Deianira and Nessus." In *John Gower's Literary Transformations,* ed. Beidler, 15–19.

Bullón-Fernández, María. *Fathers and Daughters in Gower's Confessio Amantis: Authority, Family, State, and Writing.* Cambridge: D.S. Brewer, 2000.

Burger, Glenn, and Steven. F. Kruger, eds. *Queering the Middle Ages.* Minneapolis: University of Minnesota Press, 2001.

Burrow, J. A. "The Portrayal of Amans in *Confessio Amantis.*" In *Gower's Confessio Amantis,* ed. Minnis, 5–24.

Butler, Judith. *Gender Trouble: Feminism and the Subversion of Identity.* London: Routledge, 1990.

Butterfield, Ardis. "French Culture and the Ricardian Court." In *Essays on Ricardian Literature in Honour of J. A. Burrow,* ed. A. J. Minnis, Charlotte C. Morse, and Thorlac Turville-Petre, 82–120. Oxford: Clarendon Press, 1997.

———. "Articulating the Author: Gower and the French Vernacular Codex." *Yearbook of English Studies* 33 (2003): 79–96.

Bynum, Caroline Walker. *Holy Feast and Holy Fast: The Religious Significance of Food to Medieval Women.* Berkeley: University of California Press, 1987.

Cadden, Joan. *The Meanings of Sex Difference in the Middle Ages: Medicine, Science, and Culture.* Cambridge: Cambridge University Press, 1993.

Camille, Michael. "The Pose of the Queer: Dante's Gaze, Brunetto Latini's Body." In *Queering the Middle Ages,* ed. Burger and Kruger, 57–86.

Cary, George. "Petrarch and Alexander the Great." *Italian Studies* 5 (1950): 43–55.

————. *The Medieval Alexander.* Cambridge: Cambridge University Press, 1956.

Chambers, A. B. "'Sin' and 'Sign' in *Paradise Lost.*" *Huntington Library Quarterly* 26 (1963): 381–82.

Chatten, Nicola. "'With Diverse Spieces'—Eating Death: John Gower's Re-Digestion of an Ovidian Cannibal(istic) Myth." Paper delivered at the conference, Virile Women, Consuming Men: Gender and Monstrous Appetites in the Middle Ages and Renaissance, University of Wales, Aberystwyth, 25–27 April 2000.

Cixous, Hélène. "The Laugh of the Medusa." Trans. K. Cohen and P. Cohen. *Signs* 1 (1976): 875–99.

————. "Sorties: Out and Out: Attacks / Ways Out / Forays." In Hélène Cixous and Catherin Clément, *The Newly Born Woman,* trans. Betsy Wing, intro. Sandra M. Gilbert, 63–132. London: I.B. Tauris, 1996.

Coffman, George R. "John Gower, Mentor for Royalty: Richard II." *PMLA* 69 (1954): 953–64.

————. "John Gower in His Most Significant Role." Reprinted in *Gower's Confessio Amantis,* ed. Nicholson, 40–48. (First published in *Elizabethan Studies and Other Essays in Honor of George F. Reynolds,* ed. George Fullmer Reynolds, University of Colorado Studies B, vol. 2, no. 4 [Boulder, CO: University of Colorado, 1945], 52–61.)

Coleman, Joyce. *Public Reading and the Reading Public in Late Medieval England and France.* Cambridge: Cambridge University Press, 1996.

Colish, Marcia L. "Cosmetic Theology: The Transformations of a Stoic Theme." *Assays* 1 (1981): 3–14.

Constans, L. *La Légende d'Oedipe.* Paris: Maisonneuve, 1881.

Cooper, Helen. "Gender and Personification in *Piers Plowman.*" *Yearbook of Langland Studies* 5 (1991): 31–48.

Copeland, Rita. *Rhetoric, Hermeneutics, and Translation in the Later Middle Ages.* Cambridge: Cambridge University Press, 1991.

Cox, Catherine S. "'Grope wel bihynde': The Subversive Erotics of Chaucer's Summoner." *Exemplaria* 7 (1995): 145–77.

Crane, Susan. "The Writing Lesson of 1381." In *Chaucer's England,* ed. Hanawalt, 201–21.

Craun, Edwin D. *Lies, Slander and Obscenity in Medieval English Literature: Pastoral Rhetoric and the Deviant Speaker.* Cambridge: Cambridge University Press, 1997.

Curtius, Ernst Robert. *European Literature and the Latin Middle Ages.* Trans. Willard R. Trask. London: Routledge, 1953.

Dean, James M. *The World Grown Old in Later Medieval Literature.* Cambridge: Medieval Academy of America, 1997.

Deanesly, Margaret. *The Lollard Bible and Other Medieval Biblical Versions.* Cambridge: Cambridge University Press, 1920.

Derrida, Jacques. *Of Grammatology.* Trans. Gayatri Chakravorty Spivak. Baltimore: The Johns Hopkins University Press, 1976.

de Lauretis, Teresa. "Desire in Narrative." In her *Alice Doesn't: Feminism, Semiotics, Cinema,* 103–57. London: Macmillan, 1984.

Dinshaw, Carolyn. "Rivalry, Rape, and Manhood: Chaucer and Gower." In *Chaucer and Gower,* ed. Yeager, 130–52.

———. *Getting Medieval: Sexualities and Communities, Pre- and Postmodern*. Durham, NC: Duke University Press, 1999.

Donaldson, Ian. *The Rapes of Lucretia: A Myth and Its Transformations*. Oxford: Clarendon Press, 1982.

Donavin, Georgiana. *Incest Narratives and the Structure of Gower's Confessio Amantis*. English Literary Studies Monograph Series 56. Victoria, BC: University of Victoria Press, 1993.

Doob, Penelope B. R. *Nebuchadnezzar's Children: Conventions of Madness in Middle English Literature*. New Haven: Yale University Press, 1974.

Doyle, A. I. "English Books In and Out of Court from Edward III to Henry VII." In *English Court Culture in the Later Middle Ages*, ed. V. J. Scattergood and J. W. Sherborne, 163–81. London: Duckworth, 1983.

Doyle, A. I., and M. B. Parkes. "The Production of Copies of the *Canterbury Tales* and the *Confessio Amantis* in the Early Fifteenth Century." In *Medieval Scribes, Manuscripts, and Libraries: Essays Presented to N. R. Ker*, ed. M. B. Parkes and Andrew G. Watson, 163–210. London: Scolar Press, 1978.

Driver, Martha W. "Printing the *Confessio Amantis*: Caxton's Edition in Context." In *Re-Visioning Gower*, ed. Yeager, 269–304.

Eaglestone, Robert. *Ethical Criticism: Reading After Levinas*. Edinburgh: Edinburgh University Press, 1997.

Eberle, Patricia J. "The Politics of Courtly Style at the Court of Richard II." In *The Spirit of the Court: Selected Proceedings of the Fourth Congress of the International Courtly Literature Society (Toronto 1983)*, ed. Glyn S. Burgess and Roberta A. Taylor, 168–79. Cambridge, D.S. Brewer, 1985.

———. "Miniatures as Evidence of Reading in a Manuscript of *The Confessio Amantis* (Pierpont Morgan MS. M.126)." In *John Gower*, ed. Yeager, 311–64.

Echard, Siân. "Pre-texts: Tables of Contents and the Reading of John Gower's *Confessio Amantis*." *Medium Ævum* 66 (1997): 270–87.

———. *Arthurian Narrative in the Latin Tradition*. Cambridge: Cambridge University Press, 1998.

———. "With Carmen's Help: Latin Authorities in the *Confessio Amantis*." *Studies in Philology* 95 (1998): 1–40.

———. "Designs for Reading: Some Manuscripts of Gower's *Confessio Amantis*." *Trivium* 31 (1999): 59–72.

———. "Glossing Gower: In Latin, in English, and *in absentia*: The Case of Bodleian Ashmole 35." In *Re-Visioning Gower*, ed. Yeager, 237–56.

———. "Dialogues and Monologues: Manuscript Representations of the Conversation of the *Confessio Amantis*." In *Middle English Poetry: Texts and Traditions*, ed. A. J. Minnis, 57–75. Woodbridge, Suffolk: York Medieval Texts, 2001.

Economou, Georges. "The Two Venuses and Courtly Love." In *The Pursuit of Perfection: Courtly Love and Medieval Literature*, ed. Joan M. Ferrante and G. Economou, 17–50. Port Washington, NY, and London: Kennikat Press, 1975.

———. "The Character Genius in Alan de Lille, Jean de Meun, and John Gower." Reprinted in *Gower's Confessio Amantis*, ed. Nicholson, 109–16. (First published in *Chaucer Review* 4 [1970]: 203–10.)

16

BIBLIOGRAPHY

Edmunds, Lowell. "Oedipus in the Middle Ages." *Antike und Abendland* 22 (1976): 140–55.

Edwards, A. S. G. "Selection and Subversion in Gower's *Confessio Amantis.*" In *Re-Visioning Gower,* ed. Yeager, 257–68.

Edwards, A. S. G., and T. Takamiya. "A New Fragment of Gower's *Confessio Amantis.*" *Modern Language Review* 96 (2001): 931–36.

Emmerson, Richard K. "Reading Gower in a Manuscript Culture: Latin and English in Illustrated Manuscripts of the *Confessio Amantis.*" *Studies in the Age of Chaucer* 21 (1999): 143–86.

Enders, Jody. "Delivering Delivery: Theatricality and the Emasculation of Eloquence." *Rhetoric* 15 (1997): 253–78.

Fanger, Claire. "Signs of Power and the Power of Signs: Medieval Modes of Address to the Problem of Magical and Miraculous Signifiers." Ph.D diss., University of Toronto, 1993.

———. "Magic and the Metaphysics of Gender in Gower's 'Tale of Circe and Ulysses.'" In *Re-Visioning Gower,* ed. Yeager, 203–19.

Ferster, Judith. *Fictions of Advice: The Literature and Politics of Counsel in Late Medieval England.* Philadelphia: University of Pennsylvania Press, 1996.

Fish, Stanley. *Is There a Text in This Class? The Authority of Interpretative Communities.* Cambridge, Mass.: Harvard University Press, 1980.

Fisher, John H. *John Gower, Moral Philosopher and Friend of Chaucer.* London: Methuen, 1965.

Fisher, John H., R. Wayne Hamm, Peter G. Beidler, and Robert F. Yeager. "John Gower." In *A Manual of the Writings in Middle English, 1050–1500,* gen. eds. J. Burke Severs and Albert E. Hartung, 8 vols., 7:2195–2210 and 2399–2418. New Haven: Connecticut Academy of Arts and Sciences, 1967–89.

Fleming, John V. *The Roman de la Rose: A Study in Allegory and Iconography.* Princeton: Princeton University Press, 1969.

Foucault, Michel. *The History of Sexuality.* Vol. 1, *An Introduction.* Trans. Robert Hurley. London: Allen Lane, 1979.

———. "The Confession of the Flesh." In *Power/Knowledge: Selected Interviews and Other Writings 1972–1977,* ed. Colin Gordon, trans. Colin Gordon, Leo Marshall, John Mepham, and Kate Soper, 194–228. Brighton: Harvester, 1980.

Fradenburg, Louise, and Carla Freccero, eds. *Premodern Sexualities.* London: Routledge, 1996.

Frank, Robert Worth, Jr. "The Legend of Good Women, Some Implications." In *Chaucer at Albany,* ed. Rossell Hope Robbins, 63–76. New York: Burt Franklin, 1975.

Frantzen, Allen J. "The Disclosure of Sodomy in *Cleanness.*" *PMLA* 111 (1996): 451–64.

———. *Before the Closet: Same-Sex Love from Beowulf to Angels in America.* Chicago: University of Chicago Press, 1998.

Fredell, Joel. "Reading the Dream Miniature in the *Confessio Amantis.*" *Medievalia et Humanistica,* n.s. 22 (1995): 61–93.

Freud, Sigmund. "The Psychogenesis of a Case of Homosexuality in a Woman." In *Collected Papers,* authorized translation under the supervision of Joan Riviere. London: Hogarth Press, 1924.

———. *Totem and Taboo: Resemblances between the Psychic Lives of Savages and Neurotics.* Trans. A. A. Brill. Harmondsworth: Pelican, 1938.

———. *The Interpretation of Dreams.* Trans. James Strachey. Pelican Freud Library 4. Harmondsworth: Penguin, 1976.

———. *Art and Literature: Jensen's Gradiva, Leonardo Da Vinci and Other Works.* Trans. James Strachey. Penguin Freud Library 14. London: Penguin, 1990.

———. "A Seventeenth-Century Demonological Neurosis." In *Art and Literature,* trans. Strachey, 383–423.

———. "The Uncanny." In *Art and Literature,* trans. Strachey, 339–76.

———. "Femininity." In *New Introductory Lectures on Psychoanalysis,* trans. James Strachey, Penguin Freud Library 2, 145–69. London: Penguin, 1991.

———. *Introductory Lectures on Psychoanalysis.* Trans. James Strachey. Penguin Freud Library 1. London: Penguin, 1991.

———. "The Libido Theory and Narcissism." In *Introductory Lectures,* trans. Strachey, 461–81.

———. "On Narcissism: An Introduction." In *On Metapsychology: The Theory of Psychoanalysis,* trans. James Strachey, Penguin Freud Library 11, 65–97. London: Penguin, 1991.

———. "Parapraxes." In *Introductory Lectures,* trans. Strachey, 39–108.

Galbraith, V. H. "A New Life of Richard II." *History* 26 (1942): 223–39.

Galinsky, G. Karl. *The Herakles Theme: The Adaptations of the Hero in Literature from Homer to the Twentieth Century.* Oxford: Basil Blackwell, 1972.

Gallacher, Patrick J. *Love, the Word, and Mercury: A Reading of John Gower's Confessio Amantis.* Albuquerque: University of New Mexico Press, 1975.

Galloway, Andrew. "Gower in His Most Learned Role and the Peasants' Revolt of 1381." *Mediaevalia* 16 (1993 [for 1990]): 329–47.

Garbárty, Thomas J. "A Description of the Confession Miniatures for Gower's *Confessio Amantis* with Special Reference to the Illustrator's Role as Reader and Critic." *Mediaevalia* 19 (1996): 319–43.

Garber, Marjorie. *Vested Interests: Cross-Dressing and Cultural Anxiety.* London: Penguin, 1993.

Gaunt, Simon. "Bel Acueil and the Improper Allegory of the *Romance of the Rose.*" In *New Medieval Literatures,* vol. 2, ed. Wendy Scase, Rita Copeland, and David Lawton, 65–93. Oxford: Clarendon Press, 1998.

Gilroy-Scott, Neil. "John Gower's Reputation: Literary Allusions from the Early Fifteenth Century to the Time of 'Pericles.'" *The Yearbook of English Studies* 1 (1971): 30–47.

Goolden, P. "Antiochus's Riddle in Gower and Shakespeare," *Review of English Studies,* n.s., 6 (1955): 245–51.

Grady, Frank. "The Lancastrian Gower and the Limits of Exemplarity." *Speculum* 70 (1995): 552–75.

———. "Gower's Boat, Richard's Barge, and the True Story of *Confessio Amantis:* Text and Gloss." *Texas Studies in Literature and Language* 44 (2002): 1–15.

Greene, Richard Firth. "Women in Chaucer's Audience." *The Chaucer Review* 18 (1983): 146–54.

Griffiths, Jeremy. "*Confessio Amantis:* The Poem and Its Pictures." In *Gower's Confessio Amantis,* ed. Minnis, 163–78.

Griffiths, Jeremy, Kate Harris, Derek Pearsall, and Jeremy Smith, eds. *Descriptive Catalogue of the Manuscripts of the Works of John Gower.* Forthcoming.

Griffiths, Lavinia. *Personification in Piers Plowman.* Cambridge: D.S. Brewer, 1985.

Halberstam, Judith. *Female Masculinity.* London: Duke University Press, 1998.

Hamilton, George L. "Studies in the Sources of Gower." *The Journal of English and Germanic Philology* 26 (1927): 491–520.

Hanawalt, Barbara A. ed. *Chaucer's England: Literature in Historical Context.* Minneapolis: University of Minnesota Press, 1992.

Hanrahan, Michael. "Speaking of Sodomy: Gower's Advice to Princes in the *Confessio Amantis.*" *Exemplaria* 14 (2002): 423–46.

Harbert, Bruce. "Lessons from the Great Clerk: Ovid and John Gower." In *Ovid Reviewed,* ed. Charles Martindale, 83–97. Cambridge: Cambridge University Press, 1988.

Harris, Kate. "John Gower's *Confessio Amantis:* The Virtues of Bad Texts." In *Manuscripts and Readers in Fifteenth-Century England: The Literary Implications of Manuscript Study,* ed. Derek Pearsall, 27–40. Cambridge: D.S. Brewer, 1983.

———. "Patrons, Buyers, and Owners: The Evidence for Ownership and the Rôle of Book Owners in Book Production and the Book Trade." In *Book Production and Publishing in Britain 1375–1475,* ed. Jeremy Griffiths and Derek Pearsall, 163–99. Cambridge: Cambridge University Press, 1989.

———. "Ownership and Readership: Studies in the Provenance of the Manuscripts of Gower's *Confessio Amantis.*" D.Phil. thesis, University of York, 1993.

———. "The Longleat House Extracted Manuscript of Gower's *Confessio Amantis.*" In *Middle English Poetry: Texts and Traditions,* ed. A. J. Minnis, 77–90. Woodbridge, Suffolk: York Medieval Press, 2001.

Hatton, Thomas J. "John Gower's Use of Ovid in Book III of *Confessio Amantis.*" *Mediaevalia* 13 (1987): 257–74.

Holsinger, Bruce W. "Sodomy and Resurrection: The Homoerotic Subject of the *Divine Comedy,*" in *Premodern Sexualities,* ed. Fradenburg and Freccero, 243–74.

Hudson, Anne. "Lollardy: The English Heresy?" Reprinted in her *Lollards and Their Books,* 140–63. London: Hambledon Press, 1985.

Huizinga, Johan. *The Waning of the Middle Ages.* Harmondsworth: Penguin, 1955.

Irigaray, Luce. *The Sex Which Is Not One.* Trans. Catherine Porter and Carolyn Burke. Ithaca, NY: Cornell University Press, 1985.

Iser, Wolfgang. *The Act of Reading: A Theory of Aesthetic Response.* London: Routledge and Kegan Paul, 1978.

Jaeger, C. Stephen. *The Origins of Courtliness: Civilizing Trends and the Formation of Courtly Ideals 939–1290.* Philadelphia: University of Pennsylvania Press, 1985.

———. *Ennobling Love: In Search of a Lost Sensibility.* Philadelphia: University of Pennsylvania Press, 1999.

Jones, Richard H. *The Royal Policy of Richard II: Absolutism in the Later Middle Ages.* Oxford: Basil Blackwell, 1968.

Jordan, Mark D. *The Invention of Sodomy in Christian Theology.* Chicago: University of Chicago Press, 1997.

Justice, Steven. *Writing and Rebellion: England in 1381.* Berkeley: University of California Press, 1994.

Kantorowicz, Ernst H. *The King's Two Bodies: A Study in Medieval Political Theology.* Princeton, NJ: Princeton University Press, 1957.

Kay, Sarah. "The Birth of Venus in the *Roman de la Rose.*" *Exemplaria* 9 (1997): 7–37.

Keiser, Elizabeth B. *Courtly Desire and Medieval Homophobia: The Legitimation of Sexual Pleasure in Cleanness and Its Contexts.* New Haven: Yale University Press, 1997.

Kelly, Henry Ansgar. *Love and Marriage in the Age of Chaucer.* Ithaca, NY: Cornell University Press, 1975.

Kerby-Fulton, Kathryn, and Steven Justice. "Langlandian Reading Circles and the Civil Service in London and Dublin, 1380–1427." In *New Medieval Literatures,* vol. 1, ed. Wendy Scase, Rita Copeland, and David Lawton, 59–83. Oxford: Clarendon Press, 1997.

King, Katherine Callen. *Achilles: Paradigms of the War Hero from Homer to the Middle Ages.* Berkeley: University of California Press, 1987.

Kinneavy, Gerald. "Gower's *Confessio Amantis* and the Penitentials." *The Chaucer Review* 19 (1984): 144–61.

Klindienst, Patricia. "The Voice of the Shuttle Is Ours." In *Literary Theory: An Anthology,* ed. Julie Rivkin and Michael Ryan, 216–29. Oxford: Blackwell, 1998.

Lamos, Colleen. "The Ethics of Queer Theory." In *Critical Ethics: Text, Theory, and Responsibility,* ed. Dominic Rainsford and Tim Woods, 141–51. Basingstoke: Macmillan, 1999.

Laqueur, Thomas. *Making Sex: Body and Gender from the Greeks to Freud.* London: Harvard University Press, 1990.

Lawton, David. "Dullness and the Fifteenth Century." *English Literary History* 54 (1987): 761–99.

Lees, Clare A. "Gender and Exchange in *Piers Plowman.*" In *Class and Gender in Early English Literature: Intersections,* ed. Britton J. Harwood and Gillian R. Overing, 112–30. Bloomington: Indiana University Press, 1994.

Lerer, Seth. *Chaucer and His Readers: Imagining the Author in Late-Medieval England.* Princeton: Princeton University Press, 1993.

Lichtenstein, Jacqueline. "Making Up Representation: The Risks of Femininity." *Representations* 20 (1987): 77–87.

Lochrie, Karma. *Covert Operations: The Medieval Uses of Secrecy.* Philadelphia: University of Pennsylvania Press, 1999.

Lynch, Kathryn L. *The High Medieval Dream Vision: Poetry, Philosophy, and Literary Form.* Stanford: Stanford University Press, 1988.

Macaulay, G. C. "The *Confessio Amantis.*" Reprinted in *Gower's Confessio Amantis,* ed. Nicholson, 6–14. (First published in *The Cambridge History of English Literature,* vol. 2, *The End of the Middle Ages,* ed. A. W. Ward and A. R. Waller, 166–76. Cambridge: Cambridge University Press, 1908.)

McCann, Graham. "Distant Voices, Real Lives: Authorship, Criticism, Responsibility." In *What Is an Author?,* ed. Maurice Biriotti and Nicola Miller, 72–82. Manchester: Manchester University Press, 1993.

McDonald, Nicola F. "John Gower's *Medea Genetrix.*" Paper presented at the annual meeting of the Gender and Medieval Studies Group, Gender and Creativity, St. Hilda's College, Oxford, 6 January 1998.

————. "Violence and the Gender of Space in an Illuminated *Confessio Amantis*." Paper presented at the annual meeting of the Gender and Medieval Studies Group, Gender and Space, University of York, 6 January 2001.

Machan, Tim William. "Language Contact in *Piers Plowman*." *Speculum* 69 (1994): 359–85.

————. "Thomas Berthelette and Gower's *Confessio Amantis*." *Studies in the Age of Chaucer* 18 (1996): 143–67.

McKisack, May. *The Fourteenth Century 1307–1399*. Oxford: Oxford University Press, 1959.

McNally, John J. "The Penitential and Courtly Tradition in Gower's *Confessio Amantis*." *Studies in Medieval Culture* 1 (1964): 74–94.

Mahoney, Dhira B. "Gower's Two Prologues to *Confessio Amantis*." In *Re-Visioning Gower*, ed. Yeager, 17–37.

Mainzer, Conrad. "John Gower's Use of the 'Mediaeval Ovid' in *Confessio Amantis*." *Medium Ævum* 41 (1972): 215–22.

Mainzer, H. C. "A Study of the Sources of the *Confessio Amantis* of John Gower." Unpublished D.Phil thesis, University of Oxford, 1967.

Manzalaoui, M. A. "'Noght in the Registre of Venus': Gower's English Mirror for Princes." In *Medieval Studies for J. A. W. Bennett Ætatis Suæ LXX*, ed. P. L. Heyworth, 159–83. Oxford: Clarendon Press, 1981.

Marcus, Jane. "Liberty. Sorority, Misogyny." In *The Representation of Women in Fiction*, ed. Carolyn G. Heilbrun and Margaret R. Higonnet, 60–97. Baltimore: Johns Hopkins University Press, 1983.

Mathew, Gervase. *The Court of Richard II*. London: John Murray, 1968.

Merivale, Patricia. *Pan the Goat-God: His Myth in Modern Times*. Cambridge MA: Harvard University Press, 1969.

Middleton, Anne. "The Idea of Public Poetry in the Reign of Richard II." *Speculum* 53 (1978): 94–114.

————. "Chaucer's 'New Men' and the Good of Literature in the *Canterbury Tales*." In *Literature and Society: Selected Papers from the English Institute, 1978*, n.s., 3, ed. Edward W. Said, 15–56. Baltimore: The Johns Hopkins University Press, 1980.

————. "Narrative and the Invention of Experience: Episodic Form in *Piers Plowman*." In *The Wisdom of Poetry*, ed. Larry D. Benson and Siegfried Wenzel, 91–122. Kalamazoo: Medieval Institute Publications, 1982.

————. "William Langland's 'Kynde Name': Authorial Signature and Social Identity in Late Fourteenth-Century England." In *Literary Practice and Social Change*, ed. Patterson, 15–82.

Minnis, A. J. "The Influence of Academic Prologues on the Prologues and Literary Attitudes of Late Medieval English Writers." *Mediaeval Studies* 43 (1981): 342–83.

————. "'Moral Gower' and Medieval Literary Theory." In *Gower's Confessio Amantis*, ed. Minnis, 50–78.

————. *Medieval Theory of Authorship: Scholastic Literary Attitudes in the Later Middle Ages*. Aldershot, Hants.: Scholar Press, 1988.

————. "*De Vulgari Auctoritate*: Chaucer, Gower, and the Men of Great Authority." In *Chaucer and Gower*, ed. Yeager, 36–74.

———. "John Gower, *Sapiens* in Ethics and Politics." Reprinted in *Gower's Confessio Amantis*, ed. Nicholson, 158–80. (First published in *Medium Ævum* 49 [1980]: 207–29.)

———. ed. *Gower's Confessio Amantis: Responses and Reassessments.* Cambridge: D.S. Brewer, 1983.

Minnis, A. J., and A. B. Scott, eds., with David Wallace. *Medieval Literary Theory and Criticism c.1100–c.1375: The Commentary Tradition.* Oxford: Oxford University Press, 1988.

Moi, Toril. *Sexual/Textual Politics: Feminist Literary Theory.* London: Methuen, 1985.

Morton, Donald. "Birth of the Cyberqueer." *PMLA* 110 (1995): 369–81.

Murphy, Colette. "Lady Holy Church and Meed the Maid: Re-Envisioning Female Personifications in *Piers Plowman*." In *Feminist Readings in Middle English Literature: The Wife of Bath and All Her Sect,* ed. Ruth Evans and Lesley Johnson, 140–64. London: Routledge, 1994.

Murphy, James J. "John Gower's *Confessio Amantis* and the First Discussion of Rhetoric in the English Language." *Philological Quarterly* 41 (1962): 401–11.

Murray, Jacqueline. "Twice Marginal and Twice Invisible: Lesbians in the Middle Ages." In *Handbook of Medieval Sexuality,* ed. Vern L. Bullough and James A. Brundage, 191–222. New York: Garland, 1996.

———. "Gendered Souls in Sexed Bodies: The Male Construction of Female Sexuality in Some Medieval Confessors' Manuals." In *Handling Sin: Confession in the Middle Ages,* ed. Peter Biller and A. J. Minnis, 79–93. Woodbridge, Suffolk: Boydell and Brewer, 1998.

Nicholson, Peter. "The Dedications of Gower's *Confessio Amantis*." *Mediaevalia* 10 (1984): 159–80.

———. "Gower's Revisions in the *Confessio Amantis*." *The Chaucer Review* 19 (1984): 123–43.

———. "Poet and Scribe in the Manuscripts of Gower's *Confessio Amantis*." In *Manuscripts and Texts: Editorial Problems in Later Middle English Literature,* ed. Derek Pearsall, 130–42. Cambridge: D.S. Brewer, 1987.

———. "Chaucer Borrows from Gower: The Sources of the *Man of Law's Tale*." In *Chaucer and Gower,* ed. Yeager, 85–99.

———. ed. *Gower's Confessio Amantis: A Critical Anthology.* Cambridge: D.S. Brewer, 1991.

Nicolas, H. N. "Gower, the Poet." *Retrospective Review,* 2d series, 2 (1827): 103–17.

Nitzsche, Jane Chance. *The Genius Figure in Antiquity and the Middle Ages.* New York: Columbia University Press, 1975.

Norbrook, David. "The Emperor's New Body? *Richard II*, Ernst Kantorowicz, and the Politics of Shakespeare Criticism." *Textual Practice* 10 (1996): 329–57.

Norris, Christopher. *Deconstruction and the Interests of Theory.* London: Pinter, 1988.

———. *Truth and the Ethics of Criticism.* Manchester: Manchester University Press, 1994.

Norton, Rictor. "Lovely Lad and Shame-Faced Catamite." Section 5 of *The Homosexual Pastoral Tradition* (1974; 1997), published on Norton's website at www.infopt.demon.co.uk.

Olsson, Kurt. *John Gower and the Structures of Conversion: A Reading of the Confessio Amantis.* Cambridge: D.S. Brewer, 1992.

———. "Reading, Transgression, and Judgement: Gower's Case of Paris and Helen." In *Re-Visioning Gower,* ed. Yeager, 67–92.

Papka, Claudia. "Prophecy and Heresy: Dante and the Dangers of Vernacular Religion." Paper delivered at the conference on Vernacularity: The Politics of Language and Style, University of Western Ontario, 4–7 March 1999.

Parker, Patricia. "Virile Style." In *Premodern Sexualities*, ed. Fradenburg and Freccero, 201–22.

Parkes, M. B. "Patterns of Scribal Activity and Revisions of the Text in Early Copies of Works by John Gower." In *New Science Out of Old Books: Studies in Manuscripts and Early Printed Books in Honour of A. I. Doyle*, ed. Richard Beadle and A. J. Piper, 81–121. Aldershot, Hants: Scolar Press, 1995.

Patterson, Lee. *Negotiating the Past: The Historical Understanding of Medieval Literature.* Madison, WI: University of Wisconsin Press, 1987.

———. *Chaucer and the Subject of History.* London: Routledge, 1991.

———. ed. *Literary Practice and Social Change in Britain, 1380–1530.* Berkeley: University of California Press, 1990.

Payer, Pierre J. "Sex and Confession in the Thirteenth Century." In *Sex in the Middle Ages: A Book of Essays*, ed. Joyce E. Salisbury, 126–41. New York: Garland, 1991.

Pearce, Lynne. *Feminism and the Politics of Reading.* London: Arnold, 1997.

Pearsall, Derek. "The Gower Tradition." In *Gower's Confessio Amantis*, ed. Minnis, 179–97.

———. "Gower's Latin in *Confessio Amantis*." In *Latin and Vernacular: Studies in Late-Medieval Texts and Manuscripts*, ed. A. J. Minnis, 13–25. Cambridge: D.S. Brewer, 1989.

———. *The Life of Geoffrey Chaucer: A Critical Biography.* Oxford: Blackwell, 1992.

Peck, Russell A. *Kingship and Common Profit in Gower's Confessio Amantis.* Carbondale: Southern Illinois University Press, 1978.

———. "John Gower and the Book of Daniel." In *John Gower*, ed. Yeager, 159–87.

Pequigney, Joseph. "Sodomy in Dante's *Inferno* and *Purgatorio*." *Representations* 36 (1991): 22–42.

Pickles, J. D., and J. L. Dawson, eds. *A Concordance to John Gower's Confessio Amantis.* Cambridge: D. S. Brewer, 1987.

Pittenger, Elizabeth. "Explicit Ink." In *Premodern Sexualities*, ed. Fradenburg and Freccero, 223–42.

Porter, Elizabeth. "Gower's Ethical Microcosm and Political Macrocosm." In *Gower's Confessio Amantis*, ed. Minnis, 135–62.

Propp, Vladimir. "Oedipus in the Light of Folklore." In *Oedipus: A Folkore Casebook*, ed. Lowell Edmunds, 76–121. New York and London: Garland, 1983.

Purkiss, Diane. *The Witch in History: Early Modern and Twentieth-Century Representations.* London: Routledge, 1996.

Putter, Ad. "Arthurian Literature and the Rhetoric of Effeminacy." In *Arthurian Romance and Gender: Selected Proceedings of the XVIIth International Arthurian Congress*, ed. Friedrich Wolfzettel, 34–49. Amsterdam: Rodopi, 1995.

Rank, Otto. *The Incest Theme in Literature and Legend: Fundamentals of a Psychology of Literary Creation.* Trans. Gregory C. Richter. Baltimore: Johns Hopkins University Press, 1992.

Ricks, Christopher. "Metamorphosis in Other Words." In *Gower's Confessio Amantis*, ed. Minnis, 25–49.

Robins, William. "Romance, Exemplum, and the Subject of the *Confessio Amantis*." *Studies in the Age of Chaucer* 19 (1997): 157–81.

Rowe, Donald W. *Through Nature to Eternity: Chaucer's Legend of Good Women*. Lincoln: University of Nebraska Press, 1988.

Rubin, Gayle. "The Traffic in Women: Notes on the 'Political Economy' of Sex." In *Toward an Anthropology of Women*, ed. Rayna R. Reiter, 157–210. New York: Monthly Review Press, 1975.

Saenger, Paul. "Silent Reading: Its Impact on Late Medieval Script and Society." *Viator* 13 (1982): 367–414.

Salisbury, Eve. "Remembering Origins: Gower's Monstrous Body Politic." In *Re-Visioning Gower*, ed.Yeager, 159–84.

Saul, Nigel. *Richard II*. New Haven: Yale University Press, 1997.

Scanlon, Larry. *Narrative, Authority, and Power: The Medieval Exemplum and the Chaucerian Tradition*. Cambridge: Cambridge University Press, 1994.

———. "The Riddle of Incest: John Gower and the Problem of Medieval Sexuality." In *Re-Visioning Gower*, ed. Yeager, 93–127.

Schibanoff, Susan. "Sodomy's Mark: Alan of Lille, Jean de Meun, and the Medieval Theory of Authorship." In *Queering the Middle Ages*, ed. Burger and Kruger, 28–56.

Schmitz, Götz. "Rhetoric and Fiction: Gower's Comments on Eloquence and Courtly Poetry." Reprinted in *Gower's Confessio Amantis*, ed. Nicholson, 117–42. Revised and translated by the author from "Rhetorik und Poetik: Gowers Äusserungen zur Rede- und Dichtkunst." In his *The Middel Weie: Stil- und Aufbauformen in Jown Gowers "Confessio Amantis,"* Studien zur Englischen Literatur, Band 11, 27–54. Bonn: Bonvier, 1974.

Scott, Kathleen L. "Lydgate's *Lives of Saints Edmund and Fremund:* A Newly-Located Manuscript in Arundel Castle." *Viator* 13 (1982): 335–66.

———. *Later Gothic Manuscripts, 1390–1490*. Vol. 2. London: Harvey Miller, 1996.

Sedgwick, Eve Kosofsky. *Between Men: English Literature and Male Homosexual Desire*. Columbia: Columbia University Press, 1985.

Shahar, Shulamith. *Childhood in the Middle Ages*. Trans. Chaya Galai. London: Routledge, 1992.

Simpson, James. *Sciences and the Self in Medieval Poetry: Alan of Lille's Anticlaudianus and John Gower's Confessio Amantis*. Cambridge: Cambridge University Press, 1995.

———. "Ethics and Interpretation: Reading Wills in Chaucer's *Legend of Good Women*." *Studies in the Age of Chaucer* 20 (1998): 73–100.

Somerset, Fiona. "Answering the *Twelve Conclusions:* Dymmok's Halfhearted Gestures Towards Publication." In *Lollardy and Gentry in the Later Middle Ages*, ed. Margaret Aston and Colin Richmond, 52–76. Stroud: Sutton, 1997.

Spearing, A. C. "Canace and Machaire." *Mediaevalia* 16 (1993 [for 1990]): 211–21.

Staley, Lynn. "Gower, Richard II, Henry of Derby, and the Business of Making Culture." *Speculum* 75 (2000): 68–96.

Stallybrass, Peter, and Allon White. *The Politics and Poetics of Transgression*. London: Methuen, 1985.

Steadman, John M. "Milton and St. Basil: The Genesis of Sin and Death." *Modern Language Notes* 73 (1958): 83–84.

———. "Grosseteste on the Genealogy of Sin and Death." *Notes and Queries* 204 (1959): 367–68.

Steele, Anthony. *Richard II*. Cambridge: Cambridge University Press, 1941. Reprint 1962.

Stierle, Karlheinz. "Interpretations of Responsibility and Responsibilities of Interpretation." *New Literary History* 25 (1994): 853–67.

Stock, Brian. "The Self and Literary Experience in Late Antiquity and the Middle Ages." *New Literary History* 25 (1994): 839–52.

Stow, George B. "Richard II in Thomas Walsingham's Chronicles." *Speculum* 59 (1984): 68–102.

———. "Richard II in John Gower's *Confessio Amantis:* Some Historical Perspectives," *Mediaevalia* 16 (1993 [for 1990]), 3–31.

Strohm, Paul. "Chaucer's Audience." *Literature in History* 5 (1977): 26–41.

———. "Form and Social Statement in *Confessio Amantis* and *The Canterbury Tales.*" *Studies in the Age of Chaucer* 1 (1979): 17–40.

———. "Chaucer's Fifteenth-Century Audience and the Narrowing of the 'Chaucer Tradition.'" *Studies in the Age of Chaucer* 4 (1982): 3–32.

———. "A Note on Gower's Persona." In *Acts of Interpretation: The Text in Its Contexts, 700–1600,* ed. Mary J. Carruthers and Elizabeth D. Kirk, 293–98. Norman, OK: Pilgrim Books, 1982.

———. "Chaucer's Audience(s): Fictional, Implied, Actual." *The Chaucer Review* 18 (1983): 137–45.

———. *Social Chaucer*. Cambridge: Harvard University Press, 1989.

———. "Politics and Poetics: Usk and Chaucer in the 1380s." In *Literary Practice and Social Change,* ed. Patterson, 83–112.

———. *Hochon's Arrow: The Social Imagination of Fourteenth-Century Texts.* Princeton: Princeton University Press, 1992.

Sullivan, William L. "Chaucer's Man of Law as a Literary Critic." *Modern Language Notes* 68 (1953): 1–8.

Summers, Joanna. "Gower's *Vox Clamantis* and Usk's *Testament of Love.*" *Medium Ævum* 68 (1999): 55–62.

Tambling, Jeremy. *Confession: Sexuality, Sin, the Subject.* Manchester: Manchester University Press, 1990.

Tatlock, John S. P. "The Epilog of Chaucer's *Troilus.*" *Modern Philology* 18 (1921): 625–59.

Taylor, Andrew. "Anne of Bohemia and the Making of Chaucer." *Studies in the Age of Chaucer* 19 (1997): 95–119.

Taylor, J. "Richard II's Views on Kingship." *Proceedings of the Leeds Philosophical and Literary Society* 14 (1970–72): 189–205.

Thomas, Alfred. *Anne's Bohemia: Czech Literature and Society, 1310–1420.* Minneapolis: University of Minnesota Press, 1998.

Tinkle, Theresa. *Medieval Venuses and Cupids: Sexuality, Hermeneutics, and English Poetry.* Stanford: Stanford University Press, 1996.

Tuck, Anthony. *Richard II and the English Nobility.* London: Edward Arnold, 1973.

Tyrrell, William Blake. *Amazons: A Study in Athenian Mythmaking*. Baltimore: Johns Hopkins University Press, 1984.

Vance, Eugene. "The Differing Seed: Dante's Brunetto Latini." In his *Mervelous Signals: Poetics and Sign Theory in the Middle Ages*, 230–55. Lincoln: University of Nebraska Press, 1986.

Wallace, David. *Chaucerian Polity: Absolute Lineages and Associational Forms in England and Italy*. Stanford: Stanford University Press, 1997.

———. ed. *The Cambridge History of Medieval English Literature*. Cambridge: Cambridge University Press, 1999.

Warner, Marina. *Monuments and Maidens: The Allegory of the Female Form*. London: Vintage, 1996.

Watson, Nicholas. "Censorship and Cultural Change in Late-Medieval England: Vernacular Theology, the Oxford Translation Debate, and Arundel's Constitutions of 1409." *Speculum* 70 (1995): 822–64.

———. "The Politics of Middle English Writing." In *The Idea of the Vernacular*, ed. Wogan-Browne et al., 331–52.

———. "The Monstrosity of the Moral Pig and Other Unnatural Ruminations." In *Consuming Narratives: Gender and Monstrous Appetite in the Middle Ages and the Renaissance*, ed. Liz Herbert McAvoyand and Teresa Walters, 15–27. Cardiff: University of Wales Press, 2002.

Watt, Diane. "Behaving Like a Man: Incest, Lesbian Desire, and Gender Play in *Yde et Olive* and Its Adaptations." *Comparative Literature* 50 (1998): 265–85.

———. "Truth or Dare?" *English* 50 (2001): 170–73.

Watts, John. Review of Ferster's *Fictions of Advice*. *Albion* 29 (1997): 474–75.

Weiher, Carol. "Chaucer's and Gower's Stories of Lucretia and Virginia." *English Language Notes* 14 (1976): 7–9.

Wetherbee, Winthrop. "Constance and the World in Chaucer and Gower." In *John Gower*, ed. Yeager, 65–93.

———. "Latin Structure and Vernacular Space: Gower, Chaucer, and the Boethian Tradition." In *Chaucer and Gower*, ed. Yeager, 7–35.

———. "John Gower." In *The Cambridge History of Medieval English Literature*, ed. Wallace, 589–609.

White, Allon. *Carnival, Hysteria, and Writing*. Oxford: Clarendon Press, 1993.

White, Hugh. "The Sympathetic Villain in *Confessio Amantis*." In *Re-Visioning Gower*, ed. Yeager, 221–35.

———. *Nature, Sex, and Goodness in a Medieval Literary Tradition*. Oxford: Oxford University Press, 2000.

Whiting, Bartlett Jere, and Helen Wescott Whiting. *Proverbs, Sentences, and Proverbial Phrases from English Writings Mainly Before 1500*. London: Oxford University Press, 1968.

Wogan-Browne, Jocelyn. "Chaste Bodies: Frames and Experiences." In *Framing Medieval Bodies*, ed. Sarah Kay and Miri Rubin, 24–42. Manchester: Manchester University Press, 1996.

Wogan-Browne, Jocelyn, Nicholas Watson, Andrew Taylor, and Ruth Evans, eds. *The Idea of the Vernacular: An Anthology of Middle English Literary Theory, 1280–1520*. University Park: Pennsylvania State University Press, 1999.

Woolf, Rosemary. "Moral Chaucer and Kindly Gower." in *J. R. R. Tolkien, Scholar and Storyteller: Essays in Memoriam,* ed. Mary Salu and Robert T. Farrell, 221–45. Ithaca: Cornell University Press, 1979.

Wright, Sylvia. "The Author Portraits in the Bedford Psalter-Hours: Gower, Chaucer, and Hoccleve." *British Library Journal* 18 (1992): 190–201.

Yeager, R. F. "'Oure englisshe' and Everyone's Latin: The *Fasciculus Morum* and Gower's *Confessio Amantis.*" *South Atlantic Review* 46 (1981): 41–53.

———. "'O Moral Gower': Chaucer's Dedication of Troilus and Criseyde." *The Chaucer Review* 19 (1984): 87–99.

———. "English, Latin, and the Text as 'Other': The Page as Sign in the Work of John Gower." *Text* 3 (1987): 251–67.

———. "*Pax Poetica:* On the Pacifism of Chaucer and Gower." *Studies in the Age of Chaucer* 9 (1987): 97–121.

———. "Did Gower Write *Cento?*" In *John Gower,* ed. Yeager, 113–32.

———. *John Gower's Poetic: The Search for a New Arion.* Cambridge: D.S. Brewer, 1990.

———. "Learning to Read in Tongues: Writing Poetry for a Trilingual Culture." In *Chaucer and Gower,* ed. Yeager, 115–29.

———. ed. *John Gower: Recent Readings.* Kalamazoo, MI: Medieval Institute Publications, 1989.

———. ed., *Chaucer and Gower: Difference, Mutuality, Exchange.* Victoria, BC: University of Victoria Press, 1991.

———. ed. *Re-Visioning Gower.* Asheville, NC: Pegasus, 1999.

Ziolkowski, Jan. *Alan of Lille's Grammar of Sex: The Meaning of Grammar to a Twelfth-Century Intellectual.* Cambridge: Medieval Academy of America, 1985.

MEDIEVAL CULTURES

Index

Achilles, 71–73, 75, 78, 81
Achilles and Deidamia, Tale of, 69, 71–73, 94, 95
Acteon, Tale of, 98
Adam, 43
Adam of Usk, 173n. 57
Aers, David, 31, 157, 159
Alain de Lille, 77, 78; *Anticlaudianus*, 72; *De Planctu Naturae*, xvi, 28, 46, 49–51, 52, 84, 169n. 24, 172n. 38
Alceste, 80
Alexander and the Pirate, Tale of, 114, 115, 117, 118
Alexander the Great, 41, 108, 114–19, 125, 146; birth of, 101–2, 114, 116; education of, xvii–xviii, 45, 114–17, 138–39, 149, 154
Allen, Elizabeth, xii–xiii, 5, 159
Amans, 14, 78, 119; and Christianity, 84; confession of, 41, 64, 65, 68, 78–80; and Cupid, 65–68, 80–81, 98, 176n. 41; and Genius, xvii, 15, 65, 103, 156; and Gower, xviii, 103, 153–54; and Gower as *senex amans*, 14–16, 55–56, 58, 127–28, 154–55; oedipal struggle of, 128; as reader, xii, xv; and Venus, 65, 67, 103, 127, 152, 154
Ambrose, Saint, 34, 47–48
Amnon, 133
Amorality, xi–xiii, xviii, 156–60
Anne of Bohemia, 80, 147
Antichrist, 109, 114
Anticlericalism, 29–30, 35, 157, 169nn. 29–30

Antiochus, 23, 122; and Amans, 128; and Apollonius, 123, 140–41, 185n. 54; and rape, 8–9, 128–31, 134–40, 142; and Richard II, 146–47
Apius Claudius, 122–24
Apocalypticism, 108, 111–12, 113
Apollonius: and Antiochus, 123, 140–41, 185n. 54; and Artestrathes, 137–38; flight of, 137; quests of, 129–30, 136, 142, 144; and Richard II, 148; sins of, xviii, 123, 138–40, 148; and Thaise, 132, 143
Apollonius of Tyre, Tale of, 6, 8–9, 82, 88, 90, 128; absence of women in, 131–34; female desire in, xviii, 140–45, 147; political interpretation of, xviii, 123, 145–48; riddles in, 23, 129–31, 134–36, 140–42; search for the father in, 134–40
Aquinas, Thomas, Saint, 171n. 4, 174n.6
Archibald, Elizabeth, 146
Arion, 155
Aristotle, 55, 152, 171–72n. 22; and Alexander the Great, xvii–xviii, 45, 116–17, 154
Arrons, 120–22, 124
Arundel, Thomas (archbishop of Canterbury), 30
Augustine of Hippo, Saint: *The City of God*, 182n. 34
Authorial self-representation, xvi–xviii, 22–23, 55–58, 153–56, 186n. 88. *See also* Amans, and Gower; Genius, and Gower
Authorial signatures, 127–28, 148

211

Diane Watt is senior lecturer in English at the University of Wales, Aberystwyth. She is the author of *Secretaries of God: Women Prophets in Late Medieval and Early Modern England;* editor of the collection *Medieval Women in Their Communities;* and coeditor of two volumes of essays, *Decentring Sexualities: Politics and Representations beyond the Metropolis* and *The Arts of Seventeenth-Century Science.*